SIMPLY JAVA:
AN INTRODUCTION TO
JAVA PROGRAMMING

SIMPLY JAVA:

AN INTRODUCTION TO JAVA PROGRAMMING

JAMES R. LEVENICK

WILLAMETTE UNIVERSITY

CHARLES RIVER MEDIA, INC.
Hingham, Massachusetts

Acquisitions Editor: James Walsh
Cover Design: Tyler Creative

CHARLES RIVER MEDIA, INC.
10 Downer Avenue
Hingham, Massachusetts 02043
781-740-0400
781-740-8816 (FAX)
info@charlesriver.com
www.charlesriver.com

This book is printed on acid-free paper.

James Levenick. *Simply Java: An Introduction to Java Programming*.
ISBN: 1-58450-426-9

Library of Congress Cataloging-in-Publication Data
Levenick, James, 1952-
  Simply Java : an introduction to Java programming / James Levenick.
     p. cm.
  Includes index.
  ISBN 1-58450-426-9 (pbk. with cd-rom : alk. paper)
  1. Java (Computer program language) I. Title.
  QA76.73.J38L475 2005
  005.13'3--dc22
                            2005014814

05 7 6 5 4 3 2 First Edition

CHARLES RIVER MEDIA titles are available for site license or bulk purchase by institutions, user groups, corporations, etc. For additional information, please contact the Special Sales Department at 781-740-0400.

Contents

Preface

Why write yet another introductory Java book? The answer is simple; I was unable to find a suitable textbook for teaching introductory Java programming. This is for three main reasons. First, every Java textbook I looked at, or taught from, was too tedious to read. I could not justify asking my students to read something that *I* was incapable of reading. Second, every text I reviewed piled on so much detail in the beginning, that the essential issues of object programming were obscured. It was as if every author embraced the C and C++ tradition of teaching if-else and iteration before graphics and inheritance; this text breaks with that tradition. Third, I have found that introductory programming students do better in the long run (i.e., in upper level CS courses) when they learn a modern IDE from the beginning. Very few texts incorporate treatment of an IDE. I wanted to use a modern, freely available IDE, and NetBeans™ works quite well. This text teaches NetBeans in addition to Java.

Here at Willamette University, we have used a preliminary version of this text in four introductory programming courses, and the students like it very much.

THE INTENTION OF THIS BOOK

This book is intended as a first course in Java programming. Java is an object language. Programming in an object language is mostly about writing classes, so class design and implementation are presented from the beginning.

However, it takes three or four weeks for most people to gain enough expertise to understand classes, so the first several chapters (after the introduction) are written in a quasi-tutorial style. The reader/student is directed, repeatedly, to put down the book and go to the screen to try the code. This is essential. Programming can't be learned without practice. It is a process skill, and process skills must be practiced.

COURSE INSTRUCTION

The principal difficulty in teaching the beginning of an introductory programming class is that there are too many things to learn all at once. Until students are aware of what an editor, file, compiler, and runtime environment are, they will have trouble accomplishing anything. Once those components become somewhat familiar, the more difficult task of learning to program may be undertaken.

The initial difficulty in teaching Java is that a number of concepts must be grasped first; but they are interdependent, and each must be explained by reference to the others. Until they are all understood, at least vaguely, programming remains mysterious (see the end of Chapter 5, "Toward Consistent Classes," for a list). Traditional linear Java texts start just like procedural programming texts, with a main program doing algebra. This is typically followed by methods and/or control structure. User defined classes involve yet another set of novel concepts, and are simply too much to teach at the same time as the rest of the traditional introductory material; they appear somewhere after page 500.

By contrast, this book uses a spiral approach. User defined classes and working programs are presented from the beginning, which helps students view class design as central to the activity of programming (a useful notion for them to acquire). Chapters 2 through 4 present programs to enter and run without explanations of all the Java constructs involved. This is done to allow students to run some programs, see what they do, and experiment with them a bit, before presenting a huge helping of detail. This approach makes computing more palatable for many beginning students, and provides familiar, concrete examples with which to illustrate the concepts in Chapter 5. As a wise man once explained to me, "You cannot teach someone the relationship between X and Y until they 'have' X and Y—and by 'have,' I mean, 'have coherent internal representations of.'"

Starting in Chapter 3, "Class Design and Implementation," user defined classes are presented, complete with accessors. This is a departure from most texts, and may require some explanation. The rationale is as follows. Encapsulation is an important feature of object programming. Accessors are a central (if elementary) part of encapsulation. They are also important conceptually. Until programmers understand, and are comfortable with, the syntax and semantics of accessors, they cannot understand other methods. Once they internalize accessors, they understand parameters, the assignment statement, instance variables, return types, and the return statement, and can apply these concepts in every class they write. In addition, accessors have a simple, regular structure that can be memorized easily, which makes them perfect for even a technophobic student to remember. They then serve as a model for every other method.

Some instructors might worry that the presentation here will lead to too much reliance on the IDE (especially if they are in the habit of programming without one). Like any good tool, an IDE may seem essential (especially if one has never programmed without it). It is rather like a person learning to drive without ever driving a manual transmission. If one day, that person were forced to drive a car with a clutch, there would be some difficulties initially, until he learned to do without the ease of an automatic transmission. Once upon a time, nearly every car had a manual transmission, and every driver learned to operate a clutch from the start—no more. Anyone can learn to operate a manual transmission; however, often, nowadays, students learn with an automatic transmission. Similarly, at one time, everyone programmed from the command line—no more. Every computing expert needs, at some point, to learn how to program without an IDE; but not first. Appendix A details how to edit, compile, and run Java programs from the command line (if this seems like something you want your students to learn).

A good way to teach from this book is to do the example programs just before your students do. That way, you will have them clearly in mind, and will have encountered many of the problems your students will run into. Carefully explaining bugs you encountered, and how you diagnosed and solved them, is invaluable to the students. Debugging is not easy; your students need a model. An excellent approach is (assuming you have a computer-equipped classroom) to actually enter and run the initial programs in class. This lets the students watch you make mistakes (which everyone does) and helps them learn the IDE (which is, initially, quite bewildering).

There are review problems and programming exercises at the end of each chapter, but it is expected that the instructor will come up with other programming problems that seem interesting and/or relevant.

If you have students who are not yet comfortable with the basics of files and directories, it would be good to provide some extra help with those—they are not covered here.

1 Programming Is Like Juggling

In This Chapter

- Computing as a Fact of Life
- The Past: A Very Brief History of Computing
- Juggling

This book is an introduction to programming in Java. Programming is an aspect of computing, but what exactly is computing?

COMPUTING AS A FACT OF LIFE

This millennium is an exciting time to be involved in computing. The Web, which did not exist 20 years ago, is an important new part of our society, our culture. Ordinary people, with no training in computing, can sit at a personal computer (PC) and access millions of other computers across the planet. Anyone with patience and the ability to follow simple instructions can make a Web page and post information that is immediately accessible from around the world. This is a

1

revolutionary development. Java is a programming language designed for programming on the Web.

Computing as Information Processing

Computing is information processing—always, and only. Although many people experience computing as Web browsing, chatting, or game playing, the underlying programs are always processing information by executing instructions.

A *program* is a series of instructions executed by the processor. Each instruction does some small task, such as moving a little information from one place to another, or adding one number to another and storing the result, or comparing one number to another and taking different actions depending on which is bigger. Although each individual action is small, a modern processor executes billions of instructions per second and so can accomplish a fair amount in a short time.

Information is stored mainly in two places: temporarily in memory, and permanently in files on disks. A file is a series of numbers. This is the same "file" you might store from a word processor or an e-mail program. When you save a file in a word processor, the information in your document (i.e., the text you have typed, along with the formatting information) is converted into a series of numbers and written to the disk along with the name of the file you select. Later, when you load that file again, the numbers are converted back into text to be displayed. The files you save (and the information in the files) remain on the disk indefinitely unless you delete them. Information in memory, by contrast, lasts only as long as the machine is on and the program using that memory is running. When the program terminates, that memory is freed for other processes. When the machine is turned off, all the information in memory is lost.

State and Its Representation

In an ordinary digital computer, memory is measured in bytes. It is common, in 2005, for machines to have a gigabyte of memory, or 2^{30} bytes. Each byte is composed of 8 bits, and is just enough memory to hold a single letter. As you have likely heard, all information in a digital computer is comprised of ones and zeros; since there are two possible values, it is called *binary*. A single **binary digit** is called a *bit*. Memory is a long sequence of numbered locations, each of which can hold one byte. The good news is, when programming in Java, you will almost never need to deal directly with bits, bytes, or memory locations.

You will, however, need to understand that information in your program is stored in variables, which are associated with particular locations in memory, and that a particular variable may take on different values at different times. The current value of a variable is referred to as its "state." This is an ordinary use of the word *state*, but perhaps not a common one. If it seems confusing, you might think of the "state of a light bulb" (i.e., either on or off), or the "State of the Union."

Definition of Algorithm

A program is an algorithm written in a particular programming language. That's fine, but what's an algorithm?

Rough definition: An algorithm is a step-by-step description of a process to solve a problem.

Thus a recipe is, roughly, an algorithm. It lists the various ingredients that should be added and in what order, and the cooking or baking process. Most recipes are not quite algorithms because they require judgment to carry out correctly.

Better definition: An algorithm is a step-by-step description of a process to solve a problem or a class of problems, where each step is described explicitly and requires no judgment.

The reason why many recipes do not fit this definition is that they include directions such as, "Bake until done," or "Cook until just tender." While any experienced cook understands these instructions, the cook must exercise judgment to follow them. People do this very well, but computers do not.

Therefore, when presented with a problem to be solved by a program, a programmer's job is first to formulate an algorithm, which will solve that problem. The second job is to convert the algorithm into a programming language, so that it can be executed (i.e., carried out) by a computer.

Action! The Only Three Statements That Do Anything

The remainder of this book concerns techniques that allow you to solve problems and implement algorithms in Java. There are several hundred pages explaining control structure, class structure, objects, expressions, methods and data structures. Oddly, in spite of all that, only three actions actually accomplish anything. Input statements and assignment statements change the state (or value) of variables, and output statements send information out of the program (usually for a human to read). That's it, three things—input, assignment, and output.

> **Input statement:** Bring information into the program.
>
> **Assignment statement:** Change the information in (state of) a variable.
>
> **Output statement:** Send information out of the program.

Everything else in a program, all the hours that a programmer spends designing, coding, and debugging, only arranges for those three things to happen the right number of times and in the right order. This may seem strange, but it is true.

Structure: Everything Else

The parts of a program besides input, assignment, and output can be divided into three categories:

Control structure: Selects which statements are executed, in what order, and how many times.

Data structure: Organizes data (information) so it is more convenient to access.

Class structure: Organizes classes so they are easier to understand, modify, and work with.

These three will be the subject of much of the rest of this text.

Computing as a Revolution

Computing, viewed from the inside, is always about information: inputting information, processing information, and outputting information. Viewed from the outside, it is an exciting and revolutionary development. It is transforming our world, our ways of communicating, learning, playing, and our understanding of ourselves. The changes computing will bring are mostly in the future; the computing revolution has not properly started yet.

The Web as a New Cultural Phenomenon

Some people think of "culture" as meaning opera or art galleries. A broader meaning includes language, education, technology, and even dating. Many everyday activities are being transformed by the Web. How we shop; how we communicate with our friends, family, and coworkers; how our cars and televisions work; and how we plan and spend our time. These and more are done differently if we have an Internet connection nearby.

People Have Never Had a Tool for Processing Information Before

We are only just beginning to learn how to use computing. Nothing is settled yet. The leading hardware and software producers come out with updates monthly. However, the way we deal with information has been changed forever. A good example is Google™. It sends bots out to collect information in the dead of night (i.e., when the Internet is not so busy), and then catalogs and indexes it so when people type queries it can respond quickly and direct them to relevant Web sites. If you're used to Google, this may seem like no big deal—but it is. Search engines and the Web allow information to be disseminated orders of magnitude faster. Even research scientists use search engines instead of spending long hours in libraries searching for paper copies of research articles. What will this mean for our culture? Who can say? However, it will certainly change it.

Automated Reasoning and Process

Computing also allows us to study process. A program is a mechanization of information processing. Before computers existed, information processing was only done by people (and other natural systems). In the short time that mechanical computers have existed, we have just begun to learn about process—who knows what the future will bring?

Artificial Intelligence?

Artificial intelligence is an exciting and alarming possibility. Might intelligent machines replace us all? There have been many projects starting in the 1950s to build programs to do language understanding, automatic translation, scene analysis, and more recently, build autonomous vehicles. Thus far, successes have been extremely limited. Computers are everywhere, they are blindingly fast and never forget, but they have *no* intelligence. Nevertheless, clever programmers can make them do some amazing things.

One reason why artificial intelligence is so difficult is that while computers can add numbers millions of times a second, and store and access millions of facts or rules without ever forgetting even one, they do not learn as people do, they do not form and apply concepts flexibly. People are the product of billions of years of evolution and we have highly developed and highly specialized information-processing capacities. Additionally, people are born with a set of unconscious patterns corresponding to important relationships and ways of thinking. Important how? Evolutionarily. Certain ways of processing information are more adaptive than others are, and all our ancestors survived long enough and did the right things to have and raise children. Our fascination with sex and violence is not accidental, and neither is our love for children. Our abilities to communicate with metaphors, to ascribe meaning, and to discern pattern in noise are beyond the reach of any computer yet programmed.

The enterprise of attempting to create intelligence in a digital computer has been likened to trying to climb a tree to the moon. Early, preliminary attempts seem to yield good progress, but eventually, frustrating impasses always seem to loom, and eventually the project is abandoned. Everyone knows you cannot climb a tree to the moon, whereas whether a digital computer could have intelligence remains to be seen.

Societal Impacts

Our culture is changing in many ways because of computing; here are just three examples.

Around the middle of the second millennium, kingdoms arose in Europe. In the days before computing, to raise an army to make war on your neighbors, or defend yourself from them, required first assembling a bureaucracy. A small army of clerks and functionaries was needed to coordinate the calling up, feeding, housing, and supplying of any army. This meant that to wage war, a ruler had to enlist or compel the cooperation of many civilians. Nowadays, one person with a $1,000 machine plus access to appropriate databases and software could coordinate much of that without assistance. Will this change warfare? Has it already? Look around. Watch and see.

Many Americans put a premium on their privacy. Americans hate the idea of anyone compiling and/or selling data about them without their permission and cherish the notion of relative anonymity in transactions on the Web. However, the nature of computing and the Web means that privacy is essentially an illusion. If you send e-mail across the country, there are copies of it on at least several mail servers; worse, there are logs. Admittedly, only system administrators can access them, but if there were a reason to, they could.

Uninformed people may imagine that you can do things anonymously on the Web. It is true that your personal identity is hidden, but where you are sitting and your ISP are definitely not a secret. If they were, there would be no way for the Web server you are receiving information from to send it to you. Even though you can't see them, there are servers and routers relaying the packets across the planet to your screen; and they are all logging all the transactions, just in case someone needs to find out who was accessing what.

Some people predict a collapse of traditional brick and mortar commerce. As more and more goods are sold over the Web, there will be less and less need for physical stores. Of course, there will always be stores, but perhaps soon there will be considerably fewer of them.

THE PAST: A VERY BRIEF HISTORY OF COMPUTING

Although it is not strictly necessary to know the history of computing before learning to program, there are some interesting perspectives one may develop by doing so. Therefore, this brief history.

Living in Scaffolding—A Cautionary Tale

A cathedral took many years to build. Imagine building a gigantic stone structure without power tools. Huge blocks of stone, high walls of stone. To place a block of stone on a wall, you must first lift it up and then set it in place, making sure it fits tightly. This requires solid, strong, more or less permanent scaffolding.

It was common for the workers to construct living quarters in the lower levels of the scaffolding (alongside the already completed walls). Perhaps this was simply a convenient place to build a shelter to cook for the workers, and for the workers to eat during inclement weather. As years turned into decades and the walls (and the vacated scaffolding next to them) grew higher, it was simply easier for the families of the workers to take up residence there. As decades turned to centuries, and construction was interrupted by wars or plagues, people were born, grew, raised children, and died, living in the scaffolding, knowing no other life. There were even cases where the original project was abandoned and the workers settled into the scaffolding as a permanent residence.

There is a danger, in any endeavor, that temporary measures, adopted as a means to an end, remain in effect for so long that practitioners no longer remember that they were not the goal of the project. This is not, generally, a good situation. Digital computers are a case in point.

Why Are We Still Using This Prototype?

This text will emphasize generic problem-solving principles, in addition to Java programming. These principles will be used in service of programming, but will typically be applicable to many other areas. The phrase "problem solving" is used in a special sense here. It is the activity that people engage in when they are trying to accomplish something and run into a problem that stops them. These problem-solving principles are for when you *don't* know how to cope with a problem. Here's the first (and perhaps the most general).

Problem Solving Principle #1: Build a Prototype

When attempting to solve a difficult problem, first build a prototype that solves a similar yet simpler or smaller problem. This is useful for several reasons. If you're stuck on a problem, sometimes a smaller or simpler version of the same problem will be easy. In addition, sometimes the reason a problem stops you is that you've never thought carefully about anything like it. The cognitive structure you generate by solving the simpler version sometimes allows you to see through the more complex problem.

Here's a problem that will perhaps stop you. Assume there are 32 people in a classroom. Each person is asked whether he has ever been snowboarding. Each comes to the desk at the front of the room, and writes his answer on a piece of paper; the first on the first line, the second on the second line, and so on. How many possible different sequences of yeses and noes are there? Perhaps you've been studying combinatorics and know the answer—if not, read on. What's the smallest we could make the problem? How many people? Right, one. One person can write one of two things—yes or no—so there are two possible sequences (if you can call one thing a sequence). The good thing about solving a problem with one thing instead of *n* things is that it is usually trivial. The bad thing is that it may not tell you much.

So, try two people. The first can write either yes or no; then, the second can write either yes or no. If the first person writes yes, the possible pairs are {yes, yes} and {yes, no}. If the first person writes no, the possible pairs are {no, yes} and {no, no}—four total.

The trick now is to generalize to *n* people, or in this case, 32. For one person, the answer was two, for two people it was four—can you discern the pattern? Commit to a pattern, and then see if it is true for three people. Here's how to do the analysis for three.

As we just saw, for the first two people there were four possible states of the list:

1. {yes, yes}
2. {yes, no}
3. {no, yes}
4. {no, no}

The third person can either add yes or no, giving these possibilities (the third person's answer is in **bold**):

1. {yes, yes, **yes**}
2. {yes, yes, **no**}
3. {yes, no, **yes**}
4. {yes, no, **no**}
5. {no, yes, **yes**}
6. {no, yes, **no**}
7. {no, no, **yes**}
8. {no, no, **no**}

There are twice as many possibilities as with two people. Therefore, the number of possible states is not twice the number of people, but rather, it starts at two and *doubles* with each additional yes or no added to the list. Thus, you can see the answer with 32 people is, 2*2*2*2...*2, 32 times, which is written 2^{32} (that's somewhat more than 4 billion). Remember this number, 2^{32}, and how it was derived; you will meet it again later.

Von Neumann's Prototype

Most digital computers we use are said to use the "von Neumann architecture." John von Neumann was among the designers of the first working digital computers; his name is attached to them because he took the time to write and publish the ideas that would lead to working computers. The second example of building a prototype of a system involves the digital computer. In the 1930s, von Neumann set out to build a thinking machine. Since the only things we know of that think are brains, he decided to study brain function first (an eminently reasonable idea). He concluded that brains had both analog and digital properties, and considered designing a machine with both. A digital machine would have elements with digital values—in binary, either 0 or 1. An analog machine might have elements with values that ranged between 0 and 1, where 0 represents all the way off, 1 all the way on, 0.5 half way on, 0.75 three quarters on, and so on. He started trying to settle on the details of this thinking machine, and found himself stuck on how to implement the analog portion. The way he conceptualized it, the accuracy of the analog portions was going to be so poor that a digital implementation seemed better and cheaper. Therefore, he decided to build a strictly digital machine first; namely, one with only two states: 0 and 1—a binary computer.

It turned out that even this simpler machine was not trivial to implement, but with time and persistence, they got it to work. Von Neumann died before he constructed an analog computer, or even started working on making a computer think—and here we are living in the scaffolding. Perhaps mechanical intelligence will require analog computers. We shall see.

Evolution of Computing

The rate of evolution in computing is astounding and is changing so rapidly for a number of reasons: a) it is new, b) hardware is improving rapidly, c) software is improving rapidly, and d) more and more people are getting involved, both as users and as programmers. Any human endeavor at its inception evolves rapidly. Early, simple, clumsy, poorly conceived systems give way to more sophisticated, better-debugged, easier-to-use systems.

Hardware

In the 60 years in which computing has existed, computers have been utterly transformed. Early computers were made with relays and vacuum tubes, like very old radios and televisions. The invention of the transistor allowed a truly digital device. The first transistors were hand-made, large, and were mounted on circuit boards and wired together. Soon, hundreds of tiny transistors were being packaged on a chip; these were called "integrated circuits" (ICs) and were mounted on similar boards. For example, in a 1960s computer, the central processing unit (CPU), or processor, which does the arithmetic and logic, was a board perhaps 18-inches square, packed with chips on one side and festooned with more wires than you'd want to count on the other. Before long, tens of thousands of transistors were being packed into a chip, a technique then called very large scale integration (VLSI). One day, someone managed to pack all the functionality for a CPU onto one chip, and the age of the microprocessor began.

A microprocessor can run much faster than any processor spread out on a board for one simple reason: the information in the processor has a shorter distance to travel. Several facts will help illuminate this. Electrical signals travel at about $0.6c$, where c is the speed of light (approximately 3×10^{10} cm/sec). Modern processors commonly have clock speeds of 4GHz or more. A clock speed of 1GHz means the clock ticks a billion times a second, the time from one tick to another is a billionth of a second, a nanosecond. Light travels about a foot in a nanosecond. Therefore, if components of the CPU were one foot apart, there is no way a signal could get from one to the other in time for the next clock cycle. That would slow down the processor. Thus, every modern processor is a microprocessor and every modern computer is a microcomputer.

Education, Language, and Culture

In spite of that, there are books and people who still talk about "mainframes." Some out-of-date (but still in publication) books include typologies of computers—including mainframes, mid-sized computers, mini-computers, and micro-computers—as if it is a spectrum from large and powerful to small and not, when the reverse is typically true. Why is this?

This is a characteristic of the slow evolution of culture and language. Language in a rapidly changing culture lags behind the phenomena it describes. An example is "floppy disks" as the name of 3-inch removable disks. They replaced the 5-inch removable disks, which were actually flexible (i.e., floppy). Another computing example is random access memory, or RAM, the main memory in computers. It was called "random access" because it supplanted tape memory, which was strictly "serial access." If the information you needed was on the other end of the tape, you had to wait for it to rewind; before there was RAM, memory was mostly serial, on tape. In time, the language will catch up—assuming computing stops changing so quickly.

Software: Programming the Hardware

As hardware has evolved, so has software. Software is the programs that control the hardware. It is pure information, the stuff of dreams, and seemingly as difficult to control. The first computers were programmed and debugged by physically connecting and reconnecting wires to components. The reason was that there was no memory to store the programs. Once memory was invented (tape, and then RAM), programs were written in binary, the machine language that the processor could execute directly. Each tiny instruction for the processor was laboriously entered by setting toggle switches (right, before keyboards). Even the simplest programs were very long and tedious to debug; there were no screens. Later, paper tape, card punches, and card readers made it possible to type programs, store them, and feed them in as many times as necessary.

Programming in machine code is laborious and unbelievably slow. Before long, some enterprising systems programmer wrote a symbolic assembler that eliminated some of the mind-numbing tedium. Assume the add instruction, in machine code, were 2; to add the number at location 143, you might write 2143. An assembler allows the programmer to move a little away from machine code, and write "add 143" instead. (Note: 2, 3, and 4 are not binary digits; the actual binary instruction would have looked more like 0010000101000011.)

Assembly code is not much fun, and is grossly inefficient to write. Once programmers had good assemblers, they realized they could write compilers. Compilers input some higher level language (like Fortran or C) and output assembly code. The assembly code then goes into the assembler, which emits machine code.

Fortran and C were great advances over assembly code, but before long, more powerful languages were invented. There are functional languages, database languages, logic languages, and object languages (among others). C++ was an early object language based on C++, and Java is a later language based on C. It was designed for programming on the Web, and eliminates some of the shortcomings of C++. There will be many other new languages as time goes on. Perhaps you will design one.

Why It's Not Quite That Simple

Perhaps you noticed that the distinction between hardware and software was not quite as clean as it might be. Hardware is something you can hold in your hand, but software is information. However, plugging and unplugging wires was the first example of software, and wires are definitely physical; although their arrrangement encodes information.

People like to create simple categories: hardware/software, us/them, nature/nurture. However, things are often not quite so simple. A hundred years ago a debate raged over how much of what animals (including people) do is determined by genetics and how much by experience. The blank slate faction said it was all experience; the instinct school claimed it was mostly built in; some cooler heads argued it was about 50/50. Now, most everyone knows that a better answer is 100/100—what we become is determined by our genetic heritage *and* our experiences. To neglect either would be a mistake.

The hardware/software dichotomy is also murky. It is possible to bake programs into silicon; there are hardware Java chips. Processors have microcode inside that governs their functions. It is even possible to build virtual machines, software simulations of hardware. Perhaps the most revolutionary aspect of Java is the Java virtual machine (JVM), which requires a bit of explanation.

The Java Virtual Machine

Different computers have different processors. For a program to run on a particular machine, it must first be translated into the machine code of the processor on that machine. Thus, if you have a program that must run on a dozen different CPUs, it must first be translated into a dozen different "binary" files. When a new CPU is invented, the program must be retranslated for that CPU. If you hope to distribute a program across the Web, having to retranslate a program for every computer is a major chore.

This problem is solved in Java by the introduction of an intermediate form, byte code. *Byte code* is a machine-independent form that runs on the JVM. The JVM for a particular machine knows how to interpret byte code and execute instructions on that machine to accomplish what the programmer intended. Once a Java program is compiled into byte code and distributed, it can then be run on any machine that has a JVM installed. The JVM must still be written for every type of processor, but it's a huge improvement to only distribute one program instead of every program.

JUGGLING

An instructor at this university juggles on the first day of his introductory programming courses. It's not quite the same, but you can watch him juggle if you go to *www.willamette.edu/~levenick/juggle/juggle.avi*. Programming is like juggling in that you can't learn to do it by watching. If you've been juggling for many years, you can easily keep three balls in the air for long periods of time without dropping them. You already know how, so it's easy. If you're trying to juggle for the first time, you will drop the balls often. If, each time you miss one, you curse yourself, or the ball, or think to yourself, "I'm just no good at juggling," you are not helping yourself learn. The appropriate response is, "Oops! Missed!" and then pick up the balls and keep practicing.

Programming is similar in that almost every program has mistakes initially; these are called *bugs*. Only novice programmers imagine that any nontrivial program will be right the first time. Experienced programmers make fewer mistakes than neophytes do, but they expect them and are better at finding them (having done it before). When you run into bugs, getting angry or imagining it reflects on you personally doesn't help you learn to program. It's normal for programs to have bugs, especially initially. However, after you've practiced for a few dozen hours, you will drop the balls far less frequently, and understand that it is a natural part of learning.

Learning to Program

Programming is also rather like writing, in many respects. They both are creative, iterative processes without any one correct way. They both have syntax (grammar) and semantics (meaning), and grammatical errors can obscure the meaning in either. Of course, no one reads programs for pleasure; on the other hand, novels do not deliver e-mail or control automated factories.

There are many different ways to teach Java programming. Some books still start by teaching the old C constructs, and only introduce user-defined classes after 6 or 10 weeks. Modern approaches introduce classes earlier. This text begins with classes and adds a cognitive component. A programming environment always includes a programmer; teachers and students of programming ignore the characteristics of programmers (and in particular, novice programmers) at their peril. Good software development methodology minimizes cognitive overhead, and thus leaves the programmer, at whatever level of expertise, with enough cognitive capacity to solve the problems that will inevitably arise—this is especially important for beginners.

Learning to program is not easy. The first several weeks can be especially frustrating. Fortunately, after five or six weeks, when you have mastered the basics of input, output, classes, and calculation, the ability to make a machine do what you want it to balances out the initial difficulty of doing so.

One of the reasons programming is difficult initially is one must learn so many details before one can construct even the simplest program. There are a number of facts and concepts (a few dozen) that one must grasp before programming begins to make sense—unfortunately, they are all interrelated, and understanding (or explaining) one requires understanding (or explaining) the rest. Therefore, at first, the whole enterprise can seem hopelessly confusing and sometimes daunting. However, with patience, persistence, and practice, you can surmount this obstacle; and once you learn to program, it can be very rewarding and remunerative. If, given these cautions, you wish to continue, read on!

The Approach Used Here: Less Is More; More Is Less

Computing is different from other fields. First, it is brand new. Mathematics, rhetoric, psychology, physics, and philosophy are thousands of years old. The first digital computer (which was as big as a house and less powerful than a modern-day low-end calculator) was developed in the 1940s. Java was released in 1995 (by Sun

Microsystems). It extends the old C language from the 1970s. Computing is evolving at an unheard of pace. Better hardware makes possible better software; better software allows programmers to build even better software; as programmers mature who have been educated in the new paradigms, they can invent even better paradigms. The synergy between faster, cheaper hardware, better programming tools, and better educated programmers will transform our lives.

Second, because computing is so new, there is no consensus on how to teach it. In biology, mathematics, or any of the long established disciplines, introductory courses have been taught to millions of students over the past 100 years or so. As a result, these disciplines have well-entrenched examples and excellent textbooks, tested on class after class after class. Some Java textbooks, by contrast, are rewritings of C++ textbooks. Others are a hodgepodge of hints and techniques. It's not that computer scientists don't know how to write, it's more that there hasn't been time, and it's not yet clear how to help people learn to program well in Java.

This text takes a different approach: less is more and more is less. Less is more, in that many extraneous details of Java are best avoided in the beginning, so the student can focus on what really matters. On the other hand, it is imperative that students begin by learning to write classes, even though this is difficult until they grasp a certain set of basics. Therefore, even though it is not easy to learn to write classes, that's where we will start; this seems like more, but in fact, after a few chapters there will be much less to learn later. Let's get to it!

CONCLUSION

This brief introduction to programming, computing, culture, and human nature introduced many of the themes that run throughout this text. With any luck, it has whetted your appetite for an introduction to Java programming, which follows immediately.

2 Programming the Simplest Java Programs

INTRODUCTION

This chapter introduces the structure of Java programs through several examples. It also presents an important problem-solving technique: learning how to define problems so you deal with the essentials instead of becoming hopelessly mired with nonessential issues. In this spirit, the examples are presented without complete explanations of the intricacies of every component; a thorough presentation is deferred until Chapter 5, "Toward Consistent Classes." This is done for two reasons: first, it is more interesting to write programs and see them work than it is to memorize long lists of details; and second, it is much easier to understand the details of a programming language after you have had some experience working with it.

Learning to Program

Once, a traveling salesperson was driving down a country road and spied a pair of coveralled legs protruding, unmoving, from under a gigantic combine. Concerned for the well-being of this prostrate farmer, she stopped her car, hopped the fence, walked up to him, and asked, "Are you okay?" "Yep, just trying to fix this combine," he replied. The salesperson studied the bewildering complexity of gears, levers, hydraulics, and wires for a moment, and then asked, "How did you learn to fix such a complicated thing?" "Don't know a thing about fixing 'em," he replied. "Then how on earth do you expect to be able to fix it?" "Well..." drawled the farmer, "...I figure a person made it."

A programming environment is a little like that combine. It is composed of many interacting parts, and at first, it certainly looks like you might never figure it out. However, once you learn how, programming is easy, and fun. Learning to program may seem a daunting task. To the uninitiated, the complexity may appear overwhelming, incomprehensible. Many interacting parts must be in the proper relationship before even the simplest program will work.

Like that combine, the Java language is large and complex, and very useful once you know how to use it. The old C programming language evolved into the object-based language C++ and then into Java, which resulted in some complicated syntax. If a novice programmer were required to understand everything in their first program, it might take weeks before that program could be written. To flatten the learning curve, this book uses a spiral approach. First, the essentials of Java are introduced by way of examples, and then those concepts are revisited in more detail in Chapter 5. This method will provide the understanding to accomplish many programming projects.

Learning to program in Java *is* possible. Learning to control the information-processing machine we call a computer is initially a lot of work, but can also be exciting and rewarding.

Problem Solving

"There are only two kinds of proofs in mathematics—trivial proofs and impossible proofs. The difference is that the trivial ones you already understand."
—*Freshman Calculus Prof.*

The author of this text is an experienced programmer who has written large, complex software in numerous programming languages. However, when he first uses a new programming language, he writes a tiny program that displays the single word "Greetings" on the screen. Why? The answer is simple, but difficult for some to learn. Do you know (without looking ahead) what it is? If you do, you already know one of the most important lessons of *problem solving*.

Definition of Problem Solving

Life is full of problems. You are already an expert problem solver; otherwise, you would not be where you are now, and you would not be reading this book. Problem solving (as used in this context) is different from ordinary functioning or coping. Every day, you find your way home to sleep, even if your car breaks, your bike is stolen, you've sprained your ankle, there is a traffic jam or road construction, or a train blocks the way. You deal with those problems and get home anyway, but that's mostly simple coping. Problem solving is what you do when you are stuck, when you're stopped and don't know what to do next. That's never a pleasant position to be in, but can be made more comfortable with good problem-solving skills.

Details

Fact: When you first learn to program, you get stuck frequently. Why? Because programming requires familiarity with a large number of details. Worse, when you are starting out, since you don't really understand what you are doing, that mass of details doesn't really mean anything, so there's no way to remember them all. Later, as you become familiar with the process, and develop good programming habits, dealing with many of those details will become second nature. However, initially, even though the individual details are small and not especially interesting, each must be correct for your program to work.

It's a little like when you move to a new city. At first you only know where a few places are, and getting anywhere is a mystery and takes concentration. Then you learn a few places and routes, but anytime you get off them, you are lost. In time, it becomes familiar and you don't even have to think about how to get places. But at First it's all new and confusing. Programming too. But it *does* improve.

Bugs

Errors that occur when a program runs are called *bugs*. There's a story that one early computer didn't work for days until someone discovered a dead moth between a contact. The story may be apocryphal, but the term is here to stay. An accomplished programmer has much experience solving the problems that arise in the course of programming. In other words, part of learning to program is learning to deal with bugs, both finding and fixing them (and the former is sometimes harder than the latter).

A Tool Kit for Solving Problems

This text includes a number of problem-solving techniques. Some of these are specific to programming in Java, but the majority are more generic. Think of these techniques as tools. If you learn these techniques, then when you confront problems, both programming and otherwise, you may feel better prepared—as if you've acquired a toolbox of useful problem-solving methods.

A Problem-Solving Exercise

Almost everyone has been exposed to the Pythagorean Theorem: in a right triangle, the square of the hypotenuse is equal to the sum of the squares of the other two sides. Consider Figure 2.1 as a circle centered at the origin, together with a rectangle inscribed in the upper right quadrant. The radius of the circle is r. The height of the rectangle is x. The question is, what is h? If you knew the width of the rectangle, you could use the Pythagorean Theorem, but all you know is the radius, r. Try to figure out h, but don't spend more than a few minutes on it. The answer appears later in the chapter.

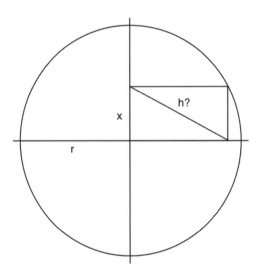

FIGURE 2.1   The radius, r, and the height of the rectangle, x, are known. What is h?

The Two Types of Java Programs: Applications and Applets

Java programs are either applets or applications, and each has unique capabilities.

Applets

Applets are programs that can run in Web browsers and are commonly used to add functionality to Web pages. When you use the Web, you will sometimes see the message "Starting Java" in the lower left corner of the screen. It is very convenient to be able to execute Java Applets from Web pages; indeed, Applets were designed for this purpose. However, there is a problem. When you go to someone's page and an `Applet` starts running, it is running on your machine. If there were no safeguards, this program could be damaging your computing system, or stealing all the information from your disk. To avoid this possibility (and thus to convince people to allow `Applets` to start up in browsers), Java has a Security Manager that limits what `Applets` are allowed to do. The most important things that `Applets` cannot do are reading and writing files on your local computer, and opening *sockets* to communicate with other machines.

Applications

Applications run independently, and do not depend on a browser (although they do require a Java Virtual Machine (JVM) to be installed). They cannot be embedded in a Web page. However, they are not prohibited from file I/O, or opening `Sockets`; they are full-fledged programs.

Components of a Java Program

What are Java programs made of? Abstractly, a program is a series of symbols that conforms to the grammatical rules (also called *synta*) of a particular programming language.

One of the big advantages of object-oriented programming is that code is reusable. *Packages* allow you to easily import classes that other people have written into your program. These classes include input/output mechanisms (to move information into and out of programs), mathematical functions, screen control, and many other things.

Class declarations include both memory declarations (which declare variables to store information) and method declarations. Method declarations explicate how members of a class respond to the messages of the same name. A useful metaphor is to think of the objects in a program as actors, and methods are the *scripts* the actors will read when they get cues (messages). The *main method* is the main script for an Application.

A Template for Every Java Main Method

Every Java Application must have a method named "main," which will be executed when the program runs. The `main()` method must have the structure shown in Listing 2.1.

LISTING 2.1   Pattern for every `Main` method.

```
1    public static void main (String [] args) {
2        General Declarations
```

```
3        Statements
4    }
```

When your program runs, it executes each line in the main() method from the top down. The general declarations may create objects and the statements may send them messages. After the last statement is executed and the closing } is reached, the main() method, and thus the application, is terminated.

Formatting

In this text, Java class names, variables, and methods are printed in Courier font to make them visually distinctive, like main() in the previous paragraph. Methods are followed by ()s, and class names start with capital letters.

EXAMPLES

This section has three examples: 1) the simplest possible Application, a robot greeter; 2) a slightly elaborated version of that, a personalized greeter; and 3) a very simple Applet.

The First Example of a Class—A Robot Greeter

Imagine you have decided to build a robot. Before going to all the work and expense of buying and assembling the motors and gears and whatnot, you wisely choose to simulate a prototype first. You decide to write a Greeter class that (recalling the previous problem-solving advice) initially does nothing but say "Greetings!" Listing 2.2 shows this code.

LISTING 2.2 A program to output "Greetings!"

```java
public class Greeter {
    public static void main (String [] args) {
        System.out.println("Greetings!");
    }
}
```

This program has only one class, Greeter, with only the main() method whose heading reads public static void main(String [] args).

That's a mouthful. Think of it as an incantation for now, like "abracadabra!" Like any language, Java contains a number of *idioms*, sequences of symbols whose meaning cannot be derived from the individual symbols, but must be learned as a whole, by rote.

This program is not particularly useful. The only reason for it is to help you learn to define classes in a simple setting where you can easily focus your attention on the essentials (which is the reason why experienced programmers write a greetings program first).

Problem Solving Technique: Build a Protootype
Create a prototype before attempting any difficult project.

If there are too many details, too many parts, too many things to keep in mind, sometimes making the problem smaller or simpler will allow you to solve it and then adapt that solution to the larger problem.

Here is the explanation of Listing 2.2 (reproduced here).

LISTING 2.2   (repris).

```
1    public class Greeter {
2        public static void main (String [] args) {
3            System.out.println("Greetings!");
4        }
5    }
```

This is the Greeter class declaration.

Line 1: Every class declaration begins with the word class. After class comes an *identifier*, the name of the class being declared. *Identifiers* must begin with a capital letter and be composed only of letters, numbers, and underscores. The name of the class is Greeter.

Lines 1–4: Next comes a pair of curly brackets containing a list of the memory and methods of this class. Here there is no memory and only one method, main(). Every Application you write must have a main() method, and that method must have the exact heading on line 2.

Line 2: public static void main (String [] args) is the heading of the main method. For now, consider this an idiom or an incantation.

Line 3: The "body," or script, of the main() method follows that heading. Like the script of every method, it is enclosed in {}s. The main script for a Greeter consists of the single line: System.out.println("Greetings!");. This is an idiom meaning, display the literal string of characters "Greetings!" on the screen.

Running Your Program

Run this program before proceeding. If you are using this book in the context of a class, your instructor will likely have explained how to do that. If you are using it in another context, now is the time to consult with an expert, or take the time to do the tutorial, or read the documentation for the Java environment you are using. Assuming you are using NetBeans, consult Appendix A, "Getting Started with Net-Beans and the Greetings Program" for instructions.

If you have never programmed, once you have compiled and run this tiny program, you will have taken a big first step. Before long, it should take a minute to do. Unfortunately, you must learn many little things, so the first time may take much longer, but should not take more than an hour. If you spend an entire hour without success, find someone to assist you.

Speaking of solving puzzles, here's a clue: The two diagonals of a rectangle are equal. Now do you know what h is (in the previous section titled "A Problem-Solving Exercise")? Sorry about the Pythagorean misdirection; the point was that how you look at a problem may determine how difficult it is to solve. If you were determined to calculate the width of the rectangle, you were doomed from the start. This is an instance of the following problem-solving technique.

Problem Solving Technique: Adopt a Different Perspective
How difficult a problem is depends on how you look at it. A problem that seems impossible from one angle sometimes is trivial from another.

Mechanics: Typing and Running Your Code

Whatever system you are using, there are three steps to running a program:

1. **Creating source files:** The Java code in the boxes is called "source code" when it is stored in a file that is called a "source file." NetBeans writes the shell of your classes for you. Since the source code declares a public class called Greeter, Java insists that it be stored in a file called Greeter.java. In addition, you must remember that case matters. If you type PUBLIC static void main, it will object. If you type (string[] args), it will not know what string is; it only understands String.
2. **Invoking the compiler:** Before your program can run, it must be converted into byte code; that is the task of the compiler after it checks the syntax.
3. **Executing the program:** If your code compiles without errors, you can then execute it. When you choose Project/Execute, NetBeans compiles and executes your code.

If you have not done so, adjourn to the keyboard to create and run this robot greeter program. Then, mysteriously you will have crossed the divide and can be labeled a "programmer"—writing (or even modifying) a class is something 99 percent of the people on this planet have never done. If your program had/has many errors, you might turn to the "What Could Go Wrong" section toward the end of the chapter for hints.

The Second Example of a Class—A Personalized RobotGreeter

This section presents a class that is able to say "Greetings, Spike!" or "Greetings, Buffy!" or "Greetings, whomever!" depending on whom you ask it to greet.

Most Java applications have a class with a main() method and little else. The main() method creates one or more objects and sends them messages; these objects and classes do the work of the program. This example, and the rest in this text, will have a class that only exists to interface with the outside world.

A Prototype

As you may recall, if a system is complex, build a prototype first; after that works, then (and only then) elaborate it. Listing 2.3 is a prototype with the desired structure that always says "Greetings!" (just like the last example).

LISTING 2.3 Prototype personalized RobotGreeter class with Main driver program.

```
1    class PersonalGreeter {
2        public static void sayHi() {
3            System.out.println("Greetings!");
4        }
5    }
6
7    public class RobotGreeter {
8        public static void main (String [] args) {
9            PersonalGreeter.sayHi();
10       }
11   }
```

Notice that the PersonalGreeter sayHi() method does exactly what the old main() method did, it displays "Greetings!" on the screen by using the idiom System.out.println("Greetings!");

There are two classes in Listing 2.3, described next.

LISTING 2.3   (repris) `PersonalGreeter` class definition.

```
1    class PersonalGreeter {
2        public static void sayHi() {
3            System.out.println("Greetings!");
4        }
5    }
```

Line 1: The `PersonalGreeter` class heading. Notice that identifiers consisting of more than one word have the first letter of the second and subsequent words capitalized.

Lines 1–5: Next comes a *block* (a pair of curly brackets and what's between them). Notice how similar it is to the `Greeter` class.

Line 2: Begins the `sayHi()` method. Unlike the `main()` method, here there is nothing in the ( ) s.

Line 3: The "body," or script, of the `sayHi()` method follows this heading. Again, like the script of every method, it is enclosed in {}s.

LISTING 2.3   (repris) `RobotGreeter` class definition.

```
7     public class RobotGreeter {
8         public static void main (String [] args) {
9             PersonalGreeter.sayHi();
10        }
11    }
```

Line 9: Sends the `sayHi()` message to the `PersonalGreeter` class. Recall that information processing in Java is accomplished by sending messages. You can tell that sayHi ( ) is a message by the ( ) s.

This prototype can only respond to one message, and its response is always to say "Greetings!" This program is useful to convince yourself that you can write a class and make it do something. (You did type in that program and test it, didn't you? If not, it's time to go to the screen and modify your previous program; just change it to be the same as Listing 2.3. Remember, programming is like juggling; can't really learn by watching, can't really learn by reading.

Elaborating the Prototype Personalized Greeter

Welcome back. Finally, let's elaborate our prototype to make it capable of greeting various people. The question, as always, is, "How best to accomplish that?" Usually, there is more than one way to approach a program. We could add a bunch of methods like sayHiToSpike() and sayHiToBuffy(), but with the use of *parameters* we could add a single method that could greet whomever we wanted it to. Listing 2.4 does just that. It is an extension of the previous listing; the changes are in **bold**, And the rest is unchanged.

LISTING 2.4   PersonalizedGreeter class and driver.

```
1    class PersonalGreeter {
2        public static void sayHi(String who) {
3            System.out.println("Greetings " + who + "!");
4        }
5    }
6
7    public class Driver {
8        public static void main (String [] args) {
9            PersonalGreeter.sayHi("Spike");
10           PersonalGreeter.sayHi("Buffy");
11       }
12   }
```

Line 1: There is no public in front of class. Java only allows one public class per file.

TIP

Free Advice
Although the access modifier —public, private, *and* protected—*are valuable in complex programs, if you simply omit them, nothing will go wrong at this stage. Feel free to leave them out for now (assuming your instructor concurs).*

The two lines that are changed in the main method both send the PersonalGreeter class the sayHi message, first with the parameter "Spike", and then with the parameter "Buffy". When the parameter is "Spike", this message causes the PersonalGreeter to display "Greetings Spike!" and when the parameter is "Buffy", it displays "Greetings Buffy!" The next section explains Strings and parameter passing; for now, it is enough to remember that things in parentheses after message names are parameters.

Quick question: How could you modify this program to greet other people?

The String Type

You will often work with literal strings of characters, like "Java" or "Hello world!" There is a class in Java called String, which is designed for just that. (Notice the capital S in String; String is the name of a class.)

DETAILS

Perhaps you are not in the mood to take on much more detail, but would rather come back and grapple with it later. That's fine. If you'd rather skip ahead to run Listing 2.4 first, feel free to do so (it's in the paragraph titled "Running the Personalized Robot Greeter" later in the chapter).

LISTING 2.4 (repris) The sayHi(String) method in the PersonalGreeter class.

```
1   class PersonalGreeter {
2       public static void sayHi(String who) {
3           System.out.println("Greetings " + who + "!");
4       }
```

Line 2: The heading for the sayHi() method. It includes the access type (public), a return type (void), the name of the method (sayHi), and a parameter (String who) enclosed in parentheses. This says that the PersonalGreeter class will respond to a sayHi() message that has a String parameter. The static after public says that this is a class method.

Line 3: The body of the sayHi method is a single message, println(String), which is sent to System.out (the screen). There is one parameter with three parts:

1. The String "Greetings "
2. The value of the parameter named who
3. The String "!";

Java treats the plus sign after a String as the *concatenation* operator, so it pastes those three things together to make a single String—"Greetings ????!"—where the ???? is the value of the String parameter passed with the sayHi(String) message.

USING PARAMETERS TO PASS INFORMATION TO A METHOD

Every time PersonalGreeter follows this script, it will display "Greetings" and "!". However, the value of the parameter, who, may be different each time the script is followed. "Greetings" and "!" are inside double quotes and so are String literals; they will be displayed literally. In contrast, who is not in double quotes, so it will not display the letters 'w'-'h'-'o', but rather the current value of the parameter named who. The value of who will be whatever string was in the parentheses where the sayHi(String) message was sent to the PersonalGreeter object. There is no way to tell what that value might be without looking there.

LISTING 2.4   (repris) The Driver class that sends PersonalGreeter the sayHi(String) twice.

```
7    public class Driver {
8        public static void main (String [] args) {
9            PersonalGreeter.sayHi("Spike");
10           PersonalGreeter.sayHi("Buffy");
11       }
12   }
```

Line 9: Sends the sayHi(String) message to PersonalGreeter with the String parameter "Spike". To repeat, this will cause the PersonalGreeter to follow (or, in technical terms, "execute") the sayHi(String) method (script), using "Spike" as the value of the String parameter named who. Thus, inside the sayHi(String) method in PersonalGreeter, "Greetings " + who + "!" will turn into "Greetings Spike!" and be sent to System.out as the parameter with the println(String) message, and thus will end up on the screen. Many small steps; the good news is that the computer carries them out tirelessly.

Line 10: Exactly the same, but with the parameter value "Buffy". Line 10 was explained very slowly; ordinarily, one might say instead: "Line 9: Sends the sayHi() message to myGreeter with the parameter "Spike"." And, to an experienced Java programmer, myGreeter.sayHi("Spike") means exactly that, and requires no explanation.

A DIGRESSION

If you have never programmed before, there are a number of new concepts in the previous example. If you did not understand it, read it again. Type it in. Get it to work. Now, read it again. Hopefully, it will make more sense. If it still doesn't, don't panic! Many concepts in any discipline cannot be grasped until you have had a certain amount of experience. When experienced programmers are trying to learn a new computer system or language, they read the entire manual or language description; it normally only takes four or five hours. Since they know little or nothing about how to use the new system or language, they can't understand much of what they read; thus, whenever they lose the thread and can't understand what they are reading, they just skip to the next section. Then they go and play with the system or language for a few days or weeks, inventing little problems to solve. This inevitably leads to numerous unsolved mysteries and frustrations. Then, they reread the manual. This second reading is often very illuminating, as now they know something of the system and have a number of questions they want to answer.

Learning to program takes time. In addition, you will find a complete explanation of parameters in Chapter 5. For now, patient reader, please put aside your reservations and proceed on the assumption that everything will become clearer shortly.

RUNNING THE PERSONALIZED ROBOT GREETER

Before reading on, go to a computer. Input and run this example (or quicker, modify the Greeter class, but remember if your class is called Foo, it must be stored in a file called Foo.java). In NetBeans, you can change the name of the class by right-clicking on it in the Filesystems pane (on the left) and selecting Rename.

After that works, insert your name and the names of several friends for the robot to greet, and then compile and run it again.

Third Example–A Minimal Applet

This example, the simplest possible class that extends Applet, illustrates the power of inheritance, and shows how to do graphics in the context of an Applet.

THE POWER OF INHERITANCE

The second kind of Java program is an applet. Instead of running independently, like applications, applets run in the context of Web pages. Thus, an applet must do a number of things to interface with the page that launches it. If you had to write the code to do those things, writing an applet would be difficult; but you don't have to. Instead, if your applet extends the built-in Java class named Applet, it can inherit all that functionality from it. Therefore, it is very easy to write small applets by extending Applet.

Object languages, like Java, allow programmers to reuse previously written classes without having to change them, or even know what is in them, by inheritance. This is a huge improvement over languages that did not allow inheritance. We cover inheritance more thoroughly in Chapter 6, "Software Reuse"; this chapter simply presents how to use it to write your own applets. Most of the details will be postponed until you have some experience running a few programs.

THE LEAST YOU CAN DO

Before writing a robot greeter applet, we will try the simplest possible `applet` *(remember, first write a prototype) as shown in Listing 2.5.

LISTING 2.5 A minimal `Applet`.

```
1    public class RobotGreeter extends java.applet.Applet {}
```

Line 1: A class declaration. It makes `RobotGreeter` extend `java.applet.Applet`; this means a `RobotGreeter` can do anything a `java.applet.Applet` can. Since there is nothing between the {}s, the `RobotGreeter` class does not add anything to, or change anything about, the `java.applet.Applet` class; it is essentially another name for that class.

You might be wondering if this class that appears to do nothing can run, or what it might do if it runs. Try it and see!

EXECUTING AN `Applet`

To run an applet ("run" is a synonym for "execute") requires four steps: 1) create the source code, 2) compile the source code to make a .class file, 3) create HTML code to start the applet, and 4) open the HTML code from a Java enabled browser. Fortunately, NetBeans handles these details for you (see the section "Creating the Simplest `Applet` in NetBeans" in Appendix A).

A GREETINGS `Applet` THAT USES A GRAPHICS CONTEXT

Now for an applet version of a robot greeter. There are a number of ways that one might make an applet that outputs `"Greetings!"` Listing 2.6 shows one way. This particular method uses `paint(Graphics)`, which is the standard method for drawing in a `Component`, and you'll be seeing it regularly later.

LISTING 2.6   An applet that writes GREETINGS! on the screen.

```
1    public class FirstApplet extends java.applet.Applet {
2
3      /** Initialization method that will be called after the applet
4       * is loaded into the browser.
5       */
6      public void init() {
7          // TODO start asynchronous download of heavy resources
8      }
9
10     public void paint(java.awt.Graphics g) {
11         g.drawString("Greetings!", 0, 100);
12     }
13   }
```

Lines 3–5, and 7: These are comments that NetBeans wrote.

Lines 6–8: The init() method, currently with an empty method body. Net-Beans writes this for you. You can add code to it as necessary.

Lines 10–12: The only change to the prototype is adding the method public void paint(Graphics); this is automatically invoked when the Applet starts.

Line 10: The method header; think of this as "abracadabra" for now.

Line 11: The only statement in paint(), draws the String "Greetings!" on the screen at location 0, 100; that's column 0 row 100 (measured in pixels from the upper left corner). Try some other numbers.

Go to the screen and try this one.

CONCLUSION

The first program that experienced programmers learning a new programming language write is one that simply says "Greetings!" or in the older C tradition, "Hello world". This is because expert programmers have learned from painful experience that if you try to do complicated things before simple ones, you can waste more hours than you might initially believe.

By writing a program that merely writes a word or two on the screen, you either encounter all the difficulties of a new programming environment in the simplest possible context, where you will know to focus your attention on the environment instead of the program, or you will discover that the programming environment is easy to use and go on to more difficult tasks immediately.

Either way, this is an example of an important problem-solving (or in this case, problem reducing) technique—build a prototype first!

This chapter presented the two types of Java greetings programs and explained roughly how they were constructed. Although numerous details were presented, many others were glossed over, or explicitly ignored. The next two chapters address some of those skipped details, and introduce more involved examples.

What Could Go Wrong?

Any number of things! When you first program, the details are legion, and any one can trip you if you forget it. The good news is that ignorance can be cured.

COMPILER ERROR MESSAGES

There are many ways to generate syntax errors. Missing a single keystroke will generate an error and can generate multiple errors. Capitalization errors can be very difficult to find. The errors here come from omitting the (after `println`:

```
examples/Greeter.java [21:1] not a statement
         System.out.println"Greetings!");
                          ^

   examples/Greeter.java [21:1] ';' expected
         System.out.println"Greetings!");
                             ^

   2 errors
   Errors compiling Greeter.
```

The next error comes from omitting the i in `public`:

```
examples/Greeter.java [11:1] 'class' or 'interface' expected
publc class Greeter {
  ^
1 error
Errors compiling Greeter.
```

The next error comes from typing an s instead of an S in `String`:

```
examples/Greeter.java [20:1] cannot resolve symbol
symbol  : class string
location: class Greeter
```

```
public static void main (string args[]) {
                        ^
1 error
Errors compiling Greeter.
```

REVIEW QUESTIONS

2.1 What are the two types of Java programs. How are they different?

2.2 How (in the context of a Java program) do you print a message on the screen?

2.3 How is information processing accomplished in Java?

2.4 What are {}s used for?

2.5 When do experienced programmers write the greetings program?

2.6 What problem-solving technique are they using when they do?

2.7 What are parameters used for?

2.8 Why is the S in `String` a capital letter?

2.9 What is public `static void main(String [] args)`?

Programming Exercises

2.10 Add these lines to your program and see what they print.

```
System.out.println("2+2");
System.out.println(2+2);
System.out.println(2+2 == 4);
System.out.println(2 > 3);
System.out.println(2 < 3);
System.out.println("backslash-t, i.e. \t is a tab\ttab\ttab");
System.out.println("backslash-n, i.e. \n is a
newline\nnewline\n");
```

2.11 Now, try these:

```
int x=17;
System.out.println(x);
System.out.println("x=" + x);
System.out.println("Which of those outputs was easier to
understand?");
System.out.println(x == 17);
x = x + 1;
System.out.println("after adding 1, x=" + x);
```

```
System.out.print("is x still 17?  No.  See? When" +
      " it compares them it says ");
System.out.println(x == 17);
```

2.12 Modify the paint method in your applet by adding these lines:

```
g.drawOval(200,200,100,100);
g.fillOval(400, 300, 75, 288);
g.setColor(java.awt.Color.RED);
g.drawRect(27, 27, 300, 10);
g.setColor(java.awt.Color.GREEN);
g.drawLine(30, 300, 400, 20);
```

It is likely you will need to enlarge the Applet window before you will see them all.

2.13 Modify paint() to draw a simple picture, instead of random stuff as in the previous question. Draw a simple house. Then, try your house, and then the front of the building in which your class meets.

3
Class Design and Implementation

In This Chapter

- Building and Testing the Prototype GUI
- A Generic Problem-Solving Technique
- Account Class: Design, Implementation, and Testing
- Creating and Testing the Finished GUI
- The Bank Class: Design, Implementation, and Testing
- Putting It All Together—Finally!

INTRODUCTION

This chapter illustrates the process of class design, coding, and testing. It starts with a description of a simple ATM simulator and concludes with a working applet that implements it. The program is grown in stages, starting with a very simple prototype and adding features only after each prototype works. The resulting Account class will be incorporated into a larger bank database system in Chapter 11, "Data Structures."

A Description of the Task

Imagine you are given this description for a programming assignment: Write a minimal ATM program that will manage three bank accounts. Each account will have a name and a balance. Allow users to display their current balances and withdraw as much (simulated) money as they want with a graphical user interface (GUI).

Before Beginning to Program: Design!

There is a strong impulse to start to program too soon. When given a problem description, some beginning programmers start typing before they have a clear idea of what they are doing. In a way, this is unavoidable, since a novice programmer knows practically nothing about the programming language. Nevertheless, it is possible to have a clear idea of *what* one is attempting to accomplish even if the *how* is a bit unclear.

It is human nature to experience confusion as pain. Experienced programmers have learned not to start typing before they have a clear understanding of what it is they are attempting. Painful, frustrating experiences have taught them to think through problems before committing to code. Therefore, between the time they read or formulate a description of a programming task, and when they actually sit down to type code, they *design*. Design can take many forms, but it always features clear, simple thinking. A coherent design supports the programming process, and can make the difference between success and failure.

One design technique is to start with the user interface; decide what the user will see and what actions the user will be provided, and then design classes that support those actions.

The User Interface

Start by drawing a picture of what the user will see when the program runs. For simplicity, start with a single bank account. To design a good user interface, you must consider what information will be presented to the user and what actions the user will take to interact with your program. What are those actions and information in this case?

If you reread the description, you will see that the user can do just two things: ask for the current balance, and withdraw funds. For a withdrawal, the user must specify how much money he wants, and that information must be input to the program. To display his balance, the user only needs to indicate that he wants to see it, so a button press will be sufficient, and then information must be output to the user.

Knowing that, what type of user interface does your ATM need? At minimum, it will need 1) a button to request the current balance, and 2) somewhere to type the amount to withdraw. The Java components for these two screen objects are `Button` and `TextField`. You are probably familiar with both of these components; they appear on many Web pages. When you fill out a form on the Web, the boxes you type in are typically TextFields, and the buttons, Buttons. Grab a piece of paper and make a quick sketch of what your user will see when your simulated ATM runs. Note that you can do this without *any* knowledge of how the program will work.

What Classes Will We Need? What Will They Do?

A principle of object design is to create classes that correspond to the things the program is modeling, and to store information in the objects corresponding to where it resides in the world. A real ATM machine communicates with a bank; user information is kept in accounts. Therefore, it is reasonable to think of having an Account class, and to store information about each person's account in a separate Account object. Note the use of the Courier typeface and the capital letters at the beginning of class names; this is to both remind you that class names begin with capital letters, and help make clear when words refer to classes (as opposed to objects in the world).

Therefore, to simulate an ATM associated with a bank that has three customers, we will need three Accounts (one to keep track of each customer's name and balance), a Bank (to contain the three Accounts), and an Applet (to handle the GUI). That would be a lot of code to write all at once, so we'll do them individually and then combine them. This situation is an example of the following problem-solving technique.

Problem Solving Technique: Stepwise Refinement
First, understand the problem, and then break it into 5+/– 2 subproblems. For each: If it is trivial, just do it; if it is not trivial, solve it by using stepwise refinement.

The first step is the most important—until you clearly understand a problem, any attempt to solve it is unlikely to succeed. Sometimes, people attempt to solve problems before understanding them, which usually results in failure and frustration.

Notice that this is a *recursive definition*, the thing being defined is used as part of its own definition. Circular definitions are bad. Recursive definitions can be very good, as long as they do not recurse forever. Since the subproblems are smaller than the original, as this recurses, eventually they become trivial and the recursion stops.

BUILDING AND TESTING THE PROTOTYPE GUI

Figure 3.1 is a rough sketch of a possible GUI for an ATM that keeps track of the balance of a single bank account. There is a Button with the label "Display" and a TextField with the text "Amount to withdraw" above it, and "Current balance" below it. The TextField will be used to both enter the amount to withdraw and display the current balance.

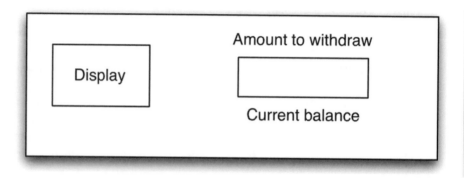

FIGURE 3.1   Rough sketch of GUI for the ATM.

The next sections explain how to build and test a GUI with those two components using NetBeans.

Getting Started

1. Start NetBeans and create a new project with a GUI Applet (see the section "Creating a GUI Applet" in Appendix A for details).
2. Add a Button with an action and test it (see the section "Adding, Connecting, and Testing a Button" in Appendix A).
3. Add a TextField to type the withdrawal amount in and to display the balance (see the section "Adding, Connecting, and Testing a TextField" in Appendix A).

Using the Button to Alter the TextField

When the user presses the Button, its actionPerformed() method will be executed. NetBeans writes the shell of the method; you, the programmer, must insert code to make it do what you want when the button is pushed. Add this line of code after line 50 (in the body of the button1ActionPerformed() method, replacing the comment //TODO add your handling code here:) in Listing A.6 in Appendix A.

```
textField1.setText("Greetings!");
```

Execute the modified program; it should make the TextField say "Greetings" when you press the button.

Simulating One Bank Account by Hand (without the Account Class)

You know how to get the text from a TextField (by using getText()), how to set the text in a TextField (by using setText(String)), and how to get control when a Button is pushed. Before going on to writing classes, let's experiment with a simple ATM with just one bank account balance stored in the Applet. You must do the following three things:

1. Create a variable to contain the current balance.
2. When the user types an amount to withdraw and presses Enter, get the withdrawal amount into the program as a number.
3. Subtract it from the balance and display the new balance.

These will be explained next; after some practice, the explanations will make more sense.

Create a Variable to Contain the Current Balance

Assume the bank account starts with $1000. The program must store the value 1000, and then decrease it when money is withdrawn. To store information (like 1000), a Java program uses a *variable*. A variable must be declared, with a name, a type, and a value, like this:

```
int balance = 1000;
```

This declares a variable whose type is int (i.e., like an integer, it stores one whole number) and sets its initial value to 1000. Figure 3.2 is an illustration of the details.

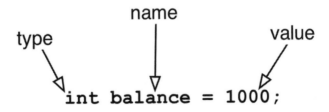

FIGURE 3.2 A declaration, with an assignment statement.

Add that line of code to your test `Applet`, outside of any method, but inside the class. You may be asking, "Where is inside the class?" The class definition is everything between the `{}`s following the name of the class. Now, you might ask, "Where is outside any method?"; this will be explained soon, for now just add it after line 14 of Listing A.6 in Appendix A that reads:

```
public class TestGUIApplet extends java.applet.Applet {
```

When the User Presses Enter, Get the Withdrawal Amount

Change the body of `textField1ActionPerformed()` by adding these lines:

```
int withdrawal = Integer.parseInt(textField1.getText());
System.out.println("withdraw=" + withdrawal);
```

The first gets the text from the `TextField` (which has type `String`), converts it to a number (`Integer.parseInt()` does that), and stores it in a variable called `withdrawal`. The second prints that value, so you can see if it worked. Try it now. (Don't forget to type a number in the `TextField`. What happens if you type anything else?)

You will soon get tired of typing `System.out.println("whatever");` every time you want to output debugging information. NetBeans provides a shortcut; simply type "sout "—the letters s-o-u-t—and then a space. This will be automatically expanded into `System.out.println("");`.

Subtract It from the Balance and Display the New Balance

Add two more lines (after the two you just added):

```
balance = balance - withdrawal;
System.out.println("new balance is: " + balance);
```

The first subtracts the value of `withdrawal` from the `balance` and stores the remainder back in `balance`. The second prints the new balance. Execute this code. Try pressing Enter more than once.

Congratulations! Three things do all the work in computing: input, assignment and output, and you have just used all three! Now, on to creating classes.

A GENERIC PROBLEM-SOLVING TECHNIQUE

Let us take a slight detour for a problem-solving technique that will be useful in thinking about the `Account` class. Try to answer this word problem (even if you don't like algebra):

Mary is twice as old as John is. Two years ago, she was three years older than he will be next year. How old is John?

Maybe you can read that, see through it, and know the answer. Perhaps you have learned a technique called "guess and check" where you try out ages and adjust them in the right direction until you stumble upon the answer. Maybe you know how to write equations to compute the answer. The first technique is great, if it works. Guess and check finds the answer, but does not give you any insight into the problem. Writing equations and solving them is a more general and useful method. However, not everyone can do this type of algebra problem. Here's a generic problem-solving technique that may help you learn to solve such problems using that more general method (and which has direct relevance to designing object programs).

NOTE

Problem Solving Technique: What are the things? What are their relationships?

By answering these two questions, you concretize your conception of the problem. Just doing that may make solving it easier because it will cause you to think carefully about it. In the context of object design, the things are potential classes, the relationships, and the potential messages.

In the problem at hand, at first glance there are several things: Mary, John, and their ages. However, if you think about it, you will soon realize that Mary and John don't matter; only their ages do. For brevity, call their ages M and J. Moreover, also of interest is Mary's age two years ago ($M-2$) and John's next year ($J+1$).

The two statements before the question state two relationships. They can be rewritten as: *Mary is twice as old as John is.* In symbols, that's $M = 2*J$; and, *Two years ago, she was three years older than he will be next year.* In symbols, that's $M-2 = (J+1)+3$. The latter simplifies to $M = J+6$, and you can then substitute $2*J$ for M to find the answer.

Account **CLASS: DESIGN, IMPLEMENTATION, AND TESTING**

Since your program must manage three bank accounts, it would be natural to create three bank account objects, where each would correspond to and hold the information for one account. To be able to create objects (like bank account objects), you must first define a class. When you define a class, you create a user-defined type. A class can then manufacture objects of that type whenever you tell it to.

Account **Class Design**

Let's apply the "things and relationships" technique to the ATM problem. The things in this problem are bank accounts, and the names and balances of each account; the relationship between those things is that each account has a name and balance associated with it. Each account will need a way to store those two pieces of information. Along with the information to be stored in each account, we must also consider what actions will be performed on, or using, that information. There are only two: display and withdraw. In the former, the balance (and perhaps the name) must be displayed; in the latter, the balance must be reduced when money is withdrawn.

The details of how to store the information in each account and how to access and change it are covered in the next section.

Converting the Design to Java Code

A class definition includes declarations of variables (where information is stored) and methods (which operate on that information).

Variables (State)

Variables encode state. This usage of "state" is very similar to a common English usage. If someone says to you, "What is the state of your bank account?" he means how much money is in it. Here are some facts about variables that you will need to know later:

Variables are containers for information. The purpose of variables is to hold information. That information may be of various types: numbers, letters, words, or even objects. Java variables are similar to, but different from, variables in algebra. As in mathematics, Java variables might contain various values. The particular values determine the state of the computation (see the section, "State and Its Representation" in Chapter 1, "Programming Is Like Juggling").

There is only one way to change the information in a variable, which is to execute an *assignment statement*. In algebra, you might encounter a formula like $x = y * 2$, and be asked, if $y = 2$, then what is x? In Java, by contrast, x = y * 2; means take the value of y, multiply it by 2, and store that value in the variable x (or, *assign* that value to x). Therefore, if the value of y was 17, and that assignment statement was executed, the value of x would become 34.

Variables hold exactly one value at a time. Whatever value had been in x before that assignment statement was executed is irretrievably lost. If you want to keep the old value, you would need another variable to hold it.

Every variable has three attributes: name, type, and value. Java is what is called a "typed" language. In addition to a name and a value, every variable in Java has a type.

For now, we will only consider variables of two built-in types. The first you have already seen; String is used to store a series of literal characters. The second, int, is used to store whole numbers, like 12, 1000000, or −37.

Adding Variables to the Account Class

To start, create an Account class in NetBeans that includes a main() method. Follow the instructions in the section "Creating a Class with a Test Driver" in Appendix A. Add the variables in Listing 3.1 after line 12 in Listing A.10 in that section (after the { in the line public class Account).

LISTING 3.1   Adding the variables to the Account class.

```
1    public class Account {
2        String name;           // a String variable called name
3        int balance;           // an int variable called balance
```

Line 3: int balance; declares a variable of type int with the name balance.

```
    // an int variable called balance"
```

is a comment meant for a person to read; Java ignores it.

So far, this class is not very useful because although each Account could store a name and a balance, there isn't any way to do anything with them. That's what methods are for.

Methods (Action)–Accessors and Withdrawal

Methods allow classes to do things, to perform actions. You can write methods to do whatever you like. The body of a method has a list of instructions to follow to accomplish whatever that method is supposed to do.

Perhaps the most common methods are *accessors*. Almost every class has accessors. Their form and usage is simple once you get used to them, and it is the same in every class. At first, until you are familiar with the Java constructs involved, they may seem a bit mysterious. For now, simply accept them as idioms without a complete understanding of every detail; in a few chapters they will seem simple and obvious.

Our Accounts are supposed to do two other things besides retaining the name and balance associated with the Account: they must allow some other method, outside of Account, to discover the value of the balance variable, and allow the balance to be changed when money is withdrawn. Therefore, the questions that must be answered are: 1) "How to get the value of a variable that's inside an object?" and 2) "How to set the value of a variable that's inside an object?"

The answer is *accessors*, methods that allow you to access the variables inside objects. These common, simple, useful methods are not easily understood at first. The problem is that even though accessors all follow the same pattern, there are many details involved in the mechanisms that implement them. Once you have programmed for a few weeks, accessors will seem easy and natural. For now, accept them as an idiom. Add the two methods, in Listing 3.2, right after the two variables you already added.

LISTING 3.2   Accessors for Balance.

```
1    public void setBalance(int nuBalance) {
2        balance = nuBalance; // set the balance
3    } // setBalance
4
5    public int getBalance() {
6        return balance;    // return the balance
7    } // getBalance
```

Lines 1–3: The setBalance() method sets the balance to the value that is sent along with the message.

Line 4: This blank line is inserted to set off the methods visually. It is a simple, but important, element of style.

Lines 5–7: The getBalance() method returns (i.e., sends back as its value) the current value of the balance variable.

This class, although very small, can now be tested. To reiterate, it is important to test your code as you develop it; that way, when something goes wrong, it is easier to isolate the error—there are simply fewer places to look.

How can you test this class? You write what is called a *driver program*, the sole purpose of which is to test your class. This may seem like a waste of time, but it is not. To convince yourself that a class works, you must test all its methods. Fortunately, there are only two: getBalance() and setBalance(int). Go to the Account class, and modify the main() method so it looks like the code in Listing 3.3.

LISTING 3.3 Testing the accessors for `Balance`.

```
1    public static void main(String[] args) {
2        Account myAccount = new Account();
3        System.out.println("Before balance=" + myAccount.getBalance());
4        myAccount.setBalance(1234);
5        System.out.println("After balance=" + myAccount.getBalance());
6    }
```

Line 2: Create and store an `Account` object, named `myAccount`.

Line 3: Check the initial balance, it should be 0. This tests `getBalance()`.

Line 4: Set the balance to 1234.

Line 5: Find out if the balance is now 1234. This tests `setBalance()` and `getBalance()`.

Now execute your program. Assuming it displays 0 and then 1234, it worked and you can move on to the `withdraw(int)` method. If you made any typing mistakes, fix them now.

Along with accessing the `balance` variable, the other action our `Account` class must take is handling withdrawals. Therefore, it will need a method, which might as well be named "withdraw." It is important to give methods (as well as classes and variables) descriptive names—fewer things to remember.

When a user types an amount to withdraw and then presses the `Enter` key, we should send our `Account` object a `withdraw()` message. Will the `withdraw()` method need any information to carry out its task? Yes, it needs to know how much to withdraw! Therefore, it will need a parameter to pass that information to the method. The amount to withdraw is a number, in whole dollars, so the type of the parameter is `int`. The name of the parameter is up to us; it can be any legal identifier—in the example, the name `amountToWithdraw` was chosen (see Listing 3.4).

How should the `withdraw()` method change the state of the `Account` object that receives it? This is the same as asking how the state of a bank account should change when a person takes money from it using an ATM. The answer is that the balance should be reduced by the amount of money withdrawn. Therefore, first our method must calculate the new balance by

```
balance - amountToWithdraw,
```

and then store that amount back in the `balance` variable. To change the value of a variable, you use an assignment statement; like this:

```
balance = balance - amountToWithdraw;
```

This assignment statement is the only line in the body of the `withdraw()` method.

LISTING 3.4   The `withdraw()` method for the `Account` class.

```
1    public void withdraw(int amountToWithdraw) {
2        balance = balance - amountToWithdraw;
3    }
```

Line 1: The method heading. There is one parameter of type `int` whose name is `amountToWithdraw`.

Line 2: An assignment statement. This will subtract whatever value is in the parameter `amountToWithdraw` from the value in the variable `balance` (inside whatever `Account` the `withdraw()` message was sent to), and then store the result of the subtraction back in that same variable (inside the `Account` object that got the `withdraw()` message).

Add this method to your `Account` class and test it. How to test? Add two more lines to your main method, possibly those in Listing 3.5.

LISTING 3.5   Testing the `withdraw()` method.

```
1    public static void main(String[] args) {
2        Account myAccount = new Account();
3        System.out.println("Before balance=" + myAccount.getBalance());
4        myAccount.setBalance(1234);
5        System.out.println("After set balance=" + myAccount.getBalance());
6        myAccount.withdraw(235);
7        System.out.println("Withdrew, balance=$" + myAccount.getBalance());
8    }
```

Assuming your program says the final balance is $999, this means all three methods work and you are ready to use your `Account` class along with your GUI to build the complete system. Well, almost ready. There's the small matter of keeping track of three accounts instead of one.

Objects and Classes

By defining a class (like the `Account` class defined in Listings 3.1, 3.2, and 3.4), you create a user-defined type. Then, you can create objects of that type (see line 2 of Listing 3.5). Novice programmers sometimes struggle with the distinction between classes and objects. It is rather like the relationship between the part of speech, noun, and individual nouns. Words like "dog," "house," and "money" are nouns (they are instances of the category "noun"). Similarly, every object is an instance of some class.

If you are just learning to program, until very recently you had never heard the terms *class* and *object* used the way they are used in the context of programming. This unfamiliarity makes determining the difference between them rather difficult, but it gets easier with practice.

To review: Classes are patterns for creating objects of that type; they define the type of information those objects will contain (variables) and the actions they can take (methods). Once the class is defined, you can create (instantiate) as many objects as you want of that type. Once you have created an object, you can send it messages to accomplish whatever task you are doing.

Cookies and Cookie Cutters Metaphor

A useful metaphor for classes and objects is cookie cutters and cookies. If you have a cookie cutter in the shape of a star, you can use it over and over to make many star-shaped cookies. After the various star cookies are cut, they can be decorated in different ways. Classes are patterns (like cookie cutters) for making objects (cookies). All objects (also called "instances") of a particular class have the same form (like all the cookies from the same cutter). Every Account you create (by saying new Account()) will have its own balance variable and its own name variable. These variables may contain different values in different objects.

It's important to remember the distinction between objects and classes; for, while cookies can be delicious, if you bite a cookie cutter you could hurt your mouth—and it wouldn't taste good.

new Account(); Instantiation! Alakazam!

Before you can send a message to an Account, you must create it, and store it in a variable. This is demonstrated in Listing 3.6. Instantiation may safely be considered magic for the present. In Chapter 5, "Toward Consistent Classes," the details will be explained, and at that point it will be essential to understand, but for now you might just think of new Account() as the incantation to make a new Account object appear.

LISTING 3.6   Instantiation. A line of code that creates an Account object.

```
1
2    Account myAccount = new Account();
```

Line 2: There are two parts here: 1) Account myAccount, which declares a variable of type Account (that's the class name) whose name is myAccount, and 2) new Account(), which instantiates an Account (i.e., creates an instance of an Account object). The equals sign between them makes these two parts into an assignment statement. The action of this assignment is to store the newly created Account in the myAccount variable.

Notice that the first character of myAccount, "m", is lowercase; the convention is that classes have uppercase first letters, and objects have lowercase—if you follow this convention, you can tell right away from the name of something whether it is an class or an object. Thus, Account is the name of the class, and myAccount is the name of the object.

Instances and Instance Variables

The Account class has two instance variables: name and balance. Therefore, every object of type Account (or instance of Account) has its own instance variables named name and balance, just as every bank account has a name and a balance associated with it. You will see an example of what this means in the next section.

Exercise: Use your Account class in conjunction with your GUI to keep track of the balance of one account. You already have all the necessary code; all you need is to understand it well enough to rearrange it to do the job.

CREATING AND TESTING THE FINISHED GUI

As always, there are two phases to creating a GUI: design and implementation.

GUI Design

We have built and tested a prototype GUI and completed the Account class. We are now ready to solve the original problem. Again, we will start with the user interface and then write the classes to support it. Designing the GUI puts our focus on the users and what actions they can take (which is a good policy), and helps us form an image of the task ahead of us.

We already have a display Button and a TextField to handle withdrawals; all we need is a means to choose between the three accounts. How should the user select the account to withdraw from or display the balance of? In a real ATM machine, the users insert their card and then enter their PIN. However, we don't have a card reader, and don't want to keep track of PINs just yet. A simple solution is to add three buttons for the three accounts. When the user pushes the Account2 button, the program will act as if the owner of the Account2 has successfully logged in; when the display button is pushed, the program will display the balance from Account2. Subsequent withdrawals will come from Account2, until another button is pushed.

GUI Implementation

Add three more Buttons to your GUI (see the section "Adding, Connecting, and Testing a Button" in Appendix A if you've forgotten how). The Buttons appear named Button2, Button3, and Button4 and are labeled the same way. These names do not remind you what they mean, and the user will object if, to select account 3, he must push the Button labeled Button4. Just as it is important to give classes, variables, and methods descriptive names so you can remember what they do, it is important to label Buttons well or the user will become confused. When there is only one button, the name is not so important, but the more there are, the more it matters. Change the labels on the Buttons to "Account1," "Account2," and "Account3" (see the section "Adding and Using a Choice" in Appendix A). Change their names to "selectAccount1Button," "selectAccount2Button," and "selectAccount3Button" (see the section "Renaming Components" in Appendix A). Make sure the Button labeled "Account1" is named "selectAccount1button"! It is very confusing and hard to figure out when the Button with the label "Account1" gives access to Account3.

Now, add actions for the three new Buttons (double-click them, remember?). They are supposed to select the current account, so have each send the Bank a message: selectAccount1(), selectAccount2(), or selectAccount3(). Naturally, the selectAccount1Button should send the bank the selectAccount1() message.

Listing 3.7 shows the actionPerformed() code NetBeans wrote for the account1Button.

LISTING 3.7 The actionPerformed() Method for the account1Button.

```
1    private void account1ButtonActionPerformed(
     java.awt.event.ActionEvent e{)
2        // Add your handling code here:
3    }
```

Notice that the name of the Button appears as part of the method name.

All you need to do is add code to tell the bank to select Account1(), as shown in Listing 3.8.

LISTING 3.8 The code to add to make the account1Button select account1.

```
1    private void account1ButtonActionPerformed(
     java.awt.event.ActionEvent e{)
2        theBank.selectAccount1();
3    }
```

Do the same for the other two Buttons. You will notice that NetBeans indicates that there is an error on each of those lines. This is because it does not know what theBank means. You will need to add the line

```
Bank theBank = new Bank();
```

outside of any method (details to follow) and create the Bank class. After doing so, the errors will go away and the program will be ready to run.

THE Bank CLASS: DESIGN, IMPLEMENTATION, AND TESTING

Just as a GUI must be designed, implemented, and then tested, so must every class.

Bank Class Design

The task of the Bank class is to simulate a tiny bank with three accounts; thus, it will need three Accounts. It must also keep track of which Account is currently in use, and make withdrawals from that Account.

There are two tasks we must accomplish: 1) create the three accounts, and 2) conceptualize and implement a technique to remember which of the accounts the user is currently working with. It turns out that declaring one more Account variable and setting it equal to whichever Account is currently in use will be sufficient.

Converting the Design to Java Code

The first thing to do is to create a Bank class with a main() method; see the section "Creating a Class with a Test Driver" in Appendix A for instructions. NetBeans will write the class shown in Listing 3.9.

LISTING 3.9   The initial Bank class.

```
 1    /*
 2     * Bank.java
 3     *
 4     * Created on April 21, 2004, 2:40 PM
 5     */
 6    public class Bank {
 7
 8        /** Creates a new instance of Bank */
 9        public Bank() {
10        }
11
```

```
12        /**
13         * @param args the command line arguments
14         */
15        public static void main(String[] args) {
16        }
17    }
```

Variables

To create the three accounts, plus the current account variable, add these four lines after line 6 in Listing 3.9. That's all it takes.

```
Account account1 = new Account();
Account account2 = new Account();
Account account3 = new Account();
Account currentAccount = account1;   // to start with
```

The first three lines declare variables called account1, account2, and account3, instantiate three Accounts, and store one Account in each variable. The fourth declares another Account variable called currentAccount, and sets it equal, initially, to account1. Thus, if you do a withdrawal before pushing any of the three buttons, it will come from account1. The modified code is shown in Listing 3.10.

LISTING 3.10   The Account declarations inserted into the Bank class.

```
1    public class Bank {
2
3        Account account1 = new Account();
4        Account account2 = new Account();
5        Account account3 = new Account();
6        Account currentAccount = account1;   // to start with
7
8        /** Creates a new instance of Bank */
9        public Bank() {
```

Line 6: The // to start with is a comment. Anything on a line after // is a comment. Comments are ignored by Java, but help people understand code.

Line 8: This is also a comment; anything between /* and */ is a comment; these block comments can span multiple lines.

Methods

The bank needs to withdraw money from the current account and display the balance of the current account; it also must be able to set the current account. Listing 3.11 shows the methods that do these things. These may be inserted anywhere in the class block of the Bank class, as long as they are outside of other methods—right after the variables would be fine.

LISTING 3.11   The method declarations for the Bank class.

```
1     public void selectAccount1() {currentAccount = account1;}
2     public void selectAccount2() {currentAccount = account2;}
3     public void selectAccount3() {currentAccount = account3;}
4
5     public int getBalance() {
6         return currentAccount.getBalance();
7     }
8
9     public void withdraw(int withdrawalAmt) {
10        currentAccount.withdraw(withdrawalAmt);
11    }
```

Both getBalance() and withdraw() just pass the buck to the Account class by sending the same message to the currentAccount object. Notice that getBalance() returns the value that comes back from Account's getBalance.

None of these methods has static in its heading. That is because they are instance methods. All methods are either instance methods or class methods. When a method uses or changes the values of variables within an instance (like withdraw() changes the value of an Account's balance variable), it must be an instance method. Otherwise, it cannot access the information in the instance. If it does not use or change any information inside an instance (like the PersonalizedGreeter sayHi() method in the previous chapter), it *may* be a class method. All methods for the next six chapters will be instance methods; you can safely forget about static for some time.

Testing

Modify the main() method in Bank as shown in Listing 3.12. Then, set the starting class to Bank (right-click the project node in the Projects window and choose Properties. Click Running Project in the left pane of the dialog box. Use the Browse button to choose the project main class.) Run the program again to make sure the Bank is working correctly.

LISTING 3.12 Test code for the Bank class.

```
1   public static void main(String[] args) {
2       Bank theBank = new Bank();
3       System.out.println("Initial acct1 balance=" + theBank.getBalance());
4       theBank.withdraw(100);
5       System.out.println("-100 acct1 balance=" + theBank.getBalance());
6       theBank.selectAccount3();
7       System.out.println(" acct3 balance=" + theBank.getBalance());
8       theBank.selectAccount1();
9       System.out.println(" acct1 balance=" + theBank.getBalance());
10  }
```

Line 2: Create a new Bank object and store it in a Bank variable named theBank.

Line 3: Display the balance of account1 (remember, currentAccount starts as account1).

Line 4: Withdraw 100 dollars from account1

Line 5: See if the balance is really −100.

Line 6: Tell theBank to change the current account to account3.

Line 7: Verify that getBalance() now returns 0 (instead of −100).

Line 8: Go back to account1.

Line 9: Verify that its balance is still −100.

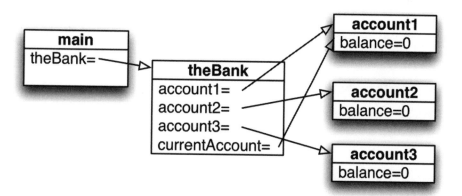

FIGURE 3.3 The state of the program after line 2 in Listing 3.12 executes. The main() method has a variable named theBank. The object called theBank has four variables. The first three point to the three Accounts. The fourth currently points to account1 as well.

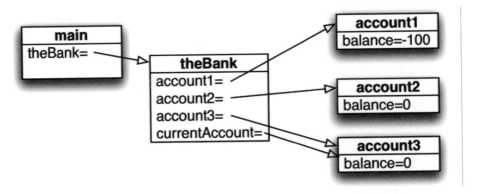

FIGURE 3.4 The only differences are the value of the balance variable in account1 and the value of currentAccount in theBank, which now points to account3 instead of account1.

Sometimes, it is helpful to draw a picture of the state of the program at various points during its execution. For instance, after line 2 in Listing 3.12 executes, the state of the program looks roughly like Figure 3.3.

After line 6 executes, the state of the program looks like Figure 3.4.

PUTTING IT ALL TOGETHER—FINALLY!

All you need to do to finish the project is to add one line to the Applet, as seen in Listing 3.13.

LISTING 3.13 Alteration to Applet code.

```
1    public class ATM_Applet extends java.applet.Applet {
2        Bank theBank = new Bank();
3    }
```

To declare the Bank variable, theBank, add this line at the beginning of the ATM_Applet class.

That's it! You are done! Now you can compile and run the Applet. Do that now (don't forget to change the main class back to ATM_Applet—see "Setting the main class" in Appendix A). Make sure it really does keep track of the three balances correctly. You will notice that everyone starts out with a balance of 0, but it still allows them to withdraw money.

Could you arrange for them to start with some other balance besides zero?

This turns out to be easy, but not obvious. The initial *default value* for every instance variable is 0, but you can set it to something else as shown in Listing 3.14 (e.g., set the initial balance for every account to $1,000,000 (change is in **bold**)). Do that now and rerun your program.

LISTING 3.14   Alteration to Listing 3.1.

```
1    public class Account {
2        String name;
3        int balance=1000000; // Every Account starts with $1,000,000!
4    }
```

Assuming you've made that program run, good work! You have done some of the most difficult programming you will ever do; working in a new language in a new IDE is incredibly difficult. There are so many details and everything is unfamiliar, so even the simplest problem can seem overwhelming. It only gets easier from here. With practice, everything you did today will become easy and effortless, and in a few weeks, you'll be amazed that this ever seemed difficult. That's how expertise works; you learn something and it seems simple. Then, it's hard to understand why everyone else can't do it. Welcome to Java programming.

CONCLUSION

Programming is always an iterative process. No one writes finished programs from scratch in one pass. Rather, it is a process of successive approximation. There are two compelling reasons for starting with a prototype, which does almost nothing, and then adding functionality after each simpler program works. First, it allows the programmer to focus on one part of the program at a time, and thus reduces cognitive overhead during the design and implementation phase. This is also an advantage of writing and testing classes one at a time. Second, it makes the task of debugging much easier. Debugging is the hardest part of programming for all levels of programmers; it can be baffling, frustrating, and exhausting. Stepwise implementation makes it much easier to find bugs when they occur, simply because a smaller part of the program is new at any time.

This chapter introduced classes; their design, implementation, testing, and incorporation into a larger program. It included various language constructs and components, including variables, the assignment statement, declarations, instantiation, accessors, parameters, and return values along with the abstract windows toolkit (AWT) Components, Button, and TextField. These various elements were presented rather telegraphically, with most of the detail omitted. A more complete and careful discussion of these topics may be found later in the book. Here, the emphasis is on constructing a working program to experiment with to get a feel for both the Java language and the process of programming.

If you are new to programming and/or Java, you may be feeling a bit confused. You probably have many questions about what you've just done, and a number of concepts about which you are unsure. If so, good! There were too many concepts and details to describe or understand all at once. However, at least you have seen the process of constructing a working Applet with several classes and a GUI. That's a lot (and it's most of what programming is about). It usually takes about three or four weeks for undergraduates in an introductory class to be able to do this type of program. Oh, and then there was all the detail of using NetBeans to build the GUI and compile/execute the program. The next chapter will fill in the detail, and if it answers any questions you might have, the details will be easier to understand and remember.

The next chapter will introduce Graphics, Color, and software reuse techniques through the development of another example. After that comes a detailed explanation of many of the concepts and programming features glossed over here. Then, some more elaborate (and interesting) examples will be undertaken.

What Could Go Wrong?

Earlier, in the section "When the User Presses Enter, Get the Withdrawal Amount," if the contents of the TextField is not an int, an Exception will be thrown.

In the section "GUI Implementation," it is very easy to get confused over which Button is which, and which ActionPerformed() should send what message. If something goes wrong with the account selection, that would be the first place to look.

REVIEW QUESTIONS

3.1 How do you create objects?

3.2 What is the difference between a class and an object?

3.3 When you declare a variable, you must specify its type and name (in that order). What are you allowed to call variables (i.e., what rules must variable names (indeed all Java identifiers) adhere to)?

3.4 Here are two legal names: something and Something. These are different, because Java is case sensitive. If you are following the convention for naming classes and objects, which of these is the name of a class and which is the name of an object?

3.5 Where is information stored in a Java program?

3.6 How do you change the value of a variable?

3.7 What is the difference between the types `int` and `String`?

3.8 What are the three attributes of every variable?

3.9 What are parameters used for?

3.10 Where do parameters go?

3.11 Is `doSomething()` a variable name or a method? How can you tell?

3.12 In `anything.everything(something)`, you can tell by the context what `anything`, `something`, and `everything` are. What are these three things? The answers are message, object, and parameter, but which is which?

3.13 Recall that computing is always information processing; in the ATM problem description, what information is processed, input, or output for each possible user action?

Programming Exercises

3.14 The instructions omitted the labels above and below the `TextField`. Add them.

3.15 Your finished `Applet` was not very user friendly. When a customer withdrew cash, and wanted to see the new balance, he had to push the display button again. It is simple (one line) to automatically display the new balance every time a withdrawal is made. Do so. Hint: write a `public void display()` method in your `Applet` (that does exactly what the display button does) and use it in `actionPerformed()` for the `TextField` right after you do the withdrawal (i.e., say `display()`).

3.16 After you do the previous exercise, you will discover a small inconvenience. If you want to withdraw the same amount repeatedly from the same account, you have to keep removing the balance and reentering the amount before you can withdraw again. Improve the usability of your interface as follows. After a withdrawal is made, move the cursor to the `TextField` and select the text so the user can simply copy the amount to be withdrawn (Ctrl-c) and then paste and press Enter repeatedly. Add the code to `actionPerformed` for the `TextField` (right after the `display()` from the previous exercise). If the name of your `TextField` was `theTF`, the code would be:

```
theTF.requestFocus();
theTF.selectAll();
```

4 Graphics and Inheritance

In This Chapter

- The Graphics Class
- The Circle Class—Design and Implementation
- Displaying a Circle Graphically
- The Color Class
- The Eye Class: Design and Implementation
- Assembling a Working Eyes Program

INTRODUCTION

"One is not likely to achieve understanding from the explanation of another."
—*Takuan Soho*

This chapter will give you more exposure to and practice with writing classes in Java. It will also illustrate how to do simple graphics, and introduce inheritance, a powerful feature of object-oriented programming. Like the last chapter, it will not present all the details of the constructs used; that will be delayed until the next chapter. For now, try to become familiar with the process of thinking a problem through, coming up with an elegant design for a solution, and then implementing and testing it—those are the important lessons that will carry over into other programming languages and possibly other areas. To learn to program, you must practice; reading about it is not good enough (as the Takuan quote implies).

A Description of the Task

Your task in this chapter will be to draw two eyes on the screen. For simplicity, you need only draw the iris and pupil. Make the iris the same color as yours. The distance between the two eyes and the size of the pupil relative to the iris should be adjustable by the user.

Creating a Prototype

In the previous chapter, you were introduced to the techniques of a) building a prototype and then gradually adding functionality, and b) sketching the GUI, and then creating and testing it before writing any other code. Do that now. First, create a new project in NetBeans (consult Appendix A, "Getting Started with NetBeans and the Greetings Program," if you've forgotten how). Add a GUI Applet called EyeApplet. Add and connect however many Buttons you will need. Compile and run your project, testing to make sure everything works so far (i.e., that each Button invokes the correct actionPerformed() method, see the section "Adding, Connecting, and Testing a Button" in Appendix A). Once you do that, you will be in a position to try the various Graphics commands as you work through the chapter.

Object Oriented Design—Choosing Classes to Implement

A decision that you must make early in the design of a problem-solving program is what classes you will use in the solution. Since your task is to draw two eyes on the screen, a natural candidate for a class would be Eye. Since an Eye consists of an iris and a pupil—two circles filled with different colors—Iris and Pupil are also candidate classes. How many classes make sense in a particular context is less than perfectly defined. For now, let's assume you will need an Eye class, and put off the decision on Iris and Pupil until you know a little more. Before designing the Eye class, you need to know several facts about Graphics and Color in Java. Often, in designing a class, you must do some experiments, play with the elements involved, and learn about the related classes Java provides, before you know enough to make informed decisions about the details of the class you are writing. These next several sections will illustrate that process; then we will return to the Eye class, and once the Eye class is done, so is our task!

THE Graphics **CLASS**

Java provides the `java.awt.Graphics` class to draw on the screen. A `Graphics` object provides a context in which Java graphics operations can be performed. In other words, to draw on the screen, you must first have a `Graphics` context in which to do so. You have already seen how to draw on the screen in an `Applet` by including a `public void paint(Graphics)` method (in the section titled "A Greetings `Applet` that Uses a Graphics Context" in Chapter 2, "Programming the Simplest Java Programs"). This section will provide a few more details.

Components **and** public void paint(java.awt.Graphics)

When you write a `public void paint(Graphics)` method in your `EyeApplet`, it overrides the default `paint()` method in `Applet`. That sentence requires a bit of explanation. Look at the heading of the `EyeApplet` class definition (in Listing 4.6). The first line of code is `public class EyeApplet extends java.applet.Applet`; thus, the class is named `EyeApplet`, it is `public`, and it is a subclass of `java.applet.Applet` (i.e., it extends `java.applet.Applet`). When you extend a class, instances of the subclass inherit all the functionality of the superclass. To add functionality, you simply add methods. To change the behavior of a method in the superclass, you write a subclass method with the same *signatur* that does something different. Because `EyeApplet` extends `Component` (actually, it extends `Applet`, which extends `Panel`, which extends `Container`, which extends `Component`, but never mind right now), it automatically inherits a `paint()` method (which does very little). If you want to paint your `Applet` differently (by drawing a circle or whatever on the screen), you write a `public void paint(java.awt.Graphics)` method in your subclass, and then that is executed instead. You will see examples of adding and modifying functionality in the `FilledCircle` class later in the chapter.

Basics of Graphics in Java

To start using graphics in Java, you must understand the `Graphics` coordinate system, and a few simple methods.

The Coordinate System

From the perspective of a Java graphics context, the drawable area is a rectangle of dots numbered from left to right and top to bottom. The dots are called **picture elements** or *pixels*. The pixel numbered (0,0) is in the upper left corner.

When you create a GUI `Applet` in NetBeans, it automatically generates an *HTML* file for a browser to use in determining how to display it. Assuming the name of your Applet is EyeApplet, the HTML file is named EyeApplet.html, and is stored in the build directory. It contains the line:

```
<APPLET code="EyeApplet.class" width=350 height=200></APPLET>
```

This specifies the width and height of the graphics context (in pixels) within the frame of the Applet (illustrated in the next section). If you want your Applet to be a different size, simply add the line setSize(400,400); in the init() method of your applet.

A Few Graphics Methods

The only method you need to draw an eye is drawOval(), but first you need to understand how drawRect() works. The drawRect() method has four parameters, all ints. The first two specify the upper left corner of the rectangle; the third and fourth, its width and height. In each pair, the first is horizontal, and the second is vertical. Thus, drawRect(x,y,width,ht) will draw a rectangle whose upper left corner is at (x,y), whose width is *width*, and whose height is *ht*.

The drawOval() method is similar. The four parameters are identical, specifying a rectangle, exactly as in drawRect(); the oval is inscribed in the specified rectangle. The drawLine() method also has four parameters; the first two specify the coordinates of one end of the line, the second two, the other. See Listing 4.1 for an illustration, and Figure 4.1 for its result.

LISTING 4.1   A paint() method.

```
1    public void paint(java.awt.Graphics g) {
2        g.drawRect(25,25,100,100);
3        g.drawOval(25,25,100,100);
4        g.drawLine(0,0,350,200);
5        g.drawString("g.drawRect(25,25,100,100);", 20, 150);
6        g.drawString("g.drawOval(25,25,100,100);", 20, 165);
7        g.drawString("g.drawLine(0,0,350,200);", 20, 180);
8    }
```

Line 2: Draws a square with sides 100 pixels long, upper left corner at (25,25).

Line 3: Draws a circle centered in it (i.e., centered at (75,75), not (25,25)).

Line 4: Draws a line from one corner of the graphics context to the other.

The coordinates of the corners of the graphics context and the square are indicated.

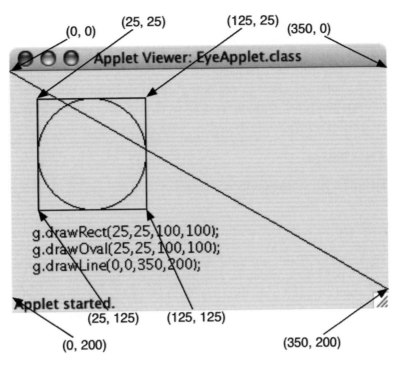

FIGURE 4.1 The result of the `paint()` method in Listing 4.1.

Notice that if we were hoping for a circle centered at (25,25), we did not get what we wanted. We will have to consider this when writing the graphical display method for the `Circle` class.

THE `Circle` CLASS—DESIGN AND IMPLEMENTATION

Circles are used to represent many things in GUIs. In a simulation, circles might represent molecules; in a game, balls; on a map, populations in cities, or incidence of infectious disease. As you have just seen, you can draw a circle in a graphics context by using `g.drawOval(int, int, int, int)`. But, if you were writing a program that displayed many circles, or if the circles moved around the screen (like the balls in a billiards game) or changed sizes (like graphics representing levels of infection), you wouldn't want to keep finding and changing the appropriate `drawOval()` code. If you tried, it would take a lot of careful attention to avoid changing the wrong one. A better solution is to hide the information about a particular circle—namely, where and how big it is—inside an object. Then, when you have multiple circles, you can just deal with them as `Circles` and let the details of where they are right now and how to draw them be handled by the `Circle` class. Additionally, if you need to change how they are drawn, there is only one piece of drawing code to change instead of numerous copies of it. Thus, you can avoid complexity and bugs at the same time. What a deal!

As with any class, in designing the `Circle` class, you must decide: 1) what information it will contain, and 2) what actions it will support, including how it will be displayed and tested.

`Circle` Class Design

To design any class, you must decide how you will specify its state and what actions it will perform.

State—What Information Completely Describes the State of a `Circle`?

To describe a circle, you must specify its center and its radius; that's it. Therefore, we will need three variables, one for its radius and two for its position (x, and y). For simplicity, and since the screen is made of discrete pixels, these can all be whole numbers, `ints`—for now. When we use `Circle` to display molecules later, it will be crucial for their positions to be able to be intermediate between pixels.

Action—What Must a `Circle` Do?

We will need accessors for all our variables so we can discover and/or change the position or size of a `Circle`. We will also need methods to display a `Circle`, both for debugging and to display it when the program is running.

Converting the Design to Java Code

The next step after designing a class is to convert that design to Java.

Creating the `Circle` Class

Create a `Circle` class (see the section "Creating a Class with a Test Driver" in Appendix A to refresh your memory, if needed).

Variables

Perhaps you already know how to declare the three variables? That would be:

```
int x;
int y;
int radius;
```

Accessors

These are just like the accessors for Account (see Listing 4.2), except the names of the variables are different. Look back at that example and try to write the accessors for x, before looking at them in Listing 4.2.

LISTING 4.2 Accessors for the Circle class.

```
1    public int getX() {return x;}
2    public int getY() {return y;}
3    public int getRadius() {return radius;}
4
5    public void setX(int nuX) {x = nuX;}
6    public void setY(int nuY) {y = nuY;}
7    public void setRadius(int nuRadius) {radius = nuRadius;}
```

The toString() Method

Java has a special method that is used almost exclusively for debugging. It is called toString(), and its signature is public String toString(). As the name implies (once you are familiar with colloquial Java-speak), it converts an object to a String. While you are testing your classes (or debugging in general), you sometimes need to know what information is in an object, whether it contains the information you expect. If you have an object called anyObject, you can always find out what's inside with:

```
System.out.println(anyObject);
```

You don't need to type .toString() because in the context of a System.out.println, Java automatically adds it for you (although you may type it if you want to).

You can write any toString() method that you choose, as long as the signature matches. Listing 4.3 shows a toString() for the Circle class that is a bit verbose. Why it is written this particular way will become obvious in the next chapter.

LISTING 4.3 toString() for the Circle class.

```
1    public String toString() {
2        String returnMe = "I am a Circle: ";
3        returnMe += "\tx=" + getX();
4        returnMe += "\ty=" + getY();
5        returnMe += "\tradius=" + getRadius();
6        return returnMe;
7    } // toString()
```

Line 2: Declare the String variable to return; set it to "I am a Circle: "

Line 3: Paste a tab (\t) onto it, followed by "x=" and the value of x.

Line 6: Return that whole String as the value of toString().

Testing Your Code

That's enough code to test. Create a Circle and check that all the methods work. To do that, after you instantiate the Circle, display it, then change all the variables and display it again. Since toString() uses getX(), getY(), and getRadius(), by doing that you have used all the methods. See Listing 4.4 for how the code might look.

LISTING 4.4   Testing the first prototype Circle class.

```
1    public static void main(String[] args) {
2        Circle aCircle = new Circle();
3        System.out.println("before" + aCircle);
4        aCircle.setX(123);
5        aCircle.setY(17);
6        aCircle.setRadius(34);
7        System.out.println("after" + aCircle);
8    }
```

Line 2: Instantiate a Circle called aCircle.

Line 3: Display it.

Lines 4–6: Set all the variables.

Type and run this test program (if you made mistakes, debug your typing). Then, once you know the Circle class can keep track of and change its variables correctly, you are ready to add the graphical display.

DISPLAYING A Circle GRAPHICALLY

To display a Circle graphically requires a method that draws the right-sized circle in the correct location. It seems this should only take one line of code. Something like:

```
g.drawOval(x,y,width,ht);
```

However, what values should we use for x, y, width, and ht? Moreover, where does the graphics context, g, come from?

public void paint(java.awt.Graphics)

A Circle knows its location and size (the location of the center is in its x and y variables, and its size is in its radius variable). The Circle will not know anything about graphics contexts, so that is best provided from the outside, by whatever method asks the Circle to display itself. This is what parameters are used for, to pass information to a method. The Applet was displayed graphically by a method called paint(); to keep down the cognitive overhead, we will use the same name, paint(), for the method that displays a Circle graphically. So, perhaps all we need is g.drawOval(x,y,radius,radius); as in Listing 4.5.

LISTING 4.5   A first try at a paint() method for Circle.

```
1    public void paint(java.awt.Graphics g) {
2        g.drawOval(x,y,radius,radius);
3    }
```

Testing the paint()Method

Add the paint() method from Listing 4.5 to your Circle class and test it by modifying your EyeApplet to create a Circle, set its x, y, and radius variables to 100, and display it graphically in paint() (see Listing 4.6).

LISTING 4.6   Creating and displaying a Circle graphically.

```
1    public class EyeApplet extends java.applet.Applet {
2        Circle aCircle = new Circle();
3
4            /** Initializes the applet EyeApplet */
5            public void init() {
6                initComponents();
7
8                aCircle.setX(100);
9                aCircle.setY(100);
10               aCircle.setRadius(100);
11           }
12
13           public void paint(java.awt.Graphics g) {
14               aCircle.paint(g);
15           }
```

Lines 8–10: Set the variables in aCircle to 100.

Unfortunately, this draws the circle that would fit inside a square of size radius, whose upper left corner is at (x,y). That has two problems: 1) it is centered at (x+radius/2, y+radius/2), and 2) its diameter is the radius of the Circle (to understand this, draw a picture labeled with coordinates).

Problem-Solving Technique: Draw a Picture

By drawing a picture, you can engage your visual-spatial processing system. Although people tend to take it for granted, the ordinary ability to walk through a crowd involves a feat of information processing. Your visual-spatial processor is more powerful than any computer on the planet, but as long as you are stuck in linguistic space, it is idle. Drawing a picture can activate it. In addition, when you look back at the picture you will remember what you were thinking.

That second problem is very easy to fix; simply pass radius*2 instead of radius for the width and height to drawOval() (see Listing 4.7).

LISTING 4.7   A second try at a paint() method for Circle.

```
1    public void paint(java.awt.Graphics g) {
2        g.drawOval(x,y,radius*2,radius*2);
3    }
```

This method gets the size right, but the circle is still in the wrong place; the center is at (x+radius,y+radius) instead of (x,y). How could you fix this? The simplest way is just to subtract the radius from x and y in the parameters you send to drawOval(), as seen in Listing 4.8.

LISTING 4.8   A correct paint() method for Circle.

```
1    public void paint(java.awt.Graphics g) {
2        g.drawOval(x-radius,y-radius,radius*2,radius*2);
3    }
```

Line 2: Draws a circle whose radius is radius, centered at (x,y). In the context of a particular Circle, x, y, and radius are variables specifying the state of that Circle.

Modify your code. Execute it to verify that the circle is displayed at the appropriate place.

More Than One Circle

Now that you have a working Circle class, you can create and display as many Circles as you want. Add another Circle, as shown in Listing 4.9. Execute it to make sure it is working properly; the circles should be concentric. Add another, intersecting `Circle` to make sure you understand the procedure (don't forget to add a line in `paint()` to display the third circle). Notice that you can add and display as many `Circles` as you want without ever looking back at the `Circle` class code. This is a huge advantage of programming with objects; once a class is written, you can forget the details inside it.

You are almost ready to design and implement the `Eye` class, as soon as you know a bit about color in Java.

LISTING 4.9 Adding a second concentric `Circle` by modifying Listing 4.6.

```
1    public class EyeApplet extends java.applet.Applet {
2        Circle aCircle = new Circle();
3        Circle bCircle = new Circle();
4
5        /** Initializes the applet EyeApplet */
6        public void init() {
7            initComponents();
8
9            aCircle.setX(100);
10           aCircle.setY(100);
11           aCircle.setRadius(100);
12           bCircle.setX(100);
13           bCircle.setY(100);
14           bCircle.setRadius(50);
15       }
16
17       public void paint(java.awt.Graphics g) {
18           aCircle.paint(g);
19           bCircle.paint(g);
20       }
```

Changes to Listing 4.6 are in bold. If you wanted a nonconcentric `Circle`, change the parameters in `setX()` and `setY()` for `bCircle`.

THE `Color` CLASS

There are several things you need to know about the `Color` class.

Setting the `Color` of the Graphics Context

A graphics context has a number of state variables, including the current color. The default color is black; however, you can change it with the accessor `setColor(Color);`. You set the color of a `Graphics` object by sending it a `setColor()` message with a `Color` as the parameter, just as you set the balance of an `Account` by sending it the `setBalance()` message with an `int` as the parameter, or the radius of a `Circle` using `setRadius()`.

Built-in `Colors`

The `Color` class has about a dozen colors predefined. To set the color to red, you would say `g.setColor(java.awt.Color.RED);`. Add that line between lines 18 and 19 in Listing 4.9 and execute the `Applet`. Notice that only the second circle is red; if you move the `setColor()` before line 18, both `Circles` will be red.

Creating Your Own `Colors`

There are millions of colors possible in Java. You can create any of them with:

```
java.awt.Color myColor = new java.awt.Color(red, green, blue);
```

The three `int` parameters to the `Color` constructor set the intensities of red, green, and blue. All three must have values in the range 0 to 255.

Exactly how many colors are available?

You can calculate this from the fact that there are three parameters, each of which can take on 256 different values. It's very much like the analysis in "Problem Solving Principle #1," in Chapter 1, "Programming Is Like Juggling."

RGB Color Model

Java has two color models, but the simpler is the RGB model. RGB stands for red-green-blue. The color of each pixel is determined by the amount of illumination in those three colors. Any combination of values for red, green, and blue is legal. To get pure red, you say `new java.awt.Color(255, 0, 0);`, thus passing 255, 0, and 0 as the parameters to `new java.awt.Color()`; 255 for red (all the way on), 0 for green and blue (all the way off). Purple is a mixture of red and blue. So, for bright purple, you would pass (255,0,255); for dark purple, perhaps (50,0,50).

The Difference between Pigment and Light

The RGB values set the intensity of light emitted in each color. You are probably more used to mixing pigments than light. Light and pigment are not identical. If you mix blue paint with red paint, you get purple. If you then add yellow, you get muddy brown (or possibly even black). When you mix red light with blue light you also get purple, but if you then add green, you get white! A combination of all colors of light yields white light. Think of a prism, which breaks white light into its constituents. If there is no pigment, white paper remains white; if there is no light, everything is black. So, `new java.awt.Color(255,255,255)` is white, and `new java.awt.Color(0,0,0)` is black.

THE Eye CLASS: DESIGN AND IMPLEMENTATION

As always, before writing a class, you should decide what it will do and how it will do it; this is referred to as design.

Designing an Eye Class

For your purposes here, an `Eye` is two concentric `Circle`s, the larger (the iris) filled with the color of your eyes (some shade of brown, blue, or green), the smaller (the pupil) filled with black. If you wanted two unfilled black circles, the `Eye` class could have two `Circle` variables and you'd be almost done.

For the user interface, you must allow the user to move at least one eye horizontally, and adjust the size of the pupils. The simplest way to do this is with two `Button`s to move one eye right and left, and two more to grow and shrink the pupils (if your interface uses some other scheme, that's fine). Thus, you will need methods to change the size and location of the eye. Fortunately, these will be very easy. Assume an `Eye` had two `Circle` variables. When the user wants to shrink the pupils, a `shrink()` message would be sent to the `Eye`. The `shrink()` method could then reduce the size of the pupil `Circle` using `getRadius()` and `setRadius()` (i.e., `iris.setRadius(iris.getRadius()-3)`). Similarly, the `moveRight()` method could adjust the locations of both `Circle`s using `getX()` and `setX()`.

The `Circle` class does almost what you need, but two things need to be modified. Instead of drawing a circle in black, you want it to fill the same circle in a particular color. One way to accomplish this would be to modify the `Circle` class. You could change `drawOval()` to `fillOval()` in `paint()`, add a `Color` variable and use it to set the color of the graphics context before you fill the circle. However, then if you wanted to be able to draw unfilled circles, you'd need to remodify the `Circle` class. Instead, we will extend the `Circle` class. That way, you won't have to change the `Circle` class, and code reuse can be illustrated by subclassing.

Inheritance: class FilledCircle extends Circle

As mentioned previously, when you extend a class, the subclass inherits the data and methods of the superclass. Thus, `FilledCircle` can use `x`, `y`, and `radius` without redeclaring them. In addition, you can add additional methods to add functionality, and override existing methods to change functionality.

Design

FilledCircle is very much like Circle; it only needs one additional variable and to override one method.

Variables

FilledCircle inherits x, y, and radius from Circle. It needs one additional variable to keep track of its color.

Methods

There must be some way to set the color of a FilledCircle, so it will need a setColor() accessor. The paint() method must be modified to fill the circle in that color instead of just drawing the outline of the circle.

Implementation

Implementation is straightforward: create the class, add the variable, and add the method.

Create a FilledCircle Class

If you need to, consult the section "Creating a Class" in Appendix A to refresh your memory.

Add a Color Variable

Here's how to declare a variable of type Color called myColor:

```
java.awt.Color myColor = new java.awt.Color(100,0,100);
```

This line auto initializes myColor to a medium purple. This default color will help in debugging; any time you see it, you will know that you forgot to set the color for this FilledCircle.

Some people don't like to type, or look at, "java.awt." repeatedly. If you would prefer, just type:

```
Color myColor = new Color(100,0,100);
```

See Listing 4.11 for a technique to allow this.

Add the Accessor to Set the Color of the FilledCircle

To be able to change the color of a FilledCircle, there must be an accessor. The standard name is setColor() and its form is identical to the other accessors you've seen; see Listing 4.10. Before long, accessors like this will be second nature. For now, realize that there is one parameter of type `Color`, named `c` (line 7, `java.awt.Color c`), and whatever value is passed through that parameter is stored in the instance variable named `myColor` (line 8, `myColor = c;`).

Override `paint()`

The heading of `paint()` is `public void paint(java.awt.Graphics g)`. Thus, the parameter is of type `Graphics` and is named `g` locally (i.e., in the `paint()` method). The body of the method must first set the `Graphics` color to the color of this particular `FilledCircle`, and then draw the filled circle. See Listing 4.10.

LISTING 4.10   The `FilledCircle` class.

```
1    public class FilledCircle extends Circle {
2        java.awt.Color myColor = new java.awt.Color(100,0,100);
3
4        /** Creates a new instance of FilledCircle */
5        public FilledCircle() {}
6
7        public void setColor(java.awt.Color c) {
8            myColor = c;
9        }
10
11       public void paint(java.awt.Graphics g) {
12           g.setColor(myColor);
13           g.fillOval(x-radius, y-radius, radius*2, radius*2);
14       }
15   }
```

Line 2: Declare a `Color` named `myColor` and initialize it to medium purple.

Lines 7–9: Accessor to set the color of a `FilledCircle`.

Lines 11–14: Paint the `FilledCircle` by setting the graphics color, and then `fillOval()`.

See Listing 4.11 for a way to avoid typing `java.awt.` over and over.

LISTING 4.11   Simplified `FilledCircle` class using `import`.

```
1    import java.awt.*;
2    public class FilledCircle extends Circle {
3        Color myColor = new Color(100,0,100);
4
```

```
5          /** Creates a new instance of FilledCircle */
6          public FilledCircle() {}
7
8          public void setColor(Color c) {
9              myColor = c;
10         }
11
12         public void paint(Graphics g) {
13             g.setColor(myColor);
14             g.fillOval(x-radius, y-radius, radius*2, radius*2);
15         }
16     }
```

Line 1: This `import` statement allows you to skip typing `java.awt.` before `Color` and `Graphics`. Compare to Listing 4.10.

Testing `FilledCircle`

Modify your existing `Applet` to test `FilledCircle`. It will be enough to simply change the `Circles` to `FilledCircles` and set the color of the smaller one to black. What will it display if it is working correctly? See Listing 4.12 for the necessary changes.

LISTING 4.12 Test code for `FilledCircle`; changes from Listing 4.9 are in bold.

```
1      public class EyeApplet extends java.applet.Applet {
2          FilledCircle aCircle = new FilledCircle();
3          FilledCircle bCircle = new FilledCircle();
4
5          /** Initializes the applet EyeApplet */
6          public void init() {
7              initComponents();
8
9              aCircle.setX(100);
10             aCircle.setY(100);
11             aCircle.setRadius(100);
12             bCircle.setX(100);
13             bCircle.setY(100);
14             bCircle.setRadius(50);
15             bCircle.setColor(java.awt.Color.BLACK);
16         }
17
18         public void paint(java.awt.Graphics g) {
```

```
19              aCircle.paint(g);
20              bCircle.paint(g);
21        }
```

Lines 2–3: Declare, instantiate, and store `FilledCircles` instead of `Circles`.

Line 15: Set the smaller's color to black so it won't be purple.

The Eye Class

Having built and tested a GUI `Applet` and a `FilledCircle` class, most of the work of building the `Eye` class is finished. Create an `Eye` class and add the following variables and methods.

Variables

An `Eye` has an iris and a pupil; these are both `FilledCircles`. Thus:

```
FilledCircle iris = new FilledCircle();
FilledCircle pupil = new FilledCircle();
```

Methods

Because an `Eye` is composed of two `FilledCircles`, most `Eye` methods will simply send the appropriate messages to those `FilledCircles`.

MoveLeft and MoveRight

To move an `Eye` left, you must move both of its `FilledCircles` left, so the `moveLeft()` method would simply set x in each to a slightly smaller number; see Listing 4.13.

LISTING 4.13 `moveLeft()` for `Eye`.

```
1    public void moveLeft() {
2        iris.setX(iris.getX()-2);
3        pupil.setX(iris.getX());
4    }
```

Line 2: Set the *x* coordinate to 2 less than it was.

Line 7: Set the `pupil` x variable to the same value.

The `moveRight()` method would be similar, except increasing x for each.

ShrinkPupil and GrowPupil

To shrink the pupil, you can simply reduce the value of the radius variable of the pupil FilledCircle; see Listing 4.14.

LISTING 4.14 shrinkPupil() for Eye.

```
1    public void shrinkPupil() {
2        pupil.setRadius(pupil.getRadius() - 2);
3    }
```

Line 2: Set the radius to 2 less than it was.

The growPupil() method is nearly identical. After you add these methods to the Eye class, go back to the actionPerfomed() method for the shrink and grow Buttons, and modify them to send those messages. There are two things you must make sure of in doing this:

1. There must be an Eye variable declared before you can send the message to it. Every message has the form someObject.someMessage();—see "The Message Statement" in Chapter 5, "Toward Consistent Classes."
2. To change what is displayed, you must invoke paint(Graphics), and to do that you must send the repaint() message. The details of this are explained in Appendix B, in the section "repaint(), paint(), and update()." For now, just use the code in Listing 4.15.

LISTING 4.15 actionPerformed() for growButton.

```
1    private void growButtonActionPerformed(java.awt.event.ActionEvent
     evt) {
2        rightEye.growPupil();
3        repaint();
4    }
```

Line 2: Send the rightEye the growPupil() message.

Line 3: Send repaint() to the Applet so you can see the new pupil size—don't forget this!

Composition and `public void paint()`

To display an `Eye`, you must display both `FilledCircles`, first the iris, and then the pupil (if you do it in the other order, the pupil will be invisible). Listing 4.16 illustrates the elegance of composition; an eye is composed of an iris and a pupil, so to paint an `Eye`, you need simply paint the `iris`, and then the `pupil`.

LISTING 4.16 `paint()` for `Eye`.

```
1    public void paint(java.awt.Graphics g) {
2        iris.paint(g);
3        pupil.paint(g);
4    }
```

That's all there is to it.

That's all the methods we need. (Or is it? Check the design to see if we did everything we planned to do. Look back at Listing 4.12, which tested the `FilledCircle` class; did it send any messages besides `paint()` to the `FilledCircles`?) Now, it's time to test.

Testing

Modify your `Applet` to create and display one `Eye`, as in Listing 4.17.

LISTING 4.17 Test code for `Eye`.

```
1    public class EyeApplet extends java.applet.Applet {
2        Eye rightEye = new Eye();
3
4        /** Initializes the applet EyeApplet */
5        public void init() {
6            initComponents();
7        }
8
9        public void paint(java.awt.Graphics g) {
10           rightEye.paint(g);
11       }
```

Note that unlike Listing 4.12, there is only one line in `init()`. What did `init()` contain in Listing 4.12?

Run it. Once you find and eliminate all the typing errors, you should notice that there's no sign of the `Eye`. Why not?

Debugging

There are many possible reasons why the Eye isn't visible. Perhaps it's never being sent paint(). Maybe it is painted in white. Perhaps it's being drawn off the screen. Maybe it is so small you can't see it. Maybe something else is being drawn on top of it. The job of the programmer, now, is to determine the cause of the problem and fix it. Assuming it is one of the reasons listed here, how could you go about determining which it is? The answer is, use the scientific method. Design and carry out experiments to verify or eliminate each of those hypothetical bugs. Until you determine what is causing the problem, it will be difficult to fix.

You might start by making the Applet window bigger; maximize it and see if the Eye appears. Alternatively, you might push the "grow pupil" Button; do it several times. This assumes that you have modified the event handling code for that Button so it sends the growPupil() method to the Eye. If you haven't added that code yet, do so now.

In the author's Applet, after he pushed the grow Button several times, he was surprised to see a quarter of a purplish circle expanding from the upper left corner. Having seen this effect before, he immediately realized that the reason he didn't see anything at first was that the radius, x, and y, were all zero. Do you know why? The default initial value of instance variables is zero (see the section "Putting it all Together—Finally!" in Chapter 3, "Class Design and Implementation."

If you compare Listing 4.12 (the Applet to test FilledCircle) and Listing 4.17 (to test Eye), you will notice that init() in the former sets x, y, and radius for both FilledCircles and sets the color of the smaller to black; in the latter it does not. Somehow, we must specify the location of the Eye and make its pupil black.

There are a number of ways we might set the initial size and location of an Eye. For now, simply add setX(), setY(), and setRadius() methods to Eye, and send these messages to the Eyes in init(). To setX() for an Eye, all you need to do is send setX() to both the iris and the pupil. For setRadius(), send setRadius() to both, but make the radius of the pupil smaller.

A maxim of object programming is for classes to know the minimum. It makes sense for the Applet to control the location of the Eye, and possibly the size. Nevertheless, every Eye will have a black pupil, so the right place to set the color of the pupil is in Eye, not Applet.

You may have noticed this code (written by NetBeans) in Eye.java.

```
/** Creates a new instance of Eye */
public Eye() {
}
```

This looks like a method without a return type, with the same name as the class. It is called the default constructor, and is invoked when you say new Eye(). If there is any initialization code for instances of a class (i.e., anything that needs to be done once, right when an instance is created), it goes in the default constructor. Therefore, that is where the code to set the color of the pupil to black goes. See Listing 4.18 for the code you should add.

LISTING 4.18   Additional code for Eye.

```
1    /** Creates a new instance of Eye */
2    public Eye() {
3        pupil.setColor(java.awt.Color.BLACK);
4    }
5
6        public void setRadius(int r) {
7            iris.setRadius(r);
8            pupil.setRadius(r/2);
9        }
10
11        public void setX(int x) {
12            iris.setX(x);
13            pupil.setX(x);
14        }
```

Line 3: Sets the color of the pupil to black (so it won't be purple).

Lines 6–9: To set the radius of the Eye, set the radius of the iris to the parameter, and set the radius of the pupil to half that.

Lines 11–14: To set x for the Eye, setX() for both its iris and pupil to the parameter.

Add that code, and then run your program again. If you've made no mistakes, it will display an Eye with a black pupil. Chances are you have made one or more mistakes. If so, figure out what's gone wrong. Don't panic! Just pick up the balls and keep practicing. Try the buttons. Do they work? Did you write code for each one?

ASSEMBLING A WORKING Eyes PROGRAM

Now that you have a working Eye class and a working Applet with buttons to adjust it, accomplishing the task of displaying two of the Eyes is trivial. Probably you already know what needs to be done. There are four things, all in the EyeApplet class.

1. Declare the second Eye (at the top).
2. Set the size and position of the second Eye (in init()).
3. Display the second Eye (in paint()).
4. Resize both pupils (in actionPerformed() for the shrink and grow Buttons).

These should all be simple since the code is already there for rightEye.

Make those changes, and test your code. The only thing remaining now is to make the Eye color match yours. You could experiment with changing the RGB parameters on line 3 of Listing 4.11, but that means you'd have to recompile each time. A more efficient (and fun) technique is to use NetBeans' Color Editor (see the section "Using the Color Editor" in Appendix A, but all you need to do is, in the Form Editor, select a Button, then in Properties click the ... button to the right of background, click RGB, and slide the sliders).

CONCLUSION

This chapter developed a program to display two eyes the color of the programmer's in an Applet. It did so by designing and implementing a Circle class, extending that to a FilledCircle, and finally building an Eye class that was composed of two FilledCircles. It thus illustrated both mechanisms for code reuse: inheritance and composition. It also illustrated the use of simple Java Graphics and Color and walked through the process of developing a program incrementally.

A novice programmer would have spent roughly three to six hours to work through this chapter; there were so many details that needed to be correct. There is no substitute for spending the time to learn to program. Like juggling, you cannot learn to do it by reading about it or watching someone else do it.

The next chapters will review the material glossed over here in more detail. See you in the next chapter!

REVIEW QUESTIONS

4.1 Why are prototypes useful to build first?
4.2 Why is design important?
4.3 What are the first two things to do in design?
4.4 What is a graphics context?
4.5 What message do you send to an Applet to cause paint() to happen? Does it have parameters?
4.6 What are parameters for?
4.7 What are the two techniques of class reuse?

4.8 What does *pixel* mean?

4.9 How many colors (exactly) are possible in Java?

4.10 What are the parameters for `drawRect()`, `fillRect()`, `drawOval()`, `fillOval()`, `drawLine()`, and `setColor()`?

4.11 How do you change the size of the `Applet` (so it stays changed)?

4.12 What are accessors for?

4.13 How do you fix a bug you can't find?

Programming Exercises

4.14 Write the `paint()` method for `Circle`.

4.15 Write the accessors for `Circle`.

4.16 Write the `Circle` class.

4.17 Write the `FilledCircle` class.

4.18 Create a `Target` class that is displayed as alternating red and white bands of color. Hint: draw the biggest `fillOval` first and work in.

5 Toward Consistent Classes

In This Chapter

- Details I—Statements in Java: Syntax and Semantics
- The Basics of Classes
- Constructors
- Details II—Types, Operators, and Expressions
- Recapitulation

INTRODUCTION

"When facing a tree, if you look at a single one of its red leaves, you will not see all the others. When the eye is not set on any one leaf, and you face the tree with nothing at all in mind, any number of leaves are visible to the eye ..."
—*Takuan Soho*

Takuan was a Buddhist master who lived in the middle of the second millennium. You may wonder how a 500-year-old quote from a Buddhist is relevant to computing; let us explain. Buddhists had been studying human nature for 2000 years at that point; and people haven't changed in 500 years. Our culture (language, technology, education) has changed radically since, but our DNA has not; our bodies, our brains, our minds are just the same. One thing Buddhists have studied extensively is attention. They recommend paying complete attention to whatever you are doing, whether it is writing code or washing the dishes (this example is from the Buddhist author Thich Nhat Hanh). The resulting focus can change your life.

How is object programming different from procedural programming (from which it grew)? In this context, the leaves on Takuan's imaginary tree are classes. If you are practicing object programming correctly, when you are writing a class, you are thinking of nothing but that class. This provides tremendous power, because you are not distracted and can focus on writing a bug-free class. Once it is written and tested, you can forget what's inside and devote your attention to other matters. This is one of the most important advantages of object programming.

A major constraint on a programmer's ability to think clearly (and thus solve the problems that inevitably arise when programming) is cognitive overhead. If every class is similar, once the pattern becomes familiar, the programmer's cognitive overhead is reduced. This chapter will present a method for writing classes that will be used in every class from now on. There are many styles of programming, and no one can say that one is best for everyone. The style recommended here is simple and consistent; that's enough for now.

This chapter includes more complete explanations of the components of classes. That requires a fair amount of detail and a bit of notation. Therefore, sections presenting some of the associated details will bracket the sections describing class components. Read those detail sections briefly, but return to them in a few days; they are dull, but learning them will save you many hours later. The first introduces the syntax and semantics of Java statements in a more rigorous way.

DETAILS I—STATEMENTS IN JAVA: SYNTAX AND SEMANTICS

So far, the code in this book has only used three kinds of Java statements: assignment statements, message statements, and return statements. They can be easily distinguished. Every assignment statement has an equals sign, like `balance = 17;`. Every return statement starts with the word *return*. Every message statement has a ".", like `System.out.println("greetings");`, although sometimes the "."s are added automatically by the compiler and do not appear in the code. The good news is there are only about a dozen statements total in Java. You may be wondering what all the rest of the code so far has been composed of; mostly declarations (class, method, and variable), which will be covered in the next section.

Syntax and Semantics

Syntax is another word for grammar, and has nothing to do with meaning. The syntax of Java (or any programming language to date) is very simple compared to a natural language like English. The compiler uses what is called a context-free grammar to check the syntax and, if it is correct, then converts the source code to byte code (see the section "The Java Virtual Machine" in Chapter 1, "Programming Is Like Juggling.") A context free grammar is composed of a set of productions. The syntax of each statement is defined by a single production, as will be seen later. Once you have learned the syntax of each of the elements of Java, the mystery of syntax errors will be mostly dispelled.

Semantics is another word for meaning. In the context of programming, semantics means action (this is sometimes called operational semantics). The semantics of a statement is the action it performs when it is executed.

BNF Notation

The productions of a grammar are often represented in BNF notation, or Backus Naur Form (Backus and Naur were the originators of this representation of grammar). This is a metalanguage; it is a language that is about a language. Since you are not familiar with the Java language, but you are familiar with English, here's an introduction to BNF for a subset of English.

BNF for a Tiny Fragment of English

Consider a fragment of English where every sentence is composed of a noun phrase followed by a verb phrase. This could be written as the BNF production:

<sentence> ::= <noun phrase> <verb phrase>

The "::=" means "is defined as." So, this is read "A <sentence> is defined as a <noun phrase> followed by a <verb phrase>." Things between pointed brackets are called nonterminal symbols and must be defined somewhere in the grammar. Therefore, to complete this grammar we would need definitions of <noun phrase> and <verb phrase>. For now, let's say that the only legal verb phrases are "runs" and "jumps." In BNF:

<verb phrase> ::= runs | jumps

The vertical bar (|) means "or." Symbols without brackets, like "runs" and "jumps," are called terminal symbols and must appear literally.

Assume that a noun phrase is either a proper name, or an article followed by a noun. In BNF:

<noun phrase> ::= <proper noun> | <article> <noun>

Let the proper nouns be "Jane," "Dick," or "Spot"; the articles "a" or "the"; and the nouns "cat" or "mouse." In BNF:

<proper noun> ::= Jane | Dick | Spot
<article> ::= A | The
<noun> ::= cat | mouse

All the nonterminals have been defined (i.e., they have appeared on the left of a ::=), so the grammar is finished. What language does it generate? In other words, what are all the legal sentences in this language? Here they are, in left to right order:

Jane runs
Jane jumps
Dick runs
Dick jumps
Spot runs
Spot jumps
A cat runs
A cat jumps
A mouse runs
A mouse jumps
The cat runs
The cat jumps
The mouse runs
The mouse jumps

Therefore, there are just 14 legal sentences in the language. Let's add optional adjectives to make it a bit more interesting.

Adding Adjectives

The notation for an optional symbol is [optional thing]. Therefore, to allow the two sentences "The big cat runs" and "The cat runs," the following productions will do:

<noun phrase> ::= <proper noun> | <article> [<adjective>] <noun>
<adjective> ::= big | small | black | white | ferocious

English allows multiple adjectives to modify a noun. If we wanted to allow a sentence like "The big black ferocious cat jumps," the requisite production would be:

<noun phrase> ::= <proper noun> | <article> [<adjective>]* <noun>

Notice the "*" after the [ ]s. This means "0 or more repetitions of the symbol in the [ ]s."

Here is the grammar all collected together:

<sentence> ::= <noun phrase> <verb phrase>
<noun phrase> ::= <proper noun> | <article> [<adjective>]* <noun>
<verb phrase> ::= runs | jumps
<adjective> ::= big | small | black | white | ferocious
<proper noun> ::= Jane | Dick | Spot
<article> ::= A | The
<noun> ::= cat | mouse

How many sentences does this grammar generate?

Review the BNF notation summary in Table 5.1 to be sure you know it; the next sections depend on it.

TABLE 5.1 BNF Notation

::=	is defined as
<x>	one thing of type x
|	or
[x]	optional x
[x]*	0 or more xs

BNF, Java, and Adaptive Systems

The Java compiler, like any contemporary compiler, is literal and rigid. It insists that source code match its grammar, symbol by symbol. Any deviation will result in compiler errors; and errors prevent the compiler from producing byte code, and without byte code, you can't execute your program.

Syntax errors are just details, but they are details that can stop you. If you omit or misuse a comma in an English paper, you may be corrected by your teacher, or lose points, but your English teacher can still understand your meaning. The compiler, by contrast, will cut you no slack. If a program is missing a semicolon, or has a misspelled word, no matter how many times you compile it, it will still generate an error, and will still not run. In the person/compiler system, the person must make the adjustment, the compiler will not. Fortunately, once you know the BNF, you will at least know what the compiler is looking for.

The Assignment Statement

The assignment statement, while simple and unprepossessing, is the only one that changes the state of a program. Its grammar is shown in BNF 5.1.

BNF 5.1   The Assignment Statement

<assignment stmt> ::= <variable> = <expression>;

Semantics

1. Evaluate the <expression>
2. Assign the value to the <variable>

Every assignment statement matches this syntax. In other words, every assignment statement is a variable, followed by the *assignment operator*, followed by an expression, and finally a semicolon. This has several implications:

1. The only thing that can appear on the left of the assignment operator is a variable, and whenever you see an assignment operator, you know that whatever is to the left of it *is* a variable; otherwise, it won't compile into working code.
2. Only an expression can appear to the right of the assignment operator, and anything that appears there must be an expression, for the same reason.
3. Any other syntax is illegal.

What is not specified by the BNF, but is necessary for an error-free program, is that the type of the expression must be compatible with the type of the variable. If they are not, a compiler error will occur. The details of compatibility appear in the section "Expressions" later in this chapter.

Check which symbols in the following examples correspond to which BNF symbols.

```
balance = nuBalance;                  // see Listing 3.2
balance = balance - amountToWithdraw; // see Listing 3.4
currentAccount = account3;            // see Listing 3.11
myColor = c;                          // see Listing 4.11
```

The Message Statement

Computing is information processing. Almost all information processing in a Java program is accomplished by sending messages to objects. As BNF 5.2 shows, every message statement is an object followed by a period, followed by a message (which has parameters enclosed in parentheses).

BNF 5.2   The Message Statement

<message stmt> ::= <object>.<message>([<actual parameters>]);

Semantics

1. Perform the parameter linkage (see "Parameters (Actual, Formal, Linkage)" later in this chapter).

2. Execute the method body of the associated method, using the <object> as this.

The BNF does not specify that the method must be defined in the class the object belongs to (or one of its superclasses). Again, the compiler will catch the error if it is not.

Examples:

```
myAccount.setBalance(1234);         // from Listing 3.3
System.out.println("Greetings");    // from Listing 2.2
rightEye.growPupil();               // from Listing 4.15
```

However, here are some message statements that do not appear to match that syntax; they have nothing to match <object>.

```
initComponents();                   // from Listing 4.9
repaint();                          // from Listing 4.15
```

This is because these are shorthand for this.initComponents() and this.repaint();. The compiler fills in this for you (see "Special to Java—What Is this?" later in this chapter).

How to Generate a NullPointerException

One of the most common runtime errors is the NullPointerException. That name is a bit worrisome, but descriptive. One way to generate an error is to send a message to an object that has been auto initialized to null. Recall that Java auto initializes instance variables to zero, which, for references (and all Objects in Java are references), is considered null. Therefore, if you send a message, any message, to an object variable before you set it to reference an object, it will always generate a `NullPointerException`. Like this:

```
1    public class Broke {
2
3        private Object anObject;
4
5        public void brokeMethod() {
6            theObject.toString();  // this will be a NullPointerException
7        }
8    } // Broke
```

Line 3: Declares a `private` `Object` instance variable named `anObject`. This will be auto initialized to `null` when a `Broke` object is created.

Line 4: When a `Broke` object is sent a `brokeMethod()` message, it will attempt to send `toString()` to `anObject`, but since `anObject` is still `null`, that is equivalent to `null.toString()`, which will cause a `NullPointerException`.

Every time you have a `NullPointerException`, it means your program has tried to send a message to an `Object` that hasn't been initialized (or has been set accidentally to `null`). Every time.

See the section "Exceptions" in Appendix B for more details.

The Return Statement

Return statements are used to exit a method and can be used to pass information back to the point that the message was sent. If the return type of the method is not void, the compiler will insist that the <expression> exist and be of a type compatible with the type of the method. The syntax is shown in BNF 5.3.

BNF 5.3 The Return Statement

<return stmt> ::= return [<expression>];

Semantics

If there is no <expression>, return immediately to where the method was invoked.

If there is an <expression>:

1. Evaluate the <expression>.

2. Leave the method immediately, returning that value as the value of the message that invoked the method.

Any of the accessors that get values have exactly one line in their bodies, a `return` statement. As you can see in Listing 5.1, the type `int` appears before `getBalance()`—this is the type of the method.

Examples:

```
return balance;                          // from Listing 3.2
return currentAccount.getBalance();  // from Listing 3.11
```

Notice in the second example that the <expression> is a message; whatever its method returns is its value.

THE BASICS OF CLASSES

As discussed previously, a class declaration defines a template for objects (or instances) of that type. It includes both variable and method declarations. Variables contain information. Methods perform actions; what an object can do depends on what methods are declared and how they are implemented. Now that you have some experience with a few classes, it is possible to gain a more detailed understanding of how they work. A class may have many methods, but this section will only cover the standard methods, accessors and `toString()`; however, these will be described more or less completely.

Variables I (State)

Variables store information; the state of an object is determined by the value of its variables. Every variable has a name, type, and value. When a variable is declared, only the name and type are required. There is a variety of variables in Java, including instance, class, local, parameter, and method variables. In this section, only instance variables will be presented. Their syntax is shown in BNF 5.4. This is not the entire BNF for a variable declaration, but it is the essence of it. See BNF 5.5 for a more complete definition.

BNF 5.4 Variable Declaration 1

<variable declaration> ::= <type> <identifier>;

Semantics

1. Create a variable of the given <type> with the name <identifier>.

Examples:

```
public class Account {
    int balance;  // see Listing 5.1
    String name;
```

Recall the Account class from Chapter 3, "Class Design and Implementation" (see Listing 5.1, which has been modified to set the initial balance for every account to $1,000,000 and to set the initial value of name to "nobody" (changes are in **bold**). If you do this and then later see an account with the name "nobody", you will know you forgot to initialize the name variable to something besides the default.

LISTING 5.1 The Account class with auto initialization.

```
1   public class Account {
2       protected String name = "nobody";
3       protected int balance = 1000000;
4
5       Account(){   //empty default constructor
6       }
7
8       public int getBalance() {return balance;}
9
10      public void setBalance(int nuBalance) {balance = nuBalance;}
11
12      public void withdraw(int amountToWithdraw) {
13          balance = balance - amountToWithdraw;
14      }
15  }
```

Each Account object must keep track of the name and balance in a particular bank account. Therefore, the Account class has two variables, balance and name, which must be declared outside of any method. The type of balance is int, and the type of name is String.

The alert reader will have noticed that the two variable declarations in Listing 5.1 do *not* conform to the syntax in BNF 5.4. The protected keyword and the assignment are optional and do not appear in that BNF definition. A more complete BNF for a variable declaration is shown in BNF 5.5.

In the case of instance variables, the variable is created when the object is instantiated; for example, in Listing 5.1, the balance and name variables will be created and initialized whenever new Account() is executed. If the optional [=<expression>] is there, then the variable is initialized to the value of the <expression>; otherwise, to zero.

BNF 5.5 Variable Declaration 2

<variable decl> ::= [<access>] <type> <identifier> [=<expression>];

Semantics

1. Create a variable of type <type> with the name <identifier> with the <access> defined.

2. If the optional =<expression> is there, perform the assignment statement.

You have seen numerous examples of instance variable declarations that included initialization. In Listing 3.13 (copied here), theBank appears outside of any method in the ATM_Applet class; it is thus an instance variable. When the Applet instance is created (if you wish to convince yourself it is an instance, run any Applet and chose Clone from the menu to create another instance), its instance variables are created and initialized.

```
1    public class ATM_Applet extends java.applet.Applet {
2        Bank theBank = new Bank();
3    }
```

When the new Bank() constructor is executed, creating a new Bank instance, the four instance variables in the Bank class are created and initialized. Thus, line 2 in the preceding code causes the four instance variables in Listing 3.10 (copied here) to be created.

```
1    public class Bank {
2
3        Account account1 = new Account();
4        Account account2 = new Account();
5        Account account3 = new Account();
6        Account currentAccount = account1;    // to start with
```

All four create Account variables; the first three instantiate Account, so they each create a name and balance variable along with the instance (lines 2 and 3 in Listing 5.1).

Two more examples:

```
String returnMe = "I am a Circle: "; // see Listing 4.3
protected Color myColor = new Color(100,0,100); // Listing 4.11
```

Each instance of a class has a copy of each *instance variable*, which is why they are called *instance* variables. The balance variable in Account is a good example;

every account needs to keep track of a different balance, so every account needs its own `balance` variable to store that information.

Methods (Control)

The standard methods include two accessors for each variable and a `toString()` method for debugging. Additionally, most classes have various constructors to make initialization simple, plus other methods that expand its capabilities. This section will present the syntax of method declarations, using examples from accessors you have already seen. Then, a tool that writes these methods automatically will be introduced before the rest of the description of methods.

The syntax of every method declaration is a method heading followed by a method body as shown in BNF 5.6.

BNF 5.6   Method Declaration

<method decl> ::= <method heading> <method body>

Semantics

A method declaration is never executed; therefore, it does not have semantics in the sense of statements. Nevertheless, it does have a meaning: Create a method for the current class with the signature declared in the method heading. The body of the method is executed when the corresponding message is sent.

The method heading can take several forms since the access modifier, the return type, and the parameters are optional; the name, and parentheses are not optional (see BNF 5.7).

BNF 5.7   Method Heading

<method heading> ::= [<access>] [<return type>] <identifier> ([<formal parameters>])

Semantics

A method heading is never executed. It defines the signature of the method. Constructors do not have a return type. For ordinary methods, if the return type is not void, the method body must end with a return statement whose <expression> has a type compatible with the <return type>.

Examples (again, match the code symbols to the BNF):

```
void setBalance(int nuBalance) -- [<access>] omitted, no return, one
    int parameter
int getBalance() -- [<access>] omitted, returns an int value, no parameters
public String toString() -- access is public, returns a String, no parameters
public void paint(java.awt.Graphics g) -- access public, no return, one
    Graphics parameter.
```

The BNF for <identifier> and <formal parameters> are omitted (recall that an identifier is any series of letters, numbers, and underscores beginning with a letter). Parameters are addressed in a subsequent section, "Formal and Actual Parameters."

A method body is simply a block statement, and a block statement is zero or more statements enclosed in {}s; see BNF 5.8 and BNF 5.9.

BNF 5.8   Method Body

<method body> ::= <block statement>

Semantics

Same as the block statement.

BNF 5.9   Block Statement

<block statement> ::= { [<statement>]* }

Semantics

Execute each statement in the block in order.

Return Types

Every method that is not a constructor must have a return type. Any legal type may be a return type. If nothing is returned, the return type must be declared as void.

Accessors

Classes typically store information; other classes need to access that information, both to discover what it is and to update it. The methods that give other objects access to variables inside an object are called "accessors." These are also called "getters" and "setters," as they get and set the values of the variables they access.

Getters–Get Values

Every getter is the same, except for three symbols. Compare the two getter methods in Listing 5.2; review Listing 3.2 if these seem unfamiliar.

LISTING 5.2   Getters for Account.

```
1    public int getBalance() {
2        return balance;    // return the balance
3    }
4
5    public String getName() {
6        return name;    // return the name
7    }
```

The only differences are the return type (int or String), the name of the method (getBalance() or getName()), and the variable whose value is returned (balance or name). Both have a return statement as the only statement in the body of the method.

The int return type in getBalance() means that the getBalance() message is an expression of type int and so can appear anywhere an int expression is legal (see "Expressions" later in this chapter).

Setters–Set Values

Setters, too, are all the same shape. Compare the two in Listing 5.3.

LISTING 5.3   Setters for Account.

```
1    public void setBalance(int nuBalance) {
2        balance = nuBalance; // set the balance
3    }
4
5    public void setName(String nuName) {
6        name = nuName; // set the name
7    }
```

Both are void (meaning they return nothing), with one parameter, which is used to set the variable involved. Both have a single assignment statement as the body of the method. They are identical in form, the differences stem from the names and types of the variables being set.

Parameters (Actual, Formal, Linkage)

Parameters carry information into methods. The first step in executing a message statement is to perform the parameter linkage. To describe the parameter linkage requires a few new terms.

Formal and Actual Parameters

There are two varieties of parameters, *formal* and *actual*. Consider Listing 5.4, which is a copy of Listing 3.3 along with the setBalance() code from the Account class.

LISTING 5.4   Formal and actual parameters.

```
1    class Account {
2        ...
3        public void setBalance(int nuBalance) {
4            balance = nuBalance; // set the balance
5        }
6    } // Account class
7    ...
8
9    public static void main(String[] args) {
10       Account myAccount = new Account();
11       System.out.println("Before balance=" + myAccount.getBalance());
12       myAccount.setBalance(1234);
13       System.out.println("After balance=" + myAccount.getBalance());
14   }
```

The formal and actual parameters are shown in **bold**. The former (1234) is the actual parameter, the latter (int nuBalance) is the formal parameter.

> **Line 12:** Sends the setBalance() message to the myAccount object with the parameter 1234.
>
> **Line 3:** The method heading for setBalance() and defines a parameter of type int.

One mnemonic to help remember which type of parameter is formal and which is actual is that the formal parameter is part of the definition of the method and definitions are formal things. In addition, the actual parameter is the value that is *actually* sent along with the particular message that invokes the method.

In BNF 5.10, the first production means "<formal parameters> is defined as a <formal parameter> followed by any number of additional <formal parameter>s separated by commas."

BNF 5.10   Formal Parameters

<formal parameters> ::= <formal parameter> [, <formal parameter>]*

<formal parameter> ::= <type> <identifier>

Semantics

Declares one or more local variables that are created when the method is invoked and destroyed when it returns.

It may take a bit of thinking to realize why this BNF production generates that. The form is identical for actual parameters, as in BNF 5.11.

BNF 5.11   Actual Parameters

<actual parameters> ::= <actual parameter> [, <actual parameter>]*

<actual parameter> ::= <expression>

Semantics

Each expression is evaluated before the message is sent as part of the parameter linkage.

When there is more than one parameter, the formal and actual parameters are matched up in the order in which they appear. The first actual parameter is said to correspond with the first formal parameter, the second with the second, and so on.

Each formal parameter is a variable declaration (i.e., a type and a name), and each actual parameter is an expression of a type compatible with the corresponding actual parameter (see "Expressions" later in this chapter). Parameters of both types always appear between parentheses and are separated by commas.

Parameter Linkage

With the phrases "actual parameter," "formal parameter," and "corresponding parameter" understood, the parameter linkage operation (the first step of the semantics of a message statement) may be expressed fairly succinctly. To perform a *parameter linkag* , for each parameter:

1. Evaluate the actual parameter.
2. Assign that value to the corresponding formal parameter. Notice that this changes the value of the parameter variable, and thus, technically speaking, changes the state of the program. Thus, the claim made previously that only assignment statements change the state of the computation is not quite true. However, it is a convenient fiction.

What is the difference between this and the semantics of the assignment statement?

Example: Listing 4.14 is the `shrinkPupil()` method for the `Eye` class. Its body is a single statement:

```
pupil.setRadius(pupil.getRadius() - 2);
```

Answer these questions before reading the answers. It's okay to look back to discover the answers if you know you know, but can't remember.

What type of statement is this?

What messages are sent when it executes?

What object is each sent to?

What type is that object (i.e., what class is it an instance of)?

What is the actual parameter?

Describe the semantics of executing this statement.

If you have no idea what most of the answers are, don't feel bad, there is a tremendous amount of detail piling up here, and it's all interrelated. Maybe it's time to take a break, and then, when your head is clear and you can focus again, reread the beginning of the chapter.

```
pupil.setRadius(pupil.getRadius() - 2);
```

Assuming you could answer most of them, here are the answers. This is a message statement. It sends the `setRadius()` message to the `pupil` object (which is a `FilledCircle`, see the section "The `Eye` Class" in Chapter 4, "Graphics and Inheritance") with the actual parameter `pupil.getRadius() - 2`.

To execute that statement, Java first performs the parameter linkage, and then executes the message body. The parameter linkage has two parts: first, evaluate the expression; second, assign the value thus derived to the formal parameter. To evaluate a message statement, Java executes the method the `getRadius()` message invokes and uses what is returned as the value, so, the first thing that happens is `pupil.getRadius()` is executed.

The `getRadius()` method has no parameters, so the action is simply to execute the method body, which is one statement (`return radius;`), which sends back the value of the `radius` variable from inside the `FilledCircle` named `pupil`. Assume that its value is 50.

To complete the evaluation of `pupil.getRadius() - 2`, Java subtracts the 2 from the 50 that came back from `getRadius()`, yielding 48. That is then assigned to the `nuRadius` parameter in the `setRadius()` method. The body of that method is the assignment statement `radius = nuRadius;`, whose execution stores the value of `nuRadius` (namely, 48) back in the `radius` variable inside the `pupil` object.

That's a lot of detail! The good news is that you don't actually have to think about that when you're programming, once you understand the basics; it all disappears into expertise. You just think something like, "Hmmm, shrinkPupil() needs to make the pupil a little smaller. How about 2 pixels? Okay. pupil.setRadius(2 less than it is); Hmmm, how to find out what the radius is now? Oh yeah, getRadius(). So, pupil.setRadius(pupil.getRadius-2);"—and type that.

The toString() Method

This is the standard debugging output routine for every class. Its signature, public String toString(), conveys several pieces of information to a Java savvy reader: 1) the name of the method is toString, 2) it has no parameters, and 3) it returns a value of type String. When writing a class, you can make toString() return any information you choose, as long as it is in a String. The most obvious information to include is the type of the object (i.e., what class it instantiates) and the current value of its variables.

Listing 5.5 is the toString() method from the Circle class. The body of the method has five statements.

LISTING 5.5   The toString() method for Circle.

```
1    public String toString() {
2        String returnMe = "I am a Circle: ";
3        returnMe += "\tx=" + getX();
4        returnMe += "\ty=" + getY();
5        returnMe += "\tradius=" + getRadius();
6        return returnMe;
7    } // toString()
```

The first, line 2, is a variable declaration statement with initialization to the String "I am a Circle: ". This variable, returnMe, is not an instance variable; because it is declared in the body of a method, it is a method variable (see "Local Variables: Parameters, Method Variables, and For Loop Variables" later in this chapter). The next three concatenate: 1) a tab (\t), 2) an instance variable name, 3) an equals sign, and 4) the value of that variable, obtained through its accessor. Line 6, the last statement, is a return statement that sends back the value of returnMe as the value of the toString() message wherever it was sent.

The ClassMaker Tool

The process of programming is not simple or easy. Even after you understand the concepts, a host of details must be attended to before a program can be completed.

Many of the details a programmer must deal with stem from the rigidity of the software, which stems from the mindlessness of current computers.

However, computers are incredibly useful owing to their blinding speed and disregard for endless repetition. In this regard, they can be a pretty good complement to human skills/proclivities; tasks that always involve the exact same actions can be mechanized.

The large majority of programming time is spent selecting, designing, and implementing classes. Although the simplest programs may have only one or a few classes, any substantial project has a number of classes. Once you have mastered accessors, constructors, and toString(), writing them is less than exciting; and, as you have seen, they have the same format in every class. That means software could be written to generate them automatically.

The author has written a ClassMaker class that inputs the shell of a class, with just the name and a list of variables, and produces the constructors, accessors, and toString() from a single button press. It is publicly available for your benefit, but you are only allowed to use it after you can write those methods correctly from memory. The reason is that the mechanics of accessors, constructors, and toString() are those of the majority of all methods, and until you understand how to write them, everything else will be hopeless. Don't use the ClassMaker until you can write these methods without peeking—the easy way is not easy in the long run.

ClassMaker **Input and Output**

Once you are able to write constructors, accessors, and toString() from memory (in our classes, usually everyone can do it by the fourth or fifth week; it just takes practice), you are ready to use the ClassMaker. It takes some of the drudgery out of creating a new class, and any repetitive task that can be automated should be.

You can find the ClassMaker at: *www.willamette.edu/~levenick/classMaker/makeClass.html.*

Listing 5.6 is the input to the ClassMaker to produce the Account class in Listing 5.7.

LISTING 5.6   Input to the ClassMaker for the Account class.

```
1    class Account {
2        int balance;
3        String name;
4    }
```

LISTING 5.7 Output from the `ClassMaker` for the `Account` class.

```
1    public class Account {
2
3        protected int balance;
4        protected String name;
5
6        public Account(){}    //empty default constructor
7
8        public Account(int balance, String name) {  //init'izing constructor
9            this();
10           this.balance = balance;
11           this.name = name;
12       }
13
14       public int getBalance() {return balance;}
15       public String getName() {return name;}
16
17       public void setBalance(int balance) { this.balance = balance;}
18       public void setName(String name) { this.name = name;}
19
20       public String toString() {
21           String returnMe = "I am a Account: ";
22           returnMe += "\tbalance=" + getBalance();
23           returnMe += "\tname=" + getName();
24           return returnMe;
25       } // toString()
26   }  // Account
```

Note that it produces the default constructor, accessors for both variables, and a `toString()` method that displays the values of both variables by using their constructors. You can copy and paste from the Web page into the NetBeans editor window. Read each line of code in Listing 5.7. Become familiar with it; that means be aware of 1) the name of the class, 2) each variable (its name and type), and 3) each method (its heading and body). Do that now. Notice anything strange? The setters are different from those earlier in the text. They do exactly the same thing as the previous setters in a different way; the details are in "Special to Java—What Is `this`?" later in this chapter.

As an exercise, recreate the `ATMApplet` from scratch using the `ClassMaker` to create the frameworks for `Account`, and `Bank`. Notice how much of the code is written for you. Do the same for the `EyesApplet`. Expect this to take several hours. Sorry. It's good to practice; when trying to learn a new programming environment or language, repeat very simple tasks over and over until you can do them effortlessly without running into problems/perplexities each time—then you'll know you have mastered the process.

You will discover that it's much easier to do things the second time, and this time what you're doing will make more sense. Once the mechanics of using Net-Beans becomes more or less automatic, you will have more cognitive capacity left over for the problems that will inevitably arise while programming.

CONSTRUCTORS

A peculiarity of object-oriented programming (OOP) is that often, much of the functionality of a class is accomplished by the constructors (or constructor chains). This statement will make more sense once you have had some experience with constructors.

Syntactically, a constructor declaration is like any other method declaration, with two differences. First, there is no return type (and no value can be returned). Second, its name must be the same as the class it is in.

Executing a constructor is just like executing any other method, but it happens automatically when you create an object of that type with matching parameters.

Default Constructors

A default constructor has no parameters. When the following line is executed:

```
Account myAccount = new Account();
```

three things happen:

1. The new `Account` object is created (i.e., space is allocated for all its variables).
2. The default constructor is executed.
3. The newly constructed `Account` is returned and stored in the `myAccount` variable.

There are thus two ways to automatically initialize the value of an instance variable; either use an assignment with the declaration `int balance=1000000;`, or insert an assignment statement in the default constructor:

```
public Account() {
    balance = 17;
}
```

Assuming you did both, what would the initial value of balance be?

Account **Class Including a Constructor with Parameters**

Usually, when you create objects, you want to give them particular values. With only a default constructor, you are forced to first create the object and then set its values with accessors as in Listing 5.8.

LISTING 5.8 Initializing with accessors.

```
1    Account myAccount = new Account();
2    myAccount.setName("Frodo");
3    myAccount.setBalance(1000000000);
```

Such initialization can be compressed into one if there is a constructor that is passed initial values for the instance variables, as shown in Listing 5.9.

LISTING 5.9 Initializing with a constructor.

```
1    Circle myCircle = new Circle(200, 100, 77);
```

For a Circle, one line replaces four. Obviously, it is fewer keystrokes and clearer to use the initializing constructor, and the ClassMaker writes it for you.

Eye/FilledCircle/Circle **Classes Including a Constructor with Parameters— and Simplifications Appertaining Thereunto**

If we rewrite the Eye Applet using initializing constructors, there are a number of savings. Most obvious is where we create and initialize the Eyes as shown in Listing 5.10.

LISTING 5.10 Initializing an Eye with accessors.

```
1    Eye rightEye = new Eye();
2
3    ...
4
5    rightEye.setX(600);
6    rightEye.setY(100);
7    rightEye.setRadius(100);
8
9    vs...
10
11   Eye rightEye = new Eye(600,100,100);
```

After using the default constructor, the position and size must then be initialized; three lines of code in initComponents(). With the initializing constructor, those three lines disappear; see Listing 5.10. Better, by adding the color to the initializing constructor, the color can be initialized when the Eye is created as well; see Listing 5.11.

LISTING 5.11   Initializing an Eye with a constructor.

```
1    Eye rightEye = new Eye(600,100,100,new Color(200, 177, 200));
```

In this example, the initializing constructors for both Eye and the built-in class Color are used. The fourth parameter to new Eye() is the constructor for Color. You will recall that the parameter linkage mechanism first evaluates each actual parameter and then copies each value to the corresponding formal parameter. To evaluate the Color constructor, a new Color object is instantiated and then passed to the Eye constructor (which passes it on to the FilledCircle object that is created in it, see line 12 in Listing 5.12).

LISTING 5.12   The Eye class, improved.

```
1    import java.awt.*;
2
3    public class Eye {
4
5        protected FilledCircle iris;
6        protected FilledCircle pupil;
7
8        public Eye(){}   //empty default constructor
9
10       public Eye(int x, int y, int radius, Color myColor) {
11           this();   // invoke the default constructor
12           iris = new FilledCircle(x,y,radius, myColor);
13           pupil = new FilledCircle(x,y,radius/2, Color.black);
14       }
15
16       public FilledCircle getIris() {return iris;}
17       public FilledCircle getPupil() {return pupil;}
18
19       public void moveRight() {
20           iris.moveRight();
21           pupil.moveRight();
22       }
23
```

```
24          public void paint(java.awt.Graphics g) {
25              iris.paint(g);
26              pupil.paint(g);
27          }
28
29          public String toString() {
30              String returnMe = "I am a Eye: ";
31              returnMe += "\tiris=" + iris.toString();
32              returnMe += "\tpupil=" + pupil.toString();
33              return returnMe;
34          } // toString()
35      }  // Eye
```

This is an example of what this section mentioned at the start: the phenomenon that in object programming, much of the work can be migrated to the constructors.

Special to Java—What Is this?

The reserved word, this, has several uses.

this

The reserved word this has a special meaning in the context of an instance method; it is the object that was sent the message that caused this method to be executed, or, shorter, the current object. In the context of a constructor, this is the object that is being constructed.

The code written by the ClassMaker uses this to access instance variables. Compare the two setters in Listing 5.13, which are copied from Listings 5.4 and 5.7.

LISTING 5.13   Setters—two techniques to avoid shadowing.

```
1   public void setBalance(int nuBalance) {
2       balance = nuBalance;
3   }
4
5   public void setBalance(int balance) {
6       this.balance = balance;
7   }
```

They both do exactly the same thing: assign the value of their parameter to the instance variable named balance. In the first version, the name of the parameter is nuBalance, so line 2 assigns the value of that parameter to the instance variable balance as desired. In the second version, the parameter is named balance, just like the instance variable. Thus, in the body of the second setBalance(), there are two different variables, both with the name "balance." If the programmer, without thinking, attempted to set the instance variable named `balance` to the value of the parameter named `balance` by typing `balance = balance;` on line 6, it could cause a hard-to-find bug. When there are two variables with the same name defined in the same place, Java uses the one that is defined the closest (actually the one defined in the nearest enclosing scope, see "Variables II (Varieties and Scope)" later in this chapter). In this case, the parameter `balance` is defined closer (looking up the code from line 6), so it is used both times (it is said to *shadow* the instance variable). Therefore, the value of the parameter `balance` is retrieved and stored back in the parameter balance, leaving the instance variable `balance` unchanged. To specify the instance variable `balance`, use `this.balance`.

The code the `ClassMaker` made for `Circle` included an initializing constructor, shown in Listing 5.14.

LISTING 5.14 The initializing constructor written by the `ClassMaker`.

```
1    public class Circle {
2
3        protected int x;
4        protected int y;
5        protected int radius;
6
7        public Circle(){}   //empty default constructor
8        public Circle(int x, int y, int radius) {   //initializing constructor
9            this();   // invoke the default constructor
10           this.x = x;
11           this.y = y;
12           this.radius = radius;
13       }
14   }
```

Note the use of `this` in the initializing constructor.

Line 9: Invokes the default constructor; `this()` is the default constructor.
Lines 10–12: Sets the three variables. `this.x` is the instance variable x.

Because the parameters `x`, `y`, and `radius` are the same as the instance variables, it uses `this` to store the values in the instance variables.

The `this()` Method

If initialization tasks are being performed for every new instance of an object, they should be done in the default constructor. That way, later, when you (or other people) add additional initializing constructors, as long as they invoke the default constructor, the functionality of all the constructors can be preserved even if someone subsequently alters the default constructor. To invoke the default constructor, in another constructor, you say, this(). However, it must be the first line of the constructor body; otherwise, it will not compile.

Wait! The previous paragraph seemed to be about avoiding possible future problems if someone added initializing constructors and then after that, someone else changed the default constructor. If all you're doing is trying to learn to program and writing tiny little programs that are just going to be discarded, *who care*? Like much of Java, this only makes any appreciable difference when you are doing something big and complicated. This is what makes learning Java a bit difficult at first. If you have the feeling it's more complicated than it needs to be to accomplish simple tasks, you are right.

It's a bit as if you want to build a small, simple bird feeder, and your friend who is a machinist says, "I've got just what you need" and opens the door to a machine shop as big as a basketball arena, packed full with numeric control machines, whirring and spinning ominously—and all you really need is a hand saw and a hammer. However, if you were one day planning to build something complicated, like perhaps a Mars rover, or a better cell phone, or... you name it, then you couldn't possibly do it with the hammer and saw.

So, don't worry about those details right now, just be aware of them, so if you run into this() you won't be completely flummoxed. By the way, the three programmers—the first who wrote the class originally, the second who modified the initializing constructor, and the third who subsequently modified the default constructor—might all be the same person at different times. They might all be you.

DETAILS II–TYPES, OPERATORS, AND EXPRESSIONS

With those examples in mind, we are ready to turn to more details.

Types

In Java, a type is a primitive type, a built-in class, or a user-defined class. Some types you have worked with include int, String, Applet, Account, Circle, and Eye. The first of those is a primitive, the next two are built in, and the last three are user-defined. There are several other primitive types, many built-in classes, and potentially infinitely many user-defined classes.

Primitive Types

The primitive types are either numeric or non-numeric. There are only two non-numeric primitive types, `char` and `Boolean`, which represent character and logical values, respectively. The numeric types are either whole numbers, roughly like the integers (`long`, `int`, `short`, `byte`), or decimals, roughly like real numbers (`double`, `float`). However, there are infinitely many integers and uncountable infinite reals, whereas every primitive Java type is represented in a limited amount of space and so can only take on a finite number of values. The primitive types, along with their possible values and operators appear in Table 5.2.

TABLE 5.2 Types, Values, and Operators

Type	Range of Values	Operators
long	$-2^{63} <= x <= 2^{63}-1$	+, −, *, /, %
int	$-2^{31} <= x <= 2^{31}-1$	
short	$-2^{15} <= x <= 2^{15}-1$	
byte	$-2^{7} <= x <= 2^{7}-1$	
double	$-1.8*10^{308} < x < 1.8*10^{308}$	+, −, *, /
float	$1.4*10^{38} < x < 1.4*10^{38}$	+, −, *, /
boolean	{false, true}	!, &&, ||
char	any keyboard character	none

For most applications, `int`s will work fine for whole numbers and `double`s for fractional numbers. There is no reason to use `float`, `short`, or `byte`, unless you discover you are out of memory; and that rarely happens. If you tried to count all the people on the planet, or keep track of the national debt, `int`s are too small, as 2^{31} is only a little more than 2 billion. Fortunately, `long`s would work just fine for those. For unlimitedly large numbers, there is the `BigNumber` class.

Numeric Types, Representation: Bits, Bytes, and Powers of Two

Some people have the idea that computing is all about bits and bytes, zeros and ones; and it is, underneath. Modern computing deals very little with bits and bytes, but there are times when you need to understand them a bit. One of those times is if you want to understand how numbers are represented in Java and why they act the way they do.

The range of values for the type int is shown in Table 5.2 as $-2^{31} <= x <= 2^{31}-1$—this has several implications and an informative cause. First, it means that if you need to store numbers larger or smaller than that, you must use another type; in this case, long. Second, if you add 1 to $2^{31}-1$, instead of getting 2^{31} as you might expect, you get negative 2^{31} instead! Try it for yourself. Set a variable to 2 billion (2000000000) and then add it to itself and print the result. To do so, type these lines into a main() method, or if your Applet is still on the screen, into init():

```
int big = 2000000000;
int bigger = big + big;
System.out.println("2 billion + 2 billion=" + bigger);
```

On our machine, this code prints:

```
2 billion + 2 billion=-294967296
```

which is certainly *not* 4 billion! Why does this happen? The explanation stems from the representation of ints.

An int is represented in Java as 4 bytes. A byte is 8 bits. A bit is the smallest possible unit of information; it has only two values, 0 or 1. Therefore, a bit is just enough information to distinguish "yes" from "no." Four bytes have 8+8+8+8 bits, that's 32, so an int can take on 2^{32} different values (if you don't know why, reread "Problem Solving Principle #1: Build a Prototype" in Chapter 1, "Programming Is Like Juggling"). Half those values are used for positive numbers (zero on up), the other half for negative numbers; half of 2^{32} is 2^{31}. Since there is no negative zero (i.e., the least negative number is –1), the smallest number is -2^{31}, whereas zero is the smallest non-negative number, so that only leaves $2^{31}-1$ other positive numbers.

The types, long, short, and byte, have 8, 2, and 1 byte, respectively (that's 64, 16, and 8 bits); if you look at Table 5.2, the ranges correspond perfectly to that.

Arithmetic Operators

Table 5.2 shows four operators for doubles, the ordinary arithmetic operators, +, –, *, and /. They work just the way you would expect; when applied to two double operands, they yield a double value. Int operators when applied to two ints yield an int value. There are two int division operators, / and %. int division is the division you might have learned in third grade, where 7/3=2 with a remainder of 1. The / operator applied to two ints yields the number of times the second goes into the first evenly, 7/3=2. The % operator yields the remainder, 7%3=1.

Mixed Expressions

When the two operands of an arithmetic operator are an int and a double, the int is converted to a double and double operator is used. As you would guess, a double value results. Thus, 2*2 evaluates to int 4, but 2*2.0 evaluates to double 4.0.

The reason the int is automatically converted to a double and not vice versa is that the range of doubles is so much greater than that of ints. There are many doubles that simply cannot be represented as ints, but every int can be represented exactly as a double.

Expressions

All information in a Java program has a type: information exists in both variables and expressions. Like a variable, an expression has a type and a value; unlike a variable, it does not have a name. Expressions are not declared and sometimes it is not obvious what their type is.

In the BNF thus far, expressions have only appeared in two places: on the right of the assignment operator and as actual parameters. That means that anything appearing either on the right of an assignment operator or as an actual parameter must be an expression syntactically.

Here are some int expressions:

```
17
1 + 1
1 + 2 * 3
1 + 2 - 3 / 4 * 5
(1 + 2 -3/4) * 5
```

The values are 17, 2, 7, 3, and 15. The first three should be obvious. The value of 17 is 17, 1+1=2, and everyone knows that you do multiplication before addition. The value of the fourth hinges on how integer division works. This is because the / operator does int division, discarding any remainder. This can be the cause of very subtle bugs, as will be seen later. So, 3/4 = 0, 0*5=0, 1+2=3, and 3–0=3.

The fifth expression uses parentheses to cause the multiplication to happen last, so (3+0)*5=15.

Precedence of Operators

In an expression with multiple operators, the question arises, "Which operator is applied first?" In other words, which operation precedes which others? You are already familiar with precedence, since you know that 1 + 2 * 3 is 7. In ordinary arithmetic, multiplication precedes addition. In computing, one says, "* has higher *precedenc˙* than +"; it means just what you expect, that without parentheses, multiplication happens before addition. Precedences are shown in Table 5.3.

TABLE 5.3 Precedence of Operators

Higher Precedence Operators Are Higher in the Table

. —the message dot

(cast)

!, unary −

*, /, %, &&

+, −, ||

<, >, <=, >=, ==, !=

The safest rule is, if you're worried that precedence is a problem, use parentheses.

BNF for Expressions

You may have noticed that the BNF for expression was missing. It is shown in BNF 5.12.

BNF 5.12 Expression

```
<expression> ::= <constant>
              | <variable>
              | <message expression>
              | <expression> <binary operator> <expression>
              | (<expression> )
              | <unary operator> <expression>
A recursive BNF production.
```

Notice that this is a recursive definition (if you've forgotten the term *recursive*, see "What Classes Will We Need? What Will They Do?" in Chapter 3, "Class Design and Implementation"); it can generate arbitrarily complex expressions. Binary and unary operators take two and one expressions as operands, respectively; they are defined as in BNF 5.13 and BNF 5.14.

BNF 5.13   Binary Operators

<binary operator> ::= + | – | * | / | % | && | || | < | > | <= | >= | == | !=
&& is and || is or; these are boolean operators.

<, >, <=, >=, ==, != are relational operators, they compare their operands and yield a boolean expression. The operator == is equals, != is not equals.

BNF 5.14   Unary Operators

<unary operator> ::= – | !
  – is minus, as in –17, ! is not, as in !(x>100)

Notice that expressions may be arbitrarily complex.

Expressions Compatible with a Type

In an assignment statement, the expression on the right of the assignment operator must be compatible with the variable on the left. The same is true of actual and corresponding formal parameters.

The simplest form of compatibility is identity. In other words, an `int` expression is compatible with an `int` variable—you can always assign the value of an expression to a variable of the same type.

For now, all you need to know is that expressions of type `int` are compatible with `double` variables, so it is legal to assign an `int` value to a `double` variable (or to use an `int` expression as an actual parameter corresponding to a `double` formal parameter), but the reverse is not true (see "Mixed Expressions" earlier in this chapter). Expressions a of type completely unrelated to a variable's type can never be compatible; you can never assign a `char` or a `String` to an `int`, or an `int` or a `double` to a `String`. However, sometimes you can convert them by hand.

Converting One Type to Another

There are a number of different techniques to convert one type to another when they are incompatible.

String `to` int

When input comes from a `TextField`, it is always a `String` (the signature of `getText()` is `public String getText()`). The method that converts a `String` to an int is `Integer.parseInt(String)`, which was illustrated in the section "Building and Testing the Prototype GUI," in Chapter 3. There is a similar method for `doubles`.

Object to String

Any `Object` can be converted to a `String` using `toString()`—but, you already knew that! An `int` (or any primitive type) can be converted to a `String` by concatenating it to the empty `String`, `""` like this `""+17` becomes `"17"`. It is possible, in some situations, to force an expression to be a particular type. When you cast an expression, you are essentially saying to the compiler, "I know more than you; do what I say here!" The next section illustrates casting.

An Example—Random Circles at Random Locations

Let's say you decide to create a bunch of `Circles` at random locations and sizes and display them. There is a random number generator that you can access by saying `Math.random()`—it returns a random number in the interval [0,1] whose type is `double`. To place a `Circle` at random requires random *x* and *y* values. To make it a random size requires a random *radius* value. Assume you want `Circles` with centers in a square 500 pixels on a side with radii up to 200 pixels; then you would need two random `ints` between 0 and 499, and one between 1 and 200. Since `random()` provides `doubles` in [0,1], you need to map from that small interval to the larger ones. The best way to do that is with a method (so as not to have to write the conversion code repeatedly—and if it turns out to have a bug, you will only have to fix it one place... plus, it might be useful later).

It is easy to perform this mapping; simply multiply. 500*0 = 0, and any number < 1 times 500 is less than 500. Therefore, the method might look like Listing 5.15.

LISTING 5.15   A method to provide random `ints` with bugs.

```
1    int rand(int max) {
2        return Math.random() * max;
3    }
```

This method will not compile because the expression has type `double`, but the method heading declares the return type as `int`.

The problem is that when you multiply a `double` by an `int` you get a `double`. Casting a `double` as an `int` simply truncates anything after the decimal point, so the obvious solution is to cast that expression as an `int`; see Listing 5.16.

LISTING 5.16 A method to provide random `ints` with a precedence error.

```
1    int rand(int max) {
2        return  (int) Math.random() * max;
3    }
```

This is a precedence error; it compiles, but always returns zero. The way to understand why is to realize that `*`, `(int)`, and the dot after `Math` are all operators and will be applied in order of precedence. So, first the `random()` message will be sent, returning a value in [0,1), then the cast, `(int)` will be applied, converting the value to an int 0 (through truncation), and finally the multiplication will result in 0.

As always, the way to fix precedence problems is with parentheses, as shown in Listing 5.17. The parentheses cause the multiplication to happen before the cast, so everything is copasetic.

LISTING 5.17 A method to provide random `ints` that works!

```
1    int rand(int max) {
2        return (int) (Math.random() * max);
3    }
```

Insert this method into your revised `EyeApplet` class, and replace the body of `paint()` with the line:

```
1    (new Circle(rand(500), rand(500), rand(200)).paint(g);
```

This will draw a different `Circle` each time you resize, or drag the window, or push a button in the `Applet`. Try it. When it works, make five copies of that line as the body of `paint()` and execute that.

Random `FilledCircles`

If you feel like playing a bit more before continuing, try this. Create and display `FilledCircles` instead of `Circles`. The `FilledCircle` constructor requires a fourth parameter, of type `Color`. To generate a random `Color`, simply give it three random values in the range [0,255] as parameters, as shown in Listing 5.18. Add this method to your `EyeApplet`.

LISTING 5.18 `randColor()` returns a random `Color`.

```
1    Color randColor() {
2        return new Color(rand(256), rand(256), rand(256));
3    }
```

Then, modify `paint()` so it contains:

```
(new FilledCircle(rand(500), rand(500), rand(50),
    randColor())).paint(g);
```

as many times as you want random `FilledCircles` displayed.

If you wanted 20 `FilledCircles`, you could copy that line 20 times; or, you could write the `for` loop in Listing 5.19.

LISTING 5.19   A loop to create and display 20 random `FilledCircles`.

```
1    for (int i=0; i<20; i++)
2        (new FilledCircle(rand(500), rand(500),
                rand(50), randColor())).paint(g);
```

The details of this loop will be explained in Chapter 8, "Iterative Statements and Strings," but for now just think of it as "abracadabra." Try it with 100 `FilledCircles` (change the 20 to 100), or 1000. Does it slow down much?

Variables II (Varieties and Scope)

There are five different varieties of variables: instance variables, class variables, parameters, method variables, and loop variables. These will be addressed in order of how often they have appeared in this text so far. They differ in where they are stored, how they are initialized, how long they exist, and where they are visible. This last is referred to as their *scope*.

Instance Variables

By far, the most common variables you have seen so far, and will encounter in object programming, are instance variables. See "Variables I (State)" early in this chapter for details. They are declared outside of any method and are visible everywhere in the class. They may include an = <expression> to initialize them, but if not, they are initialized to zero when the instance is created (before the constructor is executed).

Local Variables: Parameters, Method Variables, and For Loop Variables

There are three kinds of local variables. Unlike instance variables, their scope is the method or loop in which they are declared, and only exist while it is being executed.

Formal parameters have the form of variable declarations, namely <type> <identifier>. They are visible in the method in which they exist. Their values are provided as part of parameter linkage when the method is invoked, and cannot generally be determined at *compile time*. There are many examples in the text so far, and details are in "Parameters (Actual, Formal, Linkage)" earlier in this chapter.

Method variables are declared within the body of a method. They appeared in Listing 3.12 (`Bank theBank`), Listing 5.4 (`Account myAccount`), and Listing 5.5 (`String returnMe`). They exist only in the body of the method and must be initialized.

The only `for` loop variable was in Listing 5.19, (`int i`). Loop variables only exist within the loop they are declared in, and must be initialized when declared.

Class Variables

So far, no class variables have been used. They are not used very much in elementary programming; some people program for years and never use them. They are useful in certain situations, though, and you might run into one somewhere. Syntactically, class variables are exactly like instance variables, except they have the keyword `static` in front. Class variables do not belong to any instance, but instead to the class—hence the name. They are used when there is information that must be accessible from every instance, but does not belong to the instances. A class variable exists as long as the program is running and is visible from every instance. Variables are summarized in Table 5.4.

TABLE 5.4   Variable—Types, Scopes, and Initialization

Variable Type	Scope	Initialization
instance variable	entire class	auto, to 0 or by assignment
formal parameter	body of method	by parameter linkage
method variable	body of method	must assign initial value
loop variable	body of loop	must assign initial value
class variable	all instances	like instance

Example—Serial Numbers

Some people, when they first start object programming, feel somewhat uncomfortable about having many nearly identical objects of the same class, and would like to be able to keep track of which is which. One easy way to distinguish between nearly identical objects in the world is to attach a serial number to each. The first one is number 1, the second number 2, and so on. The same may be done with Java objects. Here's how.

Each object must keep track of its serial number, so there must be an instance variable; for example, `int serialNumber;`, which will be set to 1 for the first object instantiated, 2 for the second, and so on. There must also be a class variable to keep track of the next serial number to be assigned; like this:

```
private static int nextSerialNumber=1;.
```

Then, in the default constructor, there must be one line added:

```
serialNumber = nextSerialNumber++;
```

This is shorthand for:

```
serialNumber = nextSerialNumber;
nextSerialNumber = nextSerialNumber + 1;
```

The first line assigns the current value of the class variable nextSerialNumber (1 the first time) to the instance variable serialNumber. The second line increments the class variable nextSerialNumber.

That's all it takes. To see that it works, add this line as the second in toString():

```
returnMe += " my serial number is: " + serialNumber;
```

Modify the Circle or Account class (use the one with the main() method to make your task simple), and test to see that it works.

If you try to use an instance variable to keep track of the serial number, you will discover that you cannot make the numbering work correctly. Consider this code:

```
public class BrokeSerialExample {
    private int nextSerialNumber=1;
    public BrokeSerialExample() {
        serialNumber = nextSerialNumber++;
    }
}
```

Here, the static has been deleted, so nextSerialNumber is an instance variable instead of a class variable. Thus, every instance will have a copy of the nextSerial-Number variable, and each will be initialized to 1 before being incremented, so every instance will have a serial number with a value of 1.

Conventions

There are a number of conventions that are not required by the compiler, but make it much easier to program. These are entirely arbitrary, but are pretty much standard in the industry.

Naming Conventions

Identifiers should convey information; they should tell what they are or what they do. This includes class names, method names, and variable names. Typically, variables are nouns, and methods are verbs. Accessor names start with get or set and then the variable being accessed; for example, for `balance`: `getBalance()` and `setBalance()`.

Case Conventions

Class names begin with uppercase letters. Instance names begin with lowercase letters. The second and any subsequent English word in an identifier starts with an uppercase letter. Constants are all uppercase.

The Importance of Good Names

Descriptive names can make the difference between being able to debug your program or not. The reason is simple, cognitive capacity. People can only keep in mind around five things at once. If you name your variables that mean balance and radius, Frank and Ernestine, then you are squandering two of your precious five on remembering which means which. When the program is extremely simple, this is not a big problem, but if it is just at the limit of the programmer's capacity, this could lead to disaster.

RECAPITULATION

As mentioned in Chapter 1, a few dozen concepts must be understood, at least vaguely, before a person can program in Java. Most of them have been covered in this chapter (if you're feeling a bit overwhelmed, please be patient, it gets easier). Here's a rough list; this would be suitable to read every night after programming until it is all obvious. It appears, first as a list, and then with explanations. When you can remember the explanations by looking at the list, you can stop looking at it.

Information

> types
> values
> variables
> expressions

Language Elements

classes
  variables
  methods
  constructors
objects
  statements
  identifiers
  methods/messages
  signatures
  parameters (formal/actual)
  parameter linkages
syntax
  semantics

Process

editing
  compilation
  execution
  debugging
  prototyping

Here's that same list with some explanatory text.

Information

Types

All information in a Java program has a type. There are primitive types, built-in classes, and user-defined classes. It is possible to change types by casting.

Values

Expressions have values. To compute the value of an expression, it is evaluated. Every type has a range of legal values.

Variables

Variables hold information. Every variable has a name, a type, and a value. A variable only holds one value at a time. There are five different kinds of variables: instance, parameter, method, loop, and class.

Expressions

Variables and constants may be combined in arbitrarily complex fashion to form an expression. Syntactically, expressions appear to the right of assignment operators and as actual parameters (thus far; later, you will see them in other places).

Language Elements

Classes

A class is a template for objects of that type. It includes both variables and methods. Every object of that type has all the instance variables and can use all the methods declared in it.

If a method is declared `static`, it is not an instance method, but a class method. If a method does not use any state information from an instance (i.e., any instance variables), it can be made into a class method.

Variables

Every instance of a class has its own copy of each instance variable. All instances share access to class variables, which are stored in the class itself (interestingly, classes are also objects; they are instances of the class `Class`).

Methods

Methods have a heading and a body. The heading specifies the type, name, and parameters of the method. The method body is a single block statement, which is a pair of {}s around a series of statements. To execute the method, Java executes each of those statements in order.

Constructors

Constructors are typeless methods with the same name as the class that are executed when a new object of that class is constructed.

Objects

Objects (also called *instances*) of a particular class are created by saying:

```
new ClassName();
```

This is referred to as instantiation. When an object is instantiated, the constructor corresponding to the signature of the new message is executed.

Statements

Statements are what accomplish most of the action when a program executes. So far, these statements have been presented: assignment statement, return statement, block statement, and message statement.

Identifiers

Identifiers are Java names. They start with a letter, and are composed only of letters, digits, and underscores.

Methods/Messages

When you send a message to an object, it invokes the method in that class with the same signature. First, it performs the parameter linkage, and then executes the method body.

Signatures

The signature of a method is its access type, return type, name, and parameter types.

Parameters (formal/actual)

The parameter in the method declaration is the formal parameter, the one in the message is the actual parameter.

Parameter Linkages

Each actual parameter is evaluated and its value copied to the corresponding formal parameter.

Syntax

The syntax of Java is defined by a set of BNF productions. Any source code not matching this grammar symbol for symbol is deemed to have compiler errors.

Semantics

The semantics of a statement is the action it performs when it is executed. An experienced programmer has internalized the semantics of enough of the constructs of the language that solving routine problems is easy.

Process

Editing

Editing is when the programmer is inputting or changing source code (classes).

Compilation

Compilation is when the compiler is checking the syntax of a class. Errors at this stage are compile-time errors and are either lexical or grammatical. Lexical errors happen when the compiler does not know what an identifier means; the most common causes are forgetting to declare variables, or typos. Grammatical errors occur when the syntax of the source code does not match the BNF description of the language precisely.

After verifying the syntax of a class, the compiler converts the source code to byte code. Assuming the source code is in a file called Foo.java, the byte code will be put in a file called Foo.class.

Execution

To execute a program, the byte code is interpreted by the JVM. This is when the work of the programmer comes to fruition. The semantics of the various methods are carried out to achieve some desired result. Errors here are runtime errors, and appear as `Exceptions`.

Debugging

Debugging is the process of removing errors from a program, and is the most time-consuming and frustrating aspect of programming. Any nontrivial program has multiple errors. Only novice programmers imagine that one can program without bugs. Like dropping the balls when juggling, it happens. One important skill in programming is learning to write code that is easy to debug.

Prototyping

Building simple prototypes and adding functionality as the previous prototype works is perhaps the most important way to make debugging simple; there are simply fewer places to look for the bugs.

CONCLUSION

Programming in Java is accomplished by writing classes. Classes define the information objects of that type can store (by declaring variables) and the actions those objects can carry out (by declaring methods). Methods have a heading and a body; the former defines the signature of the method, the latter defines its action.

Although there are many programming constructs and statements, the only three that alter the state of the computation, the only three that really do anything, are input, output, and assignment; all the others are organizational, organizing both the structure of the program and which of the big three are executed in what order and how many times.

The standard set of methods that all classes should have, including constructors, accessors, and toString();, are written automatically by the ClassMaker. Any others you will have to write by hand.

This chapter presented many of the details of Java programming. If it succeeded, you are beginning to understand the interplay of the two dozen odd concepts that make up most of programming. If not, our apologies; with luck, perhaps after a bit more practice, it will fall together for you.

REVIEW QUESTIONS

5.1 Why are initializing constructors useful?

5.2 What is this?

5.3 What is this()?

5.4 Why are good names important?

5.5 What will this output?

```
byte x=127;
x++;
System.out.println("x=" + x);
```

5.6 Name four varieties of variables. What are their scopes?

5.7 What does it mean for one variable to shadow another?

5.8 What is the type and value of:

```
17
3.141
0.1*30
(int) 0.1*33
(int) (0.1*33)
2+2
"2+2"
"2"+"2"
```

Integer.parseInt("2"+"2");
13/4
13%4
""
""+13%4
"(int) 1.414"

5.9 What language does this BNF generate?

<S> ::= <A> <B>
<A> ::= a | a <A> <B>
<B> ::= b

5.10 What do the symbols: ::=, |, [], <>, [x]* mean in BNF?

Programming Exercises

5.11 You can convert an int to a String by pasting it onto "". Try this by:

```
System.out.println("" + 17);
```

You should see 17 print. Now try:

```
System.out.println("" + 17 + 17);
```

What goes wrong? Hint: you can fix it with parentheses.

6 Software Reuse

In This Chapter

- Inheritance
- Composition
- Composition Programming Example: Snowpeople

INTRODUCTION

Software is a new invention, and is nearly pure information, like a story or DNA. Fortunes have been made, and will be made writing and selling software. Creating and distributing software as a commodity is very different from growing and selling soybeans, or building and shipping refrigerators. Once it is written, software can be distributed at low cost on CD-ROMs or at almost no cost over the Web, making enormous profits possible.

A peculiarity of software is that new releases, revisions, and updates are common. The extent to which the old software can be reused determines how much work these revisions entail. If even minor changes necessitate reworking large bodies of code, then they are difficult and expensive. On the other hand, if a new version of a product can be produced without extensive rewriting, it is simpler and cheaper.

Thus, the possibility of reusing software without reworking it or even looking at it would be a tremendous advantage.

Object-oriented programming makes possible software reuse by inheritance and composition. These techniques were introduced in Chapter 5, "Toward Consistent Classes," and will be revisited in more detail here.

INHERITANCE

Inheritance gives the programmer tremendous power. Once a class is written and debugged, another class can modify or enhance it without the programmer having to worry about destroying its functionality and often without even knowing what its code looks like.

For example, every user `Applet` class extends `java.applet.Applet`. The first `Applet` you wrote (Listing 2.5) had just an empty block following the heading in Listing 2.5, and it worked just fine (although it didn't do much); see Listing 6.1.

LISTING 6.1   Reprise of Listing 2.5.

```
public class RobotGreeter extends java.applet.Applet {}
```

This is because it inherited all the functionality of `java.applet.Applet`. Here, `RobotGreeter` is said to be a subclass of `java.applet.Applet`, and `java.applet.Applet` is the superclass of `RobotGreeter`.

The `Object` Class

At the top of the Java class hierarchy sits the `Object` class. Every Java class is a descendant of `Object`. All of the methods and variables in `Object` are defined in every object of any type. There are not very many methods defined in `Object` (you can check the documentation if you are curious—*http://java.sun.com/j2se/1.4.2/docs/api/*); the only one we will address here is `toString()`.

Every user-defined class extends some class. If there is no `extends` keyword after the class name, the compiler inserts `extends Object` automatically.

The Mechanics of Message Sending

By now, you are familiar with sending messages to objects. Perhaps it has begun to seem straightforward and natural; if a class has a method defined, you can send the associated message to objects of that type. If you try to send a message to an object whose class does not have the associated method defined, a compiler error is generated, and your code will not run. However, consider the `FilledCircle` class in

Listing 6.2 and the code in Listing 6.3 where iris, a FilledCircle, is being sent setX().

LISTING 6.2   The complete FilledCircle class, from Listing 4.11.

```
1    import java.awt.*;
2    public class FilledCircle extends Circle {
3        protected Color myColor = new Color(100,0,100);
4
5        /** Creates a new instance of FilledCircle */
6        public FilledCircle() {}
7
8        public void setColor(Color c) {
9            myColor = c;
10       }
11
12       public void paint(Graphics g) {
13           g.setColor(myColor);
14           g.fillOval(x-radius, y-radius, radius*2, radius*2);
15       }
16   }
```

LISTING 6.3   From Listing 4.13.

```
1    public void moveLeft() {
2        iris.setX(iris.getX()-2);
3        pupil.setX(iris.getX());
4    }
```

There is no setX() method declared in the FilledCircle class, so why does this code compile? For that matter, do you see an int x variable in FilledCircle? How can you set what doesn't exist? You probably already know the answer; if not, look at line 2 in Listing 6.2.

At runtime, when an object is sent a message, if its class declares the associated method, the JVM executes that method. If its class does not declare that method, the JVM checks its superclass; if the JVM finds it there, it executes it; if not, the search continues up the class hierarchy. When it reaches the Object class, if the method is still not found there, a NoSuchMethodException is generated (you can read about Exceptions in Appendix B, "Exceptions").

The FilledCircle class extends the user-defined Circle class; therefore, FilledCircle inherits the x, y, and radius variables plus their accessors from the

Circle class. The compiler thus allows setX() to be sent to iris because it was defined in iris' superclass.

To aid memory and facilitate communication, it is often useful to have a picture of the class hierarchy. Figure 6.1 shows two common styles of class diagram for FilledCircle (Booch on the left, UML on the right). Both show that FilledCircle extends Circle, which extends the Object class.

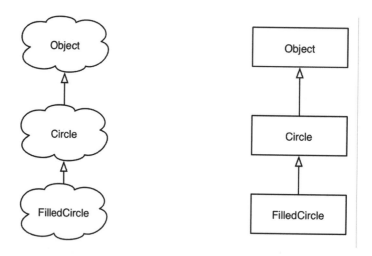

FIGURE 6.1   Booch and UML diagrams.

 You can send any object toString() and be confident it will work, why?

This Is super!

Sometimes, in a constructor, you want to invoke the superclass' constructor. The most common time is in an initializing constructor with a number of parameters, some of which are for variables in the superclass. Just as this() invokes the default constructor for this class (see the section "this" in Chapter 5), super() invokes the superclass constructor.

For example, if you wanted to write an initializing constructor for the four variables in FilledCircle and there was already one for x, y, and radius in Circle, you could write the constructor in Listing 6.4. Line 2 invokes Circle's initializing constructor to set x, y, and radius. Line 3 sets the color (!).

LISTING 6.4 Initializing constructor for `FilledCircle` using `super()`.

```
1    public FilledCircle(int x, int y, int r, Color c) {
2        super(x,y,r);
3        setColor(c);
4    }
```

The superclass initializes its three variables, and then the `color` variable is set locally. Invoking `super()` must be the first thing in the constructor.

COMPOSITION

Having one thing composed of several others is common and familiar in everyday life. A student's daily schedule is composed of classes, meetings, and meals. A face is composed of various features. Generally, we experience objects in the world as sets of features that travel around together. Containment is also familiar in the world. Dressers contain clothes of various kinds. Toolboxes are used to hold various tools. A backpack may contain books, pens, a water bottle, and a computer.

Composition in object programming shares features from both composite objects and containers in the world. It refers to a class being made up of several objects of other classes. Therefore, a composite object may be thought of as a container for other objects, or as the combination of those objects—either way can be useful in different contexts.

The `Eye` class was composed of an iris and a pupil, both `FilledCircles`. Figure 6.2 shows the class diagram for `Eye`, again in two different styles. Both show that an `Eye` extends `Object` and is composed of two `FilledCircles`, which extend `Circle`, which extends `Object`.

In the Booch diagram, each cloud represents a class. There are two kinds of arcs: arrows, representing inheritance, and lines with a dot and an h (for "has") representing composition. The class at the dotted end has or contains instances of the other. The number at the other end indicates how many instances; by default, it is one. In the UML diagram, inheritance is also represented by an arrow, but composition is represented by a horizontal arrow with a "has" label.

To write a `Face` class, you might include two `Eyes`, a `Nose`, and a `Mouth` (once you wrote `Nose` and `Mouth`). To display it, you would display each component in a particular spatial relationship to each other. You might write a `Person` class that included a `Face`, and various other body parts. Then, you could create a `Scene` involving several `Persons`.

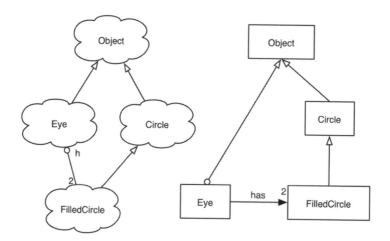

FIGURE 6.2 Booch and UML diagrams for Eye.

Composition allows you to assemble multiple objects of various types into a container. This is efficient and useful, as it allows you to group things and treat the ensemble as a single entity, thus simplifying your thinking.

COMPOSITION PROGRAMMING EXAMPLE: SNOWPEOPLE

The remainder of this chapter is a programming example.

A Description of the Task

Here is the programming task for this chapter. Write a Java Applet that will display several snowpeople of various sizes at various locations around the screen. To simulate warm weather, make the snowfolk melt some each time the user pushes a button labeled "warm sunny day." When a snowperson melts, increase the size of a gray puddle of melted snow under it.

Overall Design

Perhaps, given your experience with the Eye class, you feel that you know enough to immediately start writing code. It would be fine to write a prototype SnowPerson class immediately—that's a reasonable approach. However, before writing very much of the detailed code, it is important to think through the entire problem. What classes will you need? How will they be related? Which will do what? Carefully designing code before writing can save many hours of frustrating debugging and redesign.

As always, the first questions in GUI object design are, "What will the GUI look like?" and "What classes will be needed?" There is never one right answer to either question, and after working on the implementation some you may realize the class structure or the GUI you've chosen needs revision. Making considered choices could save a tremendous amount of time. Aim first, and then shoot.

The GUI

The interface for this problem is very simple. There is a single button that the user can push to simulate one day of melting. The only output is to display the snowpeople. It might be nice to draw some background for the snowpeople as well.

Classes

In addition to the Applet class (which, as usual, will handle the GUI), we will definitely need a SnowPerson class. We might also need a SnowBall and Puddle class, each of which would reuse FilledCircle. Or perhaps the SnowPerson could just contain four FilledCircles, named head, middle, base, and puddle.

How Many Classes Should You Have?

The right number of classes for a particular problem is somewhat ambiguous. It is perhaps a matter of taste, and as the expression goes, "there's no accounting for taste." For a large problem, having only one class would be too few; for a small problem, having more than a handful would likely be too many. Let's keep open the choice of whether to have Puddle and SnowBall classes for the present, until after considering some of the details.

SnowPerson Design

The description of the task left a number of details unspecified, including how many snowballs is a SnowPerson composed of? What are their relative sizes? What color are they? How much does a SnowPerson melt in one day? When it melts, how quickly does the puddle grow? This lack of specificity forces the programmer to either make these decisions arbitrarily, or request additional information. If someone had hired you to produce a SnowPerson Applet, you would ask him if he preferred to specify those things, or if you should make your own decisions. Imagine how upset everyone would be if you made the decisions yourself, wrote all the code, delivered it, and your customers had very different expectations. Here, these decisions have been made arbitrarily. Feel free to implement them differently.

How Many? How Big?

Let's assume that a SnowPerson is composed of three white snowballs getting smaller as they go up (as usual). Call them the base, the middle, and the head. The exact ratio of sizes is not important; let's say the radius of the middle is two-thirds the radius of the base, and the head radius is two-thirds of the middle. If you don't like how this looks, you can adjust it later.

Where Do the Three Snowballs Go?

Perhaps the most difficult decision is where to locate each of the snowballs. Recall that FilledCircles keep track of the position of their centers. Assume the Applet will specify where each SnowPerson goes using *x*- and *y*-coordinates. Should that location be used for the top of the head? Or the bottom of the base? Remember that the snowfolk are going to melt. If the location of a SnowPerson were the top of the head, as it melted, the base would rise up into the air! That could be amusing, but is hardly how real snowpeople behave. Thus, the location of a SnowPerson will be where the base touches the ground.

Given that decision, the positions of all three snowballs are fixed. The base is centered, its radius above its location. The middle is centered above that by the radius of the base plus its own radius (see Figure 6.4). The head's position is similar. The details of computing these positions are properly part of implementation.

Displaying the SnowPerson

To display a composite object, simply display each component (remember, the order of display can be important). Assuming the three snowballs and the puddle each store their color and position, this should be trivial.

Melting

This is another arbitrary decision. Let's say, for simplicity, that the radius of the base decreases by 10 percent each day, and the ratios of the radii remains two-thirds. For now, let's say the size of the puddle increases by 10 pixels each day.

Implementation

Once you understand the problem, how you will address it and what classes you will write, it is time to start implementation. Of course, depending on your level of expertise and the difficulty of the problem, the design phase may be shorter or longer (beginners tend to jump into implementation too soon).

Keeping Things Simple

Perhaps the most important skill a programmer learns is to keep every method simple. It is possible to make a program work with huge, sprawling methods, just as it is possible to build a vehicle out of spare parts, tape, and baling wire—but it is almost never a good idea, especially if you have far to go.

Strike Out on Your Own?

It won't be long before you start programming independently; coming up with your own tasks to program, or at least writing programs to complete programming assignments without being provided with the answers. The sooner you can start implementing, the better. If you are ready to jump into implementation already, do it! Try it and then come back here for hints. On the other hand, if it is still feeling a bit new and strange and you're not sure how to proceed, follow along here; but try to do the things the text recommends doing before looking at the answers. Dependence is good, but not for too long.

SnowBall? Puddle?

The decision about whether to create SnowBall and Puddle classes, or just go with four FilledCircles, must now be faced. If you decide to write SnowBall and Puddle, should they extend FilledCircle, or contain a FilledCircle (those are the two techniques to reuse software)? The answers to both those questions hinge on three things: what actions those classes must implement in addition to FilledCircle, how complicated those actions are, and how many modifications you anticipate making in the future. If this code will never be used again, there is only one additional method, and it is simple, the answer is use FilledCircle and be done with it. On the other hand, if there are many complex methods needed and extensive modifications may be required, the answer is to write subclasses.

The actions of SnowBall and Puddle are shrink, grow, and paint(). If they extend FilledCircle, they will automatically inherit paint() from FilledCircle, as well as the accessors for y and radius (which are needed for computing their new sizes and positions during melting). If they wrap up a FilledCircle (i.e., if composition is used), they would have to implement those accessors all over again. Therefore, that choice is simple: inheritance is more appropriate here.

Although it would be possible to implement a SnowPerson using four FilledCircles, composing it of three SnowBalls and a Puddle will be more elegant and allow inheritance to be illustrated.

Given that decision, the class structure for this program is illustrated in Figure 6.3.

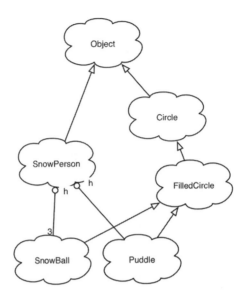

FIGURE 6.3 Booch diagram of classes.

Notice that a SnowPerson extends Object and has three SnowBalls and one Puddle. The classes SnowBall and Puddle extend FilledCircle, which extends Circle.

Implementation Plan

Here's a series of tasks that will lead to a working program. The rest of this section will detail how to implement them.

1. Create a new directory to store the code for this project.
2. Create a new project which uses that directory as the Project location.
3. Create a GUI Applet with a Button (for melting); hook up the Button.
4. Create (or better, copy) the Circle, and FilledCircle classes.
5. Create SnowBall, Puddle, and SnowPerson classes.
6. Add the chain of paint() methods so that repainting the Applet will repaint all the FilledCircles of all the SnowPersons.
7. Add the code to calculate the locations of the SnowBalls.
8. Add additional SnowPersons.
9. Add the melting code.

Naturally, after every step, test your code if you can.

You already know how to do the first three steps; come back here after you've done that. Feel free to look in Appendix A for instructions.

Creating the Classes

There are five classes in this program: Circle, FilledCircle, SnowBall, Puddle, and SnowPerson.

Circle and FilledCircle

Use the ClassMaker for Circle; that way, you will get an initializing constructor. The FilledCircle class from your Eye project does almost everything it should, except it does not have an initializing constructor; add the one in Listing 6.4.

SnowBall

The SnowBall class extends FilledCircle. Since all SnowBalls are the same color, the constructor does not need a color parameter. The only method the SnowBall class needs is melt(), which reduces the size by 10 percent; so the body of that method would be one line:

```
setRadius(getRadius()*9/10);
```

It also needs an initializing constructor, with a single line:

```
super(x,y,r,java.awt.Color.WHITE);
```

Puddle

Like SnowBall, Puddle extends FilledCircle. It needs the same initializing constructor (but that sets the color to java.awt.Color.GRAY) and a grow() method to increase its size by 10 pixels (setRadius(getRadius()+10);).

SnowPerson

The SnowPerson class has three SnowBall variables: base, middle, and head. It will need an initializing constructor that is passed the location and size. That constructor will then calculate where and how big the three SnowBalls should be. For a first prototype, let all three be the same size, as in Listing 6.5.

LISTING 6.5 Prototype initializing constructor for SnowPerson.

```
1   public SnowPerson(int x, int y, int size) {
2       base = new SnowBall(x, y, size);
3       middle = new SnowBall(x, y-size, size);
4       head = new SnowBall(x, y-size*2, size);
5   }
```

Line 2: Creates the base `SnowBall`.

Line 3: Makes the middle `SnowBall` the same size, but higher.

Line 4: Makes the head `SnowBall` the same size, and higher still.

This code centers the base at (x,y) instead of putting the bottom of the base at (x,y). However, that's good enough for now; you can adjust the locations and sizes later (after the `SnowPerson` shows up on the screen). First, build the structure of the program, and then refine it.

Adding the `paint()` Chain

You will recall from Chapter 4, "Graphics and Inheritance," that to update the way an `Applet` looks we send it `repaint()`, which causes `paint(Graphics)` to be sent to it. When the `Applet` gets the `paint()` message, it should `paint()` all the things it displays. Add a `public void paint(Graphics)` method to your `Applet` that simply sends `paint(g)` to the `SnowPerson` (see Listing 4.6). Before that will compile, you must have a `SnowPerson` to send the message to, so declare and initialize a `SnowPerson` instance variable in your `Applet`. That last instruction is completely explicit. If you don't know how to accomplish it, you might look back at the section "Variables I (State)" in Chapter 5. A big part of introductory programming expertise is familiarity with terms and concepts; the sooner you become familiar with them, the sooner programming will be easy. Perhaps you would consider rereading the section "Recapitulation" in Chapter 5?

Test that code (note that this is step 6 of the section "Implementation Plan" earlier in this chapter), and then on to making it look like a snowperson. If there are any problems, and the solutions don't jump right out at you, you might check "What Could Go Wrong?" at the end of this chapter.

Letting the Computer Do the Arithmetic

The `SnowPerson` constructor, when passed its size and position, must calculate how big the `middle` and `head` are and where the three `SnowBalls` will go. Calculating the sizes is very easy, see Listing 6.6.

LISTING 6.6 Setting the sizes of the `middle` and `head` from the `base`.

```
1    private void adjustSnowBallSizes() {
2        middle.setRadius(base.getRadius()*2/3);
3        head.setRadius(middle.getRadius()*2/3);
4    }
```

Line 2: Sets the `radius` of `middle` to two-thirds the `radius` of the `base`.

Line 3: Sets the `radius` of `head` to two-thirds the `radius` of the `middle`. Calculating the locations is more complicated.

Consider, by way of example, a `SnowPerson` of size 50, located at (200,300) (see Figure 6.4). All three `SnowBalls` have the same *x*-coordinate, but the *y*-coordinates must be calculated. The center of the `base` will be 50 pixels above the bottom (since the radius is 50) at (200, 250); the top will be 50 pixels above that. The center of the `middle` `SnowBall` will be 33 pixels above that (since 33 is two-thirds of 50) at (200,167). Similar reasoning puts the center of the `head` at (200,112).

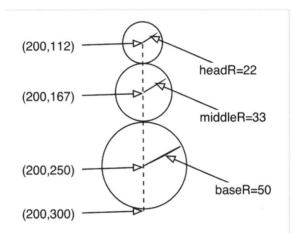

FIGURE 6.4   Locations of the three `SnowBalls`.

If, more abstractly, the SnowPerson is at (x,y), and we call the radii of the three SnowBalls baseR, middleR, and headR, then we could write the *y*-coordinate of the base as, y – baseR.

The *y*-coordinate of the middle is:

$$y - baseR*2 \ - \ middleR, \textit{ or } baseY - baseR - middleR.$$

The *y*-coordinate of the head is:

$$y - baseR*2 - middleR*2 - headR, \textit{ or } middleY - middleR - headR.$$

In Java, this looks like:

```
base.setY(y-base.getRadius());
middle.setY(y-base.getRadius()*2-middle.getRadius());
head.setY(y-base.getRadius()*2-middle.getRadius()*2-head.getRadius());
```

Notice that the *y* variables in the various SnowBalls store the *y*-coordinates as they are computed. An alternative computation is:

```
base.setY(y-base.getRadius());
middle.setY(base.gety()-base.getRadius()-middle.getRadius());
head.setY(middle.getY()-middle.getRadius()-head.getRadius());
```

Add whichever version you like better to your constructor, and check that it works. Note that the *y*-coordinate should be stored in the SnowPerson (since when the base melts, its center must be moved down to its radius above where it touches the ground). You could either type the three lines directly in the constructor, or put them in a method, called something like adjustSnowBallLocations(), and invoke that method from the constructor. Which is better? It depends on two things. Grouping code together in a method with a name helps to make obvious what it does. In addition, if it turns out you will need to use that code somewhere else in your program, you can reuse a method instead of copying and pasting the code. A completed constructor appears in Listing 6.7.

LISTING 6.7 Initializing constructor for SnowPerson.

```
1    public SnowPerson(int x, int y, int size) {
2        this.y = y;
3        base = new SnowBall(x, y-size, size);
4        middle = new SnowBall(x, y-size, size);
5        head = new SnowBall(x, y-size*2, size);
6        thePuddle = new Puddle(x,y,0);
7        adjustSnowBallSizes();
8        adjustSnowBallLocations();
9    }
```

Note that the computation of SnowBall sizes and locations is done in methods; these will be reused in melt().

Adding Additional SnowPersons

Add at least two more SnowPersons to your scene. Make them different sizes. Test to make sure they display correctly.

If you know how to that, do it. If not, read your `Applet` code (so it is in your mind). Look carefully at each line you have written. Think about what each does. Now decide how to add another `SnowPerson`.

Stop! Don't read on until you have puzzled over what to do. There are only two changes needed. First, declare and instantiate another `SnowPerson`. Second, modify `paint()` so it also draws the new one. That's it.

Making the `SnowPerson` Melt

When the user pushes the melt button, it must send the `melt()` message to however many `SnowPersons` there are and then send `repaint()` (so you can see the changes). When a `SnowPerson` gets a `melt()` message, it must both decrease the size of its `SnowBalls` (and lower them) and increase the size of its `Puddle`. You can make these changes either starting with the `Applet` and working down, or starting with `SnowPerson` and working up. The text will take the latter approach.

A number of details must be attended to in order to accomplish melting, but the `melt()` method can be written without paying any attention to them as can be seen in Listing 6.8.

LISTING 6.8 `melt()` method for `SnowPerson`.

```
1    public void melt() {
2        base.melt();
3        adjustSnowBallSizes();
4        adjustSnowBallLocations();
5        thePuddle.grow();
6    }
```

Four actions must take place: reduce the size of the base, calculate the new sizes of the middle and head, calculate the new locations of their centers, and growing the `Puddle`. The four lines of this method do that, but the details are in the methods.

Because the code to calculate the sizes of the `middle` and `head`, and the code to calculate the locations of all three `SnowBalls` were written as methods, this code is simple and easy to write.

Now add the code to send the `melt()` message to all the `SnowPersons` in the `ActionPerformed()` method of the melt `Button` and test the `melt()` method.

Displaying the *Puddle*

If you are simply following these instructions, the `Puddle` is not being displayed yet. Add the code to do that. All you need is to add `puddle.paint(g)` in `paint()` in `SnowPerson`. Does it matter where in that method it goes? Test the completed (!) code.

Congratulations! You have just completed a programming assignment more complex and sophisticated than any introductory programming text could have imagined presenting in a procedural language. You have used composition and inheritance to leverage already written classes. You have implemented a paint() chain with a GUI interface and started down the road to understanding object programming. Not everyone makes it this far.

CONCLUSION

In Java, all classes are organized into a hierarchy, called a *tree*, with the class Object at the root. Every class has Object as an ancestor; Object is a superclass (although possibly at several removes) to every other class.

Inheritance and composition allow software to be reused. This is a tremendous advantage over languages in which software cannot be reused without extensive reworking. Given a working FilledCircle class, writing SnowBall and Puddle only took a few lines of code. Once you have working SnowBall and Puddle classes, the SnowPerson class becomes simple.

In object languages, algorithmic complexity can be reduced by building an appropriate class hierarchy. The more complex the code, the harder it is to understand. Complex code is difficult to write correctly and more difficult to debug when there are errors. Simple code is easy to write correctly and easier to debug when there are errors—and there are always errors. Only neophyte programmers imagine their code will not have bugs. Experienced programmers know better. Good programmers learn techniques to make it easier to find the bugs that inevitably creep in. They develop good habits, which allow them to succeed, even in difficult situations. Well thought-out, coherent class hierarchy and incremental implementation are techniques that allow programmers to succeed.

What Could Go Wrong?

Problem 1: The SnowPerson doesn't appear on the screen.

Possible Causes: 1) paint() is never sent, 2) white FilledCircles on a white background are invisible.

Possible Solutions: 1) Send the paint message, 2) change the color of the SnowBalls or the background.

Problem 2: The SnowPerson never changes size.

Possible Causes: 1) The melt Button actionPerformed() method is not written, 2) it does not tell the SnowPerson to melt, 3) repaint() was not sent to the Applet, 4) the Snowperson melt() method is written incorrectly.

Possible Solutions: 1) Hook up the `Button`, 2) send the `melt()` message from the body of `ActionPerformed()`, 3) `send repaint()` after `melt()`.

Problem 3: The `SnowBalls` overlap in the initial `SnowPerson`.

   Possible Causes: Bad arithmetic in the `SnowPerson` constructor.

   Possible Solutions: Fix the arithmetic.

Problem 4: The `SnowPerson` is upside down.

   Possible Causes: The programmer forgot that 0 in the y direction is the top of the screen. The author made this mistake.

   Possible Solutions: Redo the code for calculating where the middle and head go, remembering which way is up.

Problem 5: After melting, the middle and/or head are floating.

   Possible Causes: 1) The programmer forgot to add the code to adjust the position of the middle and/or head after melting, 2) the programmer remembered to adjust the position, but forgot to send the message, 3) the programmer wrote the code to adjust the position after melting incorrectly.

   Possible Solutions: Add that code, and invoke it.

Problem 6: The original `SnowPerson` appears on the screen, but the second doesn't.

   Possible Causes: 1) It's on top of the first `SnowPerson`. 2) `paint()`, in the Applet does not send `paint()` to the second.

   Possible Solutions: 1) Give it different coordinates. 2) if you called it person2, add `person2.paint(g)` to `paint()` in the `Applet`.

Problem 7: The original `SnowPerson` melts, but the second doesn't.

   Possible Causes: The melt `actionPerformed()` method doesn't send `melt()` to the second one.

   Possible Solutions: Add the `melt()` message.

REVIEW QUESTIONS

6.1 What are the two techniques to reuse classes?

6.2 Write a `SnowBall` class that uses each technique to reuse `FilledCircle`. Which seems better to you? Why?

6.3 Does `SnowBall` use composition or inheritance?

6.4 How do you know if you need more classes?

6.5 How do you know if you have too many classes?

6.6 Write down, one per line, every method invoked (including the values of the parameters) when `new SnowPerson(50, 200, 300)` is executed.

6.7 Write the `melt()` method for a `SnowBall`. Make it reduce the size of the `SnowBall` by 17 percent. Do you have to worry about which order in which the operators are applied?

6.8 Describe in detail what happens when the `SnowPerson` sends `melt()` to the base. What object is this? What methods are invoked in what classes and in what order?

6.9 Describe in detail what happens when a user pushes the `Melt for a day` Button. Include every method invoked and what class it resides in, in the correct order. Pretty scary, eh?

Programming Exercises

6.10 Send `toString()` to your `Applet` and `System.out.println()` what it returns. What does it print?

6.11 Put this line in `initComponents()` in your `Applet`:

```
System.out. println(this).
```

How do you explain why it works?

6.12 Send `toString()` to an object that you know does not have it defined. What does that print?

6.13 Modify your `Applet` to display 50 `SnowPersons` of random sizes at random locations. Look at the previous chapter for how to do this.

6.14 Modify your code so that all of the `SnowPersons` move a few pixels toward the center of the screen each time you push the button (in addition to melting). Hint: You can calculate the change you should make to the x-coordinate to move right or left (depending on if it is left or right of center) arithmetically. The method `Math.abs()` will return the absolute value of an `int`.

6.15 You may notice that the `Puddle` of one `SnowPerson` covers up others. Modify the display methods so that the `Puddle`s are all in the background. Hint: Draw all the Puddles first; add a `paintPuddle()` method, and in the `Applet`, first paint all the `Puddle`s, and then the `SnowBall`s.

7 Conditional Statements

INTRODUCTION

In the old procedural paradigm, writing a program was essentially the construction of an algorithm (see "Definition of Algorithm" in Chapter 1, "Programming Is Like Juggling"). To design a program, the entire task was broken down into a series of subtasks. To implement that design, subprograms (also called *subroutines*) were written for each subtask. Typically, there was a main loop that repeatedly called various subroutines depending on conditions. Looping and conditional statements were central to understanding and building programs, so they always appeared early in programming texts; very little could be done without them.

By contrast, in the object paradigm presented here, writing a program involves designing and implementing a class structure and a GUI. The finished program still implements an algorithm, but its complexity is distributed across the various classes. In a properly implemented object program, every class and method is simple. Once classes are written, they can be reused with a minimum of labor.

Thus far, the programs in this text have accomplished conditional and repeated action by relying on the user and the event loop. The event loop is the mechanism built into the JVM to handle user events. If the user wanted to make several withdrawals, he pushed the withdraw Button several times. To move the Eye left, he pressed the moveLeft Button. Nonetheless, object programs do need looping and conditional statements. This chapter and the next will introduce those two elements of control structure.

ACTIONS DEPENDING ON CONDITIONS–CONDITIONAL EXECUTION

Every program thus far has run the same way every time. However, there are times when a program needs to choose between actions to perform based on the current conditions. For instance, ATM machines usually won't let you withdraw more money than you have in your account. The ATM in Chapter 3, "Class Design and Implementation," would pretend to give out money even if the resulting balance was negative. The code for withdraw() is shown in Listing 7.1.

LISTING 7.1 The withdraw() method for the Account class (from Listing 3.4).

```
1    public void withdraw(int amountToWithdraw) {
2        balance = balance - amountToWithdraw;
3    }
```

The if Statement–Do Something or Don't

An if statement can be used to prevent the Account from being overdrawn, as in Listing 7.2. The if statement (lines 2–3) causes the assignment on line 3 to only occur if the balance is at least as big as the amount to withdraw.

LISTING 7.2 A withdraw() method that prevents overdrafts.

```
1    public void withdraw(int amountToWithdraw) {
2        if (balance >= amountToWithdraw)
3            balance = balance - amountToWithdraw;
4    }
```

An `if` statement starts with the word `if`, then a `boolean` expression in parentheses, and then a statement to execute if that expression evaluates to `true`. This syntax is shown in BNF 7.1.

BNF 7.1   The if Statement

<if stmt> ::= if (<boolean expression>) <stmt> [else <stmt>]

Semantics:

1. Evaluate the <boolean expression>.

2. If the value of the expression is true, execute the <stmt> after <expression>.

3. If the value is false and there is an else part, execute the <stmt> in the else part.

Remember that every legal if statement must match this syntax exactly. The expression must be of type boolean (since only the values true and false make sense here) and must be enclosed in ()s. Then, there must be exactly one statement (if there are several things you want to do in the if part, you must enclose them in {}s to transform them into a single block statement).

if-else—Do One Thing or Another

An `if` statement (without an `else`) is used when you want an action performed only under certain conditions; it either executes the statement following the expression or does nothing, depending on the value of the expression. By contrast, an `if-else` statement is used to choose between two actions.

Example: Preventing Overdrafts While Alerting the Customer to the Problem

If a person tries to withdraw more money than he has, the code in Listing 7.2 would simply ignore him, which could be a bit unsettling. It might be better to let him know something had gone wrong (i.e., either make the withdrawal or print an error message). That's a choice between two things, so the construct to use is the `if-else` statement, as in Listing 7.3.

LISTING 7.3   A `withdraw()` method with an `if-else` statement.

```
1    public void withdraw(int amountToWithdraw) {
2        if (balance >= amountToWithdraw)
3            balance = balance - amountToWithdraw;
4        else System.out.println("Oops! You don't have that much!");
5    }
```

The else part (line 4) executes if `amountToWithdraw > balance`. Thus, if the user is trying to withdraw more than he has, instead of ignoring him, it will print an error message.

More Complex `boolean` Expressions

The `boolean` expression in an `if` statement may, like any expression, be arbitrarily complex. Numbers may be compared by any of the relational operators (see BNF 5.13 "Binary Operators" in Chapter 5, "Toward Consistent Classes"). Two `boolean` expressions may be conjoined with || (or), and && (and), and negated with ! (not).

Examples:

```
x>0          // true if x is >0
x>=0 && x<=100     // true if 0<=x<=100, i.e. a legal exam score
x==7 || x==11      // true if x is 7 or 11, i.e. a winner in craps
x!=7 && x!=11 && x!=2 && x!=12 //true if x is not 7, 11, 2, or 12
```

Truth Tables

It is not always obvious exactly how to write `boolean` expressions, especially in complicated situations. When in doubt, a heavy-handed but inevitably correct technique is to make a truth table. A truth table lists (or, as computer scientists like to say, enumerates) all the possible combinations of values for the `boolean` clauses in a `boolean` expression, along with the values of the expression under those conditions. For instance, assume there are two `boolean` variables, p and q. Each may take on either the value true (T) or false (F). Thus, for the pair, there are four possible values: TT, TF, FT, and FF, as shown in the leftmost two columns of Table 7.1.

TABLE 7.1 Truth Table One

p	q	p && q	p || q	!p
T	T	T	T	F
T	F	F	T	F
F	T	F	T	T
F	F	F	F	T

The rightmost column has the values for not-p ($!p$); notice that they are just the opposite of the values for p. The values for $p\&\&q$ and $p\|q$ are shown in between; notice that || is inclusive-or, it includes the case when both p and q are true. There is another or operator, exclusive-or, which is true just if p or q is true, but not both. Java's or is inclusive-or.

DeMorgan's Law

The ! operator is straightforward, it turns true to false and false to true. However, there is a peculiarity of applying ! to expressions including operators. The ! operator distributes across parentheses, but it changes || to && and && to ||. See Table 7.2 for an example.

TABLE 7.2 Truth Table Two

p	q	p && q	!(p && q)	!p && !q	!p || !q
T	T	T	F	F	F
T	F	F	T	F	T
F	T	F	T	F	T
F	F	F	T	T	T

The fact that $!(p\&\&q)=!p||!q$ and that $!(p||q)=!p\&\&!q$ is called DeMorgan's Law; forget it and you will run into some nasty bugs.

Problem-Solving Technique–Analysis by Cases

It is very common in writing a program, and in problem solving in general, that one must do different things in different cases. For instance, if you are running under a Frisbee, if it was thrown forehand, you expect it to tail off one way; if it was thrown backhand, the other. If it was thrown as a hammer (upside down), you expect it to slow down rapidly and tail off abruptly. In each case, you do different things to catch it.

Analysis by Cases (ABC for short) is a problem-solving technique designed especially for problems with multiple cases.

NOTE

Problem Solving Technique: Analysis by Cases (ABC)
Identify the various cases. For each, answer the following questions (making a table if it is complicated): 1) How can you distinguish this case? 2) What action do you wish to take in this case?

Once you have identified each case, decided how to distinguish each case from the others, and what action to perform in each case, you are ready to write code. The examples will illustrate the use of this technique.

Example–A Robot Bouncer

Imagine going to a club and encountering a robot bouncer. The job of the robot bouncer is to only let in people who are at least 18 years old and charge them each the cover charge. Write a method that is passed a `Person` as a parameter, and outputs as a message to `System.out` what the robot would say to that person. Assume that the `Person` is passed as a parameter and that a `Person` object has an `age` and a `balance` variable with standard accessors.

To start, write a method that only checks the person's age. There are just two cases here. If the person's age is greater than or equal to 18, it should say "Welcome"; otherwise, say "Sorry." That was the ABC method in a very simple context; so simple it is trivial. The two cases were under 18 and not. They are distinguished by the age of the person. To write code for this requires an `if-else` statement, as in Listing 7.4.

LISTING 7.4   Robot bouncer that only checks age.

```
1    void checkAge(Person aPerson) {
2        if (aPerson.getAge() >= 18)
3            System.out.println("Right this way!");
4        else System.out.println("I'm sorry, you must be 18 to enter.");
5    }
```

This would work fine if there were no cover charge to collect. Next, one might reason that if the person is 18 or older, then the bouncer, instead of waving him in, should check if he also has the cover charge, as shown in Listing 7.5.

LISTING 7.5   Robot bouncer that checks age and balance.

```
1    void checkAgeAndBalance(Person aPerson) {
2        if (aPerson.getAge() >= 18)
3            if (aPerson.getBalance() > 5)
4                System.out.println("Right this way!");
5            else System.out.println("Sorry, you don't have the cash");
6        else System.out.println("I'm sorry, you must be 18 to enter.");
7    }
```

This example replaces line 3 in the previous with an if-else to check if the person has the money to pay the cover charge. This is legal syntactically, since an if-else statement is a statement (check the BNF if you have any doubts about this). This would work, but it is cleaner to use a compound boolean expression to check both conditions at once. The person is allowed in if his age and his balance meet certain conditions, as illustrated in Listing 7.6.

LISTING 7.6   Robot bouncer that checks age and balance using &&.

```
1    void checkAgeAndBalance2(Person aPerson) {
2        if (aPerson.getAge() >= 18 && aPerson.getBalance > 5)
3            System.out.println("Right this way!");
4        else System.out.println("You must be 18 and have $5 to enter.");
5    }
```

Cascaded if-elses—Do One of a Number of Things

Sometimes, a program must do exactly one of a number of things. In that case, you can build a structure called a cascaded if-else by repeatedly using an if-else statement as the statement following the else. The code in Listing 7.5 could be rewritten into a cascading if-else as shown in Listing 7.7. This is exactly equivalent to Listing 7.5, but is perhaps easier to read.

LISTING 7.7   Robot bouncer that checks age and balance using a cascaded if-else.

```
1    void checkAgeAndBalance(Person aPerson) {
2        if (aPerson.getAge() < 18)
3            System.out.println("I'm sorry, you must be 18 to enter.");
4        else if (aPerson.getBalance() > 5)
5            System.out.println("Right this way!");
6        else System.out.println("Sorry, you don't have the cash");
7    }
```

The order in which conditions are checked may be important; careful thinking is required to make sure it will work properly in every case.

Example I—A Robot Aspirin Bottle

Imagine that you are assigned to program an aspirin bottle to announce the correct dosage given a person's age. The dosage for aspirin is as follows: under 5, consult with a doctor; 6–12, one; 13–65, two; over 65, one. Listing 7.8 shows this coded as a cascading if-else.

LISTING 7.8   Cascaded if-else for aspirin dosage.

```
1    if (age<6)
2        System.out.println("consult with your physician");
3    else if (age<13)
4        System.out.println("dosage=1");
5    else if (age<66)
6        System.out.println("dosage=2");
7    else System.out.println("dosage=1");
```

Notice that when you get to an `else` clause, it must be the case that the previous condition was `false` (otherwise, the `else` clause would not execute). Thus, if execution reaches line 3, age must be >=6, and if execution reaches line 7, age>=66.

Each `else-if` clause executes only if the previous `boolean` expression was `false` (because of the semantics of an `if-else`; see BNF 7.1 "The `if` Statement," if you have any doubts about this. Once you get used to this notion, it will be obvious). It is also possible to make this a bit shorter as shown in Listing 7.9.

LISTING 7.9   A slightly shorter cascaded `if-else` for aspirin dosage.

```
1    if (age<6)
2        System.out.println("consult with your physician");
3    else if (age<13 || age>65)
4        System.out.println("dosage=1");
5    else System.out.println("dosage=2");
```

Notice that if execution reaches line 5, `!(age<13 || age>65)` must be `true`, in other words, it must be true that `(age>=13 and age<=65)`.

Which is the right way to structure this? There is not one clear answer. It depends on which way makes sense to the programmer, and which way is clearer to a reader—it's a matter of style.

Example II–Reporting the Score of a Tennis Game

Imagine you were assigned to build a robot tennis score announcer. In tennis, scores of zero, one, two, and three are announced as love, fifteen, thirty, and forty, respectively. Assuming the scores are kept as `ints`, your robot score announcer would be passed two `ints`. It must convert the two `int` scores to the appropriate `String`; for example, if the score were 3 for the server and 2 for the receiver, the correct output is forty-thirty. Therefore, a method that announced the score might make use of a method that converted an `int` to a tennis score for both of the scores, as in Listing 7.10.

LISTING 7.10   An `announceScore()` method that uses `convert()` twice.

```
1    void announceScore(int serverScore, int receiverScore) {
2        System.out.println(convert(serverScore)
                        + "-" + convert(receiverScore));
3    }
```

In that case, the task is to write and test the `convert()` method. As usual, the simplest way to generate a test driver is to create a class with a `main()` method (see the section "Creating a Class" in Appendix A) as in Listing 7.11.

LISTING 7.11   Testing the `convert()` method.

```
1    public class SingleScoreConverter {
2
3        public static String convert(int score) {
4            if (score==0)
5                return "love";
6            else if (score==1)
7                return "fifteen";
8            else if (score==2)
9                return "thirty";
10           else if (score==3)
11               return "forty";
12           else return "value out of range:" + score;
13       }
14
15       public static void main(String[] args) {
16           System.out.println("0=" + convert(0));
17           System.out.println("1=" + convert(1));
18           System.out.println("2=" + convert(2));
19           System.out.println("3=" + convert(3));
20           System.out.println("4=" + convert(4));
21       }
22
23   }
```

Line 3: Since only one `SingleScoreConverter` will be needed, and it has no state (i.e., no instance variables), `convert()` can be a static method (i.e., a class method).

The main() method tests all four legal values and one that is out of range. Thus, it tests all five cases. It is important to test all the cases; otherwise, the one you didn't test will be a hard-to-find bug later.

The `convert()` method is implemented using a cascaded `if-else`. It returns the `String` representing the `int` it is passed. It does not use `System.out.println()` to display the score because `System.out.println()` is only for debugging or experimenting with code.

Class Methods

Most methods you have seen so far have been instance methods. Instance methods are invoked when a message is sent to an instance of a class; in the context of an instance method, `this` is a reference to the object to which the message was sent. Class methods, like class variables (see the section "Class Variables" in Chapter 5), have the keyword `static` in the heading; they are invoked when a message is sent to a class. Examples include:

```
int withdrawal = Integer.parseInt(textField1.getText());
```

from the section "When the User Presses Enter, Get the Withdrawal Amount," in Chapter 3, and:

```
Thread.sleep(50);
```

from section "The `step()` Method" in Chapter 9, "Simulation and Animation."

In the context of a class method, "`this`" is not declared (since the message was *not* sent to an instance but instead to a class). Therefore, in the body of `static void main()`, if `convert()` were an instance method, we couldn't write `convert(3)`. If we did, the compiler, knowing that the syntax of every message statement is `object.message (parameters)`, would append `this` on the front, to make `this.convert(3)`. Then, it would notice that `this` was not defined, and would protest.

Therefore, even though we are inside a method in the `SingleScoreConverter` class, because it is a `static` method, we cannot directly invoke instance methods in that class. Instead, we must either instantiate `SingleScoreConverter` and send the messages to the instance, or make `convert()` a class method. Some methods operate on instance variables (like `withdraw()` in the `Account` class), but `convert()` simply converts its parameter, so it can be a class method.

BNF 7.2   The Switch Statement

<switch stmt> ::= switch (<enumerable expression>) {

           [<case clause>]*

           [default: <stmt>]

     }

<case clause> ::= case <constant>: [<statement>]*
Semantics:

1. Evaluate the <enumerable expression>.

2. If the value of the expression equals any of the <constant>s in the <case clauses>, then execute the <stmt>s after that <constant>, and all the rest of the cases.

3. Otherwise, execute the <stmt>s after default (if it appears).

The Switch Statement

Another construct that selects from a number of possibilities is the switch statement. The switch statement does not add any power to the cascaded if-else, but it is a little neater and easier to read. The syntax is shown in BNF 7.2.

This is the most complicated statement in Java; it is inherited, so to speak, from C++ and old C. The convert method from Listing 7.11 is shown in Listing 7.12, and is rewritten using a switch statement in Listing 7.13.

LISTING 7.12   convert() using cascaded if-else.

```
1    private String convert(int score) {
2        if (score==0)
3            return "love";
4        else if (score==1)
5            return "fifteen";
6        else if (score==2)
7            return "thirty";
8        else if (score==3)
9            return "forty";
10       else return "value out of range:" + score;
11   }
```

LISTING 7.13   convert() using Switch.

```
1    private String convert(int score) {
2        switch (score) {
3            case 0: return "love";
4            case 1: return "fifteen";
5            case 2: return "thirty";
6            case 3: return "forty";
7            default: return "Value out of range: " + score;
8        } // switch
9    }
```

This latter convert() uses a switch statement instead of a cascaded if-else. Switch adds no power, but some people find it easier to read.

There are two difficulties with the switch statement. One is that it can only switch on types that are enumerable. Enumerable types include int and char; String and double will not work. The other difficulty is that unless the statements in each case clause end with a break or return statement, *the following cases are all executed too!* This can have surprising (and sometimes upsetting) results.

PROGRAMMING EXAMPLE: USING THE SingleScoreConverter CLASS IN A TENNIS SCOREKEEPING PROGRAM

As previously, this example will start with a description of the task, and then continue with design, implementation, and testing.

A Description of the Task

The programming task for this chapter is to write a Java Applet that will keep track of the score in a tennis match. It should announce the score before each point, and the winner of each game, set, and finally the match. The winner of a tennis match is, as in Wimbledon Women's Tennis, the first player to win two sets. A player wins a set if she has won at least six games and is at least two games ahead (we will not handle tie-breakers).

The same player serves for an entire tennis game. Before each point, the score is announced, the server's score first. A game is won when one of the players has at least five points and is at least two points ahead. If the score reaches 4–4, then, until the game is decided, the score is announced as "deuce" for ties and "advantage server" or "advantage receiver," depending on who is ahead by one.

Assume for now that the user will push one of two Buttons for each point; one if the server gets the point, and the other if the receiver gets the point.

Design

Both the GUI and the classes must be designed.

GUI Design

The GUI is simple; two Buttons and somewhere to display the output. Either a TextField or a TextArea could work for that. Which would be better? A TextField only has one line; however, the user might want to be able to see the history of points, so a TextArea seems more sensible.

Here's how to create a prototype (although, odds are you are familiar with this by now):

1. Create a new GUI AWT Applet named TennisApplet (don't forget to create a directory to store all the files in first).
2. Add, rename, relabel, resize, connect, and test two Buttons (don't forget to set the Layout to null so they don't fill the screen).
3. Add, rename, and resize a TextArea—write in the TextArea on a Button press to make sure everything is working so far.

Adding Images to the GUI (Optional)

You can make your GUI look much nicer if you add images to it. For instance, the programmer who wrote this `Applet` copied images of Maria Sharpova and Serena Williams, the two finalists in the 2004 Wimbledon tournament, and added them to his `Applet`. However, due to copyright issues, he has replaced them here with images from his photo album.

To add images to a GUI requires:

1. Find and copy the images you want to have in your GUI (save them in the same directory as the class files; otherwise, it won't work).
2. Declare an `Image` variable for each.
3. Read each image into its `Image` variable.
4. Write a `public void paint(Graphics)` method to draw them.

Step 1 can be accomplished by finding an image on the Web, right-clicking it, selecting "Save" (or some such), and then navigating to the directory your tennis code is in. Alternatively, you could copy images from *www.willamette.edu/ ~levenick/SimplyJava/images/*. The code to accomplish steps 2–4 is in Listing 7.14.

LISTING 7.14 The `TennisApplet`.

```
1    import java.awt.*;
2
3    public class TennisApplet extends java.applet.Applet {
4        Image mariaImage, serenaImage;
5
6        /** Initializes the applet TennisApplet */
7        public void init() {
8            initComponents();
9            // read from code directory
10           mariaImage = getImage(getCodeBase(), "maria.jpg");
11           serenaImage = getImage(getCodeBase(), "serena.jpg");
12       }
13
14       public void paint(Graphics g) {
15           g.drawImage(mariaImage, 250, 100, 150, 200, this);
16           g.drawImage(serenaImage, 50, 100, 150, 200, this);
17       }
18   }
```

Line 1: Imports `java.awt.*`, so it will know what `Graphics` and `Image` are.

Line 4: Declares two `Image` variables.

Lines 10–11: Read in the two images. The files must be named exactly `maria.jpg` and `serena.jpg`, or else (of course) they will not be found.

Lines 14–17: Draw the images. The four `int` parameters specify the rectangle to draw the image in; it will be scaled to that size.

You will need to arrange your `Buttons` and `TextArea` so they are not on top of the `Images`. Alternatively, you can change the `x` and `y` coordinates of the rectangles in which the `Images` are displayed—whatever works for you. If you've forgotten Java rectangles, look back at the section "Basics of Graphics in Java" in Chapter 4, "Graphics and Inheritance."

Class Design

The class structure for this problem is not obvious at first glance. Clearly, there will be an `Applet`. Perhaps there should be an `Announcer` class that uses a `SingleScoreConverter` (see Listing 7.10) that will announce the score before each point.

In a real tennis game, there are two players, so `Game` and `Player` are candidate classes. Perhaps the `Game` could do the announcing, instead of having a separate `Announcer` class. If we were going to extend the program to simulate tennis games (instead of pushing a `Button` for each point), the `Player` class might include information about a player's attributes, such as service consistency and speed, stamina, quickness, strength, or accuracy.

If the program kept track of the score for a single `Game`, the class structure might look like Figure 7.1.

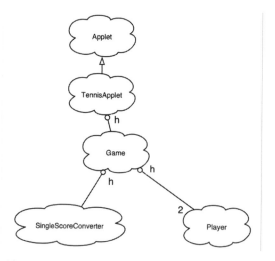

FIGURE 7.1   Booch diagram for one game of `Tennis`.
The `TennisApplet` creates a `Game` that has a
`SingleScoreConverter` and two `Players`.

To score a tennis match, something must keep track of the score in individual games, the number of games each player has won in each set, and the number of sets each player has won. At the beginning of each game, the score must be set to 0–0 and there must be code to specify the server in this game. At the beginning of each set, the games each player has won must be set to zero as well. In addition, there must be code to decide when a game, set, and match are over.

This various logic might be in one class, or distributed over several as in Figure 7.2. By building Match, Set, and Game classes, the initialization for each can be handled by constructors.

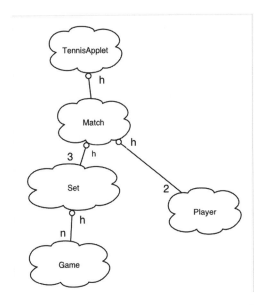

FIGURE 7.2   Booch diagram for a tennis match.
A Match has two Players and up to three Sets.
A Set has *n* Games (at least 6).

Making It Smaller; Just Play a Single Game

If the description sounds like, and the Booch diagram looks like, rather a lot to take on to start, you know what to do—make it simpler, and build a prototype first. Figure 7.1, with just a single game, seems like a reasonable place to start.

Game and Player Classes

So, create Player and Game classes; write the code and test it. The Player and Game classes are most easily made with the ClassMaker. Add a Game variable in the Applet;

initialize it in `init()`, and send it messages when the user pushes the `Buttons`. The `Game` should announce the score before each point. For now, simply have it write to `System.out`. Don't worry about deuce scoring or game ending. If you need a hint, see Listing 7.15, but try to do it yourself as much as possible.

LISTING 7.15 The `TennisApplet`.

```
1    public class TennisApplet extends java.applet.Applet {
2        Game theGame;
3
4        /** Initializes the applet TennisApplet */
5        public void init() {
6            initComponents();
7            theGame = new Game(new Player("Serena"), new Player("Maria"));
8        }
9
         ...code deleted...
10
11       private void serButtonActionPerformed(java.awt.event.ActionEvent
         evt) {
12           theGame.serverScored();
13       }
14
15       private void recButtonActionPerformed(java.awt.event.ActionEvent
         evt) {
16           theGame.receiverScored();
17       }
18   }
```

Line 2: Declares the `Game` variable.

Line 7: Instantiates a `Game` and stores it.

Lines 12 and 16: Send the appropriate message to the game when the user pushes a button.

Keep in mind that if you've added the `Image` code, your `TennisApplet` will look slightly different.

The `Game` class needs variables for each player's score, and methods to increment each when the user pushes that `Button`. It also needs a way to report the score. You probably know how to write the `Game` class. A preliminary class is in Listing 7.16.

LISTING 7.16 The preliminary Game class.

```
1    public class Game {
2        Player server, receiver;
3        int receiverScore, serverScore;
4        SingleScoreConverter theConverter;
5
6        /** Creates a new instance of Game */
7        public Game(Player server, Player receiver) {
8            this.server = server;
9            this.receiver = receiver;
10           theConverter = new SingleScoreConverter();
11       }
12
13       public void receiverScored() {
14           receiverScore++;
15           announceScore();
16       }
17
18       public void serverScored() {
19           serverScore++;
20           announceScore();
21       }
22
23       public void announceScore() {
24           System.out.println(theConverter.convert(serverScore) + "-" +
                 theConverter.convert(receiverScore));
25       }
26   }
```

Lines 2–4: Declare variables.

Lines 7–11: The constructor saves the two Players and instantiates the converter.

Lines 13–16 and 18–21: Increment the appropriate score and announce the new score.

Lines 23–25: Announces the score.

Compile and run these two classes; push Buttons until both scores are out of range. Now it is time to add the code to handle deuce games and the game being over. However, before doing that, it will be more efficient to replace the System.out.println in announceScore() with code to write to the TextArea in the Applet. That println was for debugging, and the more printlns we add, the more we'll have to change for the final product.

Establishing the Linkage Back to the Applet's TextArea

If the Game had a reference to the TextArea back in the Applet, announceScore() could write to it directly; (i.e., line 24 in Listing 7.16 could be theTA.append() instead of System.out.println(). However, where will Game get that reference? This is a common problem for beginning object programmers, but the solution can be deduced with a little careful thought, assuming you have internalized the constructs covered thus far. Maybe you know how already?

For theTA.append(...) to compile in the Game class, Game must have a variable of type java.awt.TextArea named theTA. Easy enough; add java.awt.TextArea theTA;.

However, like all instance variables, it will be initialized to 0, which, for a reference, is null. Although now theTA.append(...) will compile, when it runs it will generate the infamous, "Null pointer exception." Therefore, the question becomes, how to set theTA to actually reference theTA variable back in the Applet? The answer is very easy, once you realize it. How does one set the value of a variable in one class from another? The same as always! Use an accessor. The ClassMaker will write it for you, or you could just type it; whatever is easier.

When should you set theTA in Game? Since it only needs to be done once, it should be done in the constructor, or right after the constructor is invoked; see Listing 7.17.

LISTING 7.17   Code establishing a reference back to the TextArea from theGame.

```
1    public void init() {
2        initComponents();
3        theGame = new Game(new Player("Serena"), new Player("Maria"));
4        theGame.setTheTA(theTA);
5    }
```

Line 4: Sets theTA in theGame to theTA in the Applet (so that you can write in it from there).

Make those changes and test your code.

Adding Game-Over and Deuce-Scoring Code

The announceScore() method in Listing 7.16 assumes that the game is still in progress and the first deuce (forty-forty) has not been reached. It remains to write code to detect and announce these other two cases, so that we can write announceScore(). This is a perfect place to use the ABC method (see the problem-solving technique "Analysis by Cases (ABC)" earlier in this chapter). If you want to make sure you've learned this technique, this would be a good time to practice it. On the other hand, it is possible to delay making detailed decisions by pretending there are methods that can distinguish between the cases. This is illustrated in Listing 7.18.

LISTING 7.18 announceScore() using methods.

```
1    public void announceScore() {
2        if (gameOver())
3            announceGameOver();
4        else if (simpleScore())
5            announceSimpleScore();
6        else announceDeuceScore();
7    }
```

There are three different cases for the score in tennis: game over, simple scoring, and deuce scoring. This announceScore() distinguishes between them by using methods in a cascaded if-else.

The use of methods makes the code legible. This way, the code is simple and easy to understand; the details of whether the game is over or when we can use simple scoring is hidden in the methods.

The gameOver() Method

How to write the gameOver() method? Oddly, most of it can be written syntactically; you can do most of the work of writing it given what you know about syntax. Look at line 2 in Listing 7.18. From that you can infer the type of the gameOver() method. Since its type is not void, it must return a value of that type. If you don't know the type, look back at the syntax of an if statement (BNF 7.1 "The if Statement.") With that in mind, a prototype of gameOver() can be written while ignoring the details of its logic; see Listing 7.19.

LISTING 7.19 gameOver() prototype.

```
1    public boolean gameOver() {
2        return false;
3    }
```

The type of gameOver() must be boolean; otherwise, it could not be used in the context if(gameOver()). Since it is not void, it must return a value. This prototype method would compile and run, but would always (as you can see) return false.

Now, we must fill in the logic so the method will return true when the game is over.

Writing Simple Code

Logically, the game is over if either player has at least 4 points and is at least 2 points ahead. The first thing some programmers think to write is that the game is over:

```
        if (serverScore >= 4 && serverScore - receiverScore >=2 ||
            receiverScore >= 4 && receiverScore - serverScore >=2)
```

which is a mouthful. If you were going to write this, it would be good to enclose it in a method (see Listing 7.20) so you could use it from various places.

LISTING 7.20   gameOver() first try.

```
1    public boolean gameOver() {
2        return (serverScore >= 4 && serverScore - receiverScore >=2
3            || receiverScore >= 4 && receiverScore - serverScore >=2);
4    }
```

Logically, this method is correct, but compare it for simplicity and ease of understanding with Listing 7.21. This code is not wrong, but it is a bit complicated and difficult to read. It is more elegant to write the test more abstractly as in Listing 7.21, which is a simple, easy-to-read version of gameOver(). The game is over if the server has won or the receiver has won.

LISTING 7.21   gameOver() made simple.

```
1    public boolean gameOver() {
2        return serverWon() || receiverWon();
3    }
```

This way is less prone to errors and easier to modify when there are errors. This method is far superior in terms of debugging and clarity, but it has a price: now there are two more methods to write.

Combining Nearly Identical Methods

One's first impulse might be to simply copy and paste the logic from the two lines into the two methods as in Listing 7.22.

LISTING 7.22   serverWon() and receiverWon(), take one.

```
1    public boolean serverWon() {
2        return serverScore >= 4 && serverScore - receiverScore >=2;
3    }
4
5    public boolean receiverWon() {
6        return receiverScore >= 4 && receiverScore - serverScore >=2;
7    }
```

Notice that the logic is identical in the two methods, with the variables serverScore and receiverScore reversed. Anytime you discover nearly identical code like this you can combine it. The resulting methods are shown in Listing 7.23.

LISTING 7.23   serverWon() and receiverWon(), take two.

```
1    public boolean serverWon() {
2        return winner(serverScore, receiverScore);
3    }
4
5    public boolean receiverWon() {
6        return winner(receiverScore, serverScore);
7    }
```

The commonalities are combined by invoking the same method with the variables serverScore and receiverScore reversed.

Both methods simply return the value of winner, but with the actual parameters exchanged. This is a useful technique to learn; it has the benefit of putting the decision of whether one player or the other has won the game in the same code. This is useful because if the logic is wrong, it is only wrong in one place, and can be fixed in one place. The downside is that now winner(int, int) must be written; see Listing 7.24.

LISTING 7.24   winner(int,int).

```
1    public boolean winner(int x, int y) {
2        return x >= 4 && x >= y + 2;
3    }
```

A player with score x wins over a player with score y if x is at least 4 and is at least 2 more than y.

Notice that this method returns true just if the first parameter, x, is at least 4 and at least 2 more than the second, y. This concludes gameOver(). Writing it produced several other methods, but they are all one line long. Looking back at Listing 7.18, it remains to write announceGameOver(), simpleScore(), announce SimpleScore(), and announceDeuceScore().

The simpleScore()Method

As long as we have not reached the first deuce score, we can use the simple score announcer from before. The first deuce score is 3–3, so as long as either score is less than 3, simple scoring will work (see Listing 7.25).

LISTING 7.25 simpleScore().

```
1    public boolean simpleScore() {
2        return receiverScore < 3 || serverScore < 3;
3    }
```

AnnounceSimpleScore () method

The announceSimpleScore() method is just the old announceScore() method, as shown in Listing 7.26.

LISTING 7.26 announceSimpleScore().

```
1    public void announceSimpleScore() {
2        theTA.append(theConverter.convert(serverScore) + "-"
                    + theConverter.convert(receiverScore) + "\n");
3    }
```

The announceGameOver() and announceDeuceScore() Methods

The method announceGameOver() is shown in Listing 7.27. It checks who won and announces that.

LISTING 7.27 announceGameOver().

```
1    public void announceGameOver() {
2        if (serverWon())
3            theTA.append("Game Server!\n");
4        else theTA.append("Game Receiver!\n");
5    }
```

Finally, announceDeuceScore() is shown in Listing 7.28. There are three cases: deuce, advantage server, and advantage receiver.

LISTING 7.28 announceDeuceScore().

```
1    public void announceDeuceScore() {
2        if (receiverScore==serverScore)
3            theTA.append("Deuce\n");
4        else if(receiverScore < serverScore)
5            theTA.append("Advantage Server\n");
6        else theTA.append("Advantage Receiver\n");
7    }
```

There are three cases in deuce scoring, so the correct construct is a cascaded if-else. If it were difficult to decide how to write the code, ABC would be relevant.

That's all the code. There were quite a few methods, but they are all quite simple. There is a trade-off between writing simple, easy-to-debug code and the number of classes and methods one must type. The typing is rather tedious, but the time spent designing and implementing a simple solution will be recouped many times by the time not spent debugging, especially in complicated programs.

Testing

Now it's time to test the play one game code. After you fix all the small mistakes, you should see it displaying in the TextArea. There are two problems with the code written in the preceding section (see Figure 7.3).

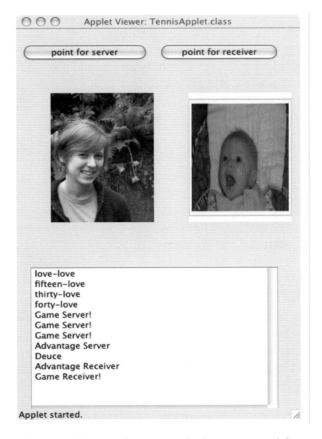

FIGURE 7.3 The complete output for four presses of the left Button, and then six of the right. Two bugs are apparent.

First, it does not announce the score before the first point; it never says "love-love." Second, after the game is over, it still allows points to be scored. The output shown is for four clicks of "point for server" and then six of "point for receiver." It would be better to stop scoring after the game is over! Fortunately, because the code is written well, these are both easy to fix.

Announcing the Score before the First Point

Fixing bugs can be easy or difficult, and the better you understand the code, the easier it is. The simpler the code, the easier it is to understand what's going wrong. Well-written code has modules that make it easy to modify.

The reason it does not announce the score before the first point is obvious if you look at the code. The only time it announces the score is when the user pushes a Button (check it, it's true). So, how to announce the score before the first point?

It would be easy to cause the game to announce the score if there was a method that announced the score in Game. Is there?

Where should the announceScore message be sent to theGame? Look at the TennisApplet code you've written. Where should you send that message? In init(), right after theGame is created; see Listing 7.29.

LISTING 7.29   Announcing the initial score before the game.

```
1    public void init() {
2        initComponents();
3        theGame = new Game(new Player("Serena"), new Player("Maria"));
4        theGame.setTheTA(theTA);
5        mariaImage = getImage(getCodeBase(), "maria.jpg");
6        serenaImage = getImage(getCodeBase(), "serena.jpg");
7        theGame.announceScore();
8    }
```

Preventing Points after the Game Is Over

When the user pushes a "point for" Button, you don't always want to add a point, only sometimes—which is what if statements are for. You should only add a point if the game is not over. Here's the payoff from having written the gameOver() method. You can use it from the Applet to check if the game is over and only add a point if it is not; see Listing 7.30.

LISTING 7.30   Only add points if the Game is not over—!over.

```
1    private void serButtonActionPerformed( java.awt.event.ActionEvent evt) {
2        if (!theGame.gameOver())
```

```
3          theGame.serverScored();
4    }
```

Line 2: Guards sending the serverScored() message with !theGame.gameOver(). In other words, if the game is over, do not send the serverScored() message.

Make these changes (guard both the Buttons!) and rerun your code. With any luck, you now have a working TennisApplet.

CONCLUSION

The if statement allows different statements to execute depending on the situation. It has two forms, if without an else and if-else. If you want your program to do something only under certain conditions, use an if statement.

```
if (condition is true)
    doSomething
```

If you want your program to do either one thing or another, use an if-else statement.

```
if (whatever condition determines when to do the first thing)
    oneThing();
else anotherThing();
```

Multiple cases can be handled either by a cascaded if-else, or a switch statement. In complex cases, the ABC technique can help clarify your thinking.

REVIEW QUESTIONS

7.1 If you want to either execute a statement or not depending on some condition, what statement do you use?

7.2 If you want to execute either one statement or another depending on circumstances, what statement do you use?

7.3 Why is the if statement called a conditional statement?

7.4 Write a statement that prints "yes" if x is greater than zero and "no" otherwise.

7.5 Reverse the logic in Listing 7.6; exchange the statements before and after the `else`, and then reverse the logic of the `boolean` expression so it still does the right thing. If in doubt, make a truth table.

7.6 Make a truth table for *(!p||q) && !(p&&!q)*.

7.7 In craps, on the first roll, if you roll 7 or 11, you win; if you roll 2 or 12, you lose. Otherwise, you must roll the same value you rolled the first time before you roll a 7 to win. Write a cascaded `if-else` statement that tests a variable `rollValue` and prints one of three things: "you win!" "sorry, you lose," or "roll again" depending on its value.

Programming Exercises

7.8 Here's some code with what may be a subtle bug. What would it print if age were 14? If age were 41? How do you fix it?

```
if (age > 18)
    System.out.println("Major");
else
    System.out.println("Minor");
    System.out.println("You may not enter!");
```

7.9 Write a method named `exclusiveOr()`, which is passed two `boolean` parameters and returns `true` if exactly one of them is `true`.

7.10 An exam is graded as follows: 91–100: A, 81–90: B, 61–70: D, <61: F. Write a method that is passed an `int` score and returns the appropriate grade as a `String`. First, use an `if-else`, and then a `switch` statement. Hint: what values would `(score-1)/10` take on for various scores? Remember how `int` division works.

7.11 Modify `announceWinner()` to announce the winner's name, like "Game Serena!" Hint: use `getName()`.

7.12 Add an error message if the user pushes a `Button` after the game is over.

7.13 A better solution is to disable the `Button`s when the game is over. Do that. Perhaps the easiest way is to send them the `setVisible(false)` message.

7.14 Modify your code so it plays a set instead of a game. Create a `Set` class; model it on `Game`. Play an entire set.

7.15 Modify your code so it plays a match instead of a set.

8 Iterative Statements and Strings

In This Chapter

- Iteration: Repeated Action
- The `while` Loop
- The `for` Loop
- Strings: A Very Brief Introduction

INTRODUCTION

Repetition is a part of life; the sun comes up, the sun goes down. Spring turns to summer; fall arrives and students gather in classrooms. Babies grow to children, mature to adults, have more babies, and die. Civilizations rise and fall, again and again. The galaxy turns, but very slowly to our eyes.

This Chapter

This chapter introduces Java statements that repeat. Together with conditional statements, these comprise the bulk of control structure in Java. Good control structure, coupled with well-designed class structure, can yield powerful and useful software.

Unlike other chapters, this one is almost devoid of classes. It focuses on the mechanics of loops and Strings. Perhaps you can learn this material simply by reading the text, but it may help these constructs stick in memory if you type them into a program and run them (and they are all essential to programming). This would also give you a chance to experiment with small changes to them, to play around with them. That's one of the best ways for most people to learn.

The previous chapter introduced conditional statements; this one will introduce the other statements that implement control structure, iterative statements. It also will discuss Strings in more detail.

ITERATION: REPEATED ACTION

Iterate is another word for *repeat*. To make a program do something a number of times, use an iterative statement. There are three iterative statements in Java; see BNF 8.1. This chapter will cover while and for.

BNF 8.1 Iterative Statement

<iterative stmt> ::= <while stmt> | <for stmt> | <do-while stmt>

THE while LOOP

The while loop is the simplest of the looping constructs.

Syntax and Semantics

The syntax and semantics of a while statement are shown in BNF 8.2.

Notice that the syntax is very much like an if statement (see BNF 7.1 "The if Statement"). The difference in semantics is that after the <stmt> is executed, the <boolean expression> is evaluated again, and if it is still true, that process repeats, possibly forever. The programmer must remember to make sure that while loops are not infinite!

BNF 8.2 The `while` Statement

> <while stmt> ::= while (<boolean expression>) <stmt>
>
> Semantics:
>
> 1. Evaluate the <boolean expression>.
> 2. If the value of the expression is true,
>
>   a) execute the <stmt> after <expression>
>
>   b) Go back to step 1.

Example 1: Counting to Ten

Listing 8.1 shows a `while` loop that prints the numbers from 1 to 10.

LISTING 8.1 Counting to 10.

```
1    int count=1;
2
3    while (count<=10) {
4        System.out.println("count=" + count);
5        count++;
6    } // while
```

Line 1: Declares an `int` variable named `count` and sets it to the value 1.

Lines 3–6: The `while` loop, which will run `while` `count` <= 10.

Line 4: Prints the value of `count` (along with a descriptive label).

Line 5: Adds one to `count`.

This loop runs over and over until the `boolean` expression `count<=10` evaluates to `false` at the top of the loop (it is only rechecked before the entire loop body executes). So, the execution of the loop is controlled by the value of `count`. Thus, `count` is the *control variable* for this loop. In this case, the control variable is also being used to display the count; sometimes the control variable only controls the number of times the loop executes. If you omit line 5, this will print `count=1`, forever! This is called an *infinite loc$_{i}$*.

One way to understand what a section of code does is analysis; simply look at it and see what it does. If that works, fine. If that doesn't work, another way to discover what it does is called *hand simulation*. To hand simulate code, you need paper and pencil. Write down the variables involved and step through the code, carrying out the semantics of each statement one by one, recording the values of the variables as you go. Table 8.1 shows the hand trace for Listing 8.1; make sure you understand it, and then do it yourself. It is slow work, but sometimes it provides insight into the mysterious inner workings of code.

TABLE 8.1 Hand Simulation for Listing 8.1

Line	Action	Count
1	declare count	1
3	count<=10? yes, do body	1
4	output count=1	1
5	count++	2
3	count<=10? yes, do body	2
4	output count=2	2
5	count++	3
3	count<=10? yes, do body	3
...	...	...
5	count++	10
3	count<=10? yes, do body	10
4	output count=10	10
5	count++	11
3	count<=10? no!, done!	11

Example 2: Doing Something 10 Times

Listing 8.2 is a generic loop to do something 10 times. Because it is in a loop that goes around 10 times, something() will be executed 10 times. What that something is, is up to the programmer.

LISTING 8.2 Doing something 10 times.

```
1    int count=1;
2
3    while (count<=10) {
4        something();
5        count++;
6    } // while
```

For example, this loop can be used to output the squares and cubes of the numbers from 1 to 10, as shown in Listing 8.3, which uses Listing 8.2 as the body of `main()`.

LISTING 8.3   Using that `while` loop to print a list of squares and cubes.

```
1    public class TestIteration {
2
3        private static void sqAndCube(int x) {
4            System.out.println("x=" + x + "x^2=" + x*x + "x^3=" +
x*x*x);
5        }
6
7        public static void main(String[] args) {
8            int count=1;
9            while (count <= 10) {
10               sqAndCube(count);
11               count++;
12           }
13       }
14   }
```

Line 3: The heading for `sqAndCube()`. Notice that it is a class method.

The control variable is passed as the value to square and cube each time. Notice that there are some formatting issues.

This code does what it is supposed to, but the output doesn't look very nice. Figure 8.1 has the output for this loop from our machine.

```
x=1x^2=1x^3=1
x=2x^2=4x^3=8
x=3x^2=9x^3=27
x=4x^2=16x^3=64
x=5x^2=25x^3=125
x=6x^2=36x^3=216
x=7x^2=49x^3=343
x=8x^2=64x^3=512
x=9x^2=81x^3=729
x=10x^2=100x^3=1000
```

FIGURE 8.1   Output from Listing 8.3
—obviously in need of spaces.

Although there are spaces in the `println()`, there are none inside the ""s. That `println()` would create better looking output if it had a few spaces, like this:

```
System.out.println("x="+ x + " x^2=" + x*x + " x^3=" + x*x*x);
```

Figure 8.2 has the output with that change.

```
x=1  x^2=1  x^3=1
x=2  x^2=4  x^3=8
x=3  x^2=9  x^3=27
x=4  x^2=16  x^3=64
x=5  x^2=25  x^3=125
x=6  x^2=36  x^3=216
x=7  x^2=49  x^3=343
x=8  x^2=64  x^3=512
x=9  x^2=81  x^3=729
x=10  x^2=100  x^3=1000
```

FIGURE 8.2 Slightly better output from Listing 8.3—still in need of tabs.

This is better, but the different widths of the larger numbers rather wreck the readability. This is a good place to use the tab character (\t):

```
System.out.println("x="+x+ "\tx^2=" + x*x + "\tx^3=" + x*x*x);
```

Output from this appears in Figure 8.3 and looks better. The general problem of formatting text from Java will be postponed indefinitely.

```
x=1        x^2=1      x^3=1
x=2        x^2=4      x^3=8
x=3        x^2=9      x^3=27
x=4        x^2=16     x^3=64
x=5        x^2=25     x^3=125
x=6        x^2=36     x^3=216
x=7        x^2=49     x^3=343
x=8        x^2=64     x^3=512
x=9        x^2=81     x^3=729
x=10       x^2=100    x^3=1000
```

FIGURE 8.3 Output from Listing 8.3—with tabs.

Example 3: Doing Something *N* Times

In the more generic loop in Listing 8.4, the control variable is compared to another variable, *N*, instead of 10.

LISTING 8.4   Code A generic `while` loop—does `something()` *N* times, suitable for memorization.

```
1    static final int N=10;
2    int count=1;
3
4    while (count<=N) {
5        something();
6        count++;
7    } // while
```

   This can make a big difference in a more complex situation. Changing a 10 to 1000 is easy, changing eight 10s to 1000s, less so; and what if you forget one of them?

Example 4: Counting to 10—Take Two

Listing 8.1 started the value of `count` at 1, as a person would. However, it is common for loops in programs to start from 0 instead, for reasons that will be seen later. Listing 8.5 shows the same loop counting from 0. There are three changes: `count` is initialized to 0, the expression is (`count<10`) instead of (`count<=10`), and lines 4 and 5 are exchanged. Convince yourself that this loop does the same thing as the other.

LISTING 8.5   Counting to 10—take two.

```
1    int count=0;
2
3    while (count<10) {
4        count++;
5        System.out.println("count=" + count);
6    } // while
```

   This also prints the numbers 1–10, but using slightly different logic.

Infinite Loops

The `while` loop gives the programmer tremendous power. However, with increased power comes increased capacity for error. If the control variable is never updated inside the loop, and the loop starts (i.e., the condition is true the first time), then it is always an infinite loop. If the control variable is not correctly updated, it may be an infinite loop.

THE for LOOP

Listing 8.6 does exactly what Listing 8.4 did, but uses a for loop instead of a while loop.

LISTING 8.6   Doing something 10 times with a generic for loop.

```
1    static final int N=10
2
3    for (int count=1; count<=N; count++) {
4        something();
5    } // for
```

Notice that initialization, checking, and incrementing the control variable all happen in the first line of the for. This makes them much more difficult to forget.

It is a bit more compact than the equivalent while loop, and until you are used to it, more confusing. One young programmer who was familiar with while loops but not for loops refused to learn for loops because "They are too complicated!" This was a mistake.

Sometimes, learning one thing makes another more difficult to learn. This is called *proactive interference*. The effect is particularly strong when you know one way to do something and someone wants you to learn another. The way you know (in that young programmer's case, the while loop) seems simple and obvious, the new way difficult and confusing. When you try to solve a problem with a new technique, you immediately know how to solve it with the old technique (which interferes with applying the new technique). Therefore, you resist the new way. This is true at all scales, from iterative statements to programming languages and paradigms, operating systems, and even lifestyles. However, change is good; if you stop learning, your life is essentially over. Oops, back to the for loop.

The syntax and semantics of a for loop is very similar to that of a while loop. As BNF 8.3 shows, it starts with the word *for*, then some things in ()s, and then a single statement.

There are three things in the ()s; the one in the middle, the continuation condition, is a boolean expression (see BNF 8.3), exactly like the while loop. The first thing, <initialization>, is done once, before anything (like initialization always is). The third, <update>, is done after the body of the loop is executed (each time it is executed). See Figure 8.4 for an illustration.

BNF 8.3   The for Statement

<for stmt> ::= for (<initialization>;<continuation condition>; <update>) <stmt>

Semantics:

1. Execute <initialization>.

2. If the value of the <continuation condition>. is true,

   a) execute the <stmt>.

   b) Execute <update>.

   c) Go back to step 2 (that's right, step 2).

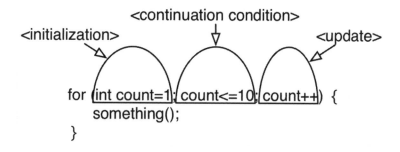

FIGURE 8.4   `for` loop illustration.

BNF 8.4   `for` Loop Details

<initialization> ::= <stmt>

<continuation condition> ::= <boolean expression>

<update> ::= <stmt>

Both <initialization> and <update> are simply statements, the <continuation condition> is simply a boolean expression.

The big advantage of a `for` loop is that the initialization and update are included in the statement. That way, they are easy to find and hard to omit accidentally.

Programming Example

Here is a slightly more complicated example.

Task

Write a program that will count to 1000 by twos, displaying the count to System.out.

Several methods might be employed to accomplish this task. First, since we already have a loop that counts to 10 by ones, we could simply change the 10 to 1000 and only print the even numbers, as in Listing 8.7.

LISTING 8.7   Counting to 1000 by twos—method one.

```
1    static final int N=1000;
2
3    for (int count=1; count<=N; count++) {
4        if (count is even)
5            System.out.println("" + count);
6    } // for
```

The for loop iterates 1000 times, with count going from 1 to 1000. Only even numbers print.

Notice here that the first part of the String parameter is "". That way, it doesn't say "count=" every time. With some compilers, if you omit that and just write System.out.println(count);, it will generate a compiler error complaining that an int is not a String (recall "int to String" in Chapter 5, "Toward Consistent Classes.")

How can we determine if count is even? Here's a hint: even numbers are evenly divisible by 2. Need another hint? The % operator yields the remainder after int division. One more hint? If a number divides another evenly, the remainder is zero. Okay?

A second approach to this problem is to change the update so that each time around the loop it adds 2 to count instead of 1 (change the count++ to count=count+2; see Listing 8.8).

LISTING 8.8   Counting to 1000 by twos—method two.

```
1    static final int N=1000;
2
3    for (int count=2; count<=N; count=count+2) {
4        System.out.println("" + count);
5    } // for
```

By changing both the initialization and the update, we get clean simple code.

Third, we could just count from 1 to 500 and print twice the count each time (see Listing 8.9), where count goes from 1–500, and count*2 is printed each time around the loop.

LISTING 8.9 Counting to 1000 by twos—method three.

```
1    static final int N=500;
2
3    for (int count=1; count<=N; count++) {
4        System.out.println("" + count*2);
5    } // for
```

Which of these methods would be better? It's a matter of style.

Cleaning Up the Output

If you run that code, it produces 500 lines of output. That's a bit excessive; it would be nicer if more than one number were printed on each line. The `println()` method ends the line after it outputs its parameter. There is another method, `print()`, that does not end the line. Thus, the simple solution would seem to be to send `print()` instead of `println()` to `System.out`; do you know what would go wrong in that case?

Using `print()`, all the numbers are concatenated, without any spaces, on one line. The beginning of the output is shown in Figure 8.5.

```
246810121416182022242628303234363840424446485052545658606264666870727476788082848688909294969810 0102104
```

FIGURE 8.5 Using `print()` instead of `println()` produces more compact output. Possibly too compact!

That's two problems. The first is very easy to solve; see Listing 8.10.

LISTING 8.10 Counting to 1000 by twos—on one line.

```
1    for (int count=2; count<=N; count=count+2) {
2        System.out.print(" " + count);
3    } // for
```

Notice the `print()` instead of `println()`. The space in the `""`s puts spaces between the numbers.

The second problem is more complicated and the solution is not obvious.

Printing 10 Numbers per Line

One idea would be to print a fixed number of numbers on each line; say 10. Pseudocode for this is shown in Listing 8.11.

LISTING 8.11 Pseudocode for printing 10 numbers on each line.

```
1    for (int count=2; count<=N; count=count+2) {
2        System.out.print(" " + count);
3        if (have printed 10 on this line)
4            System.out.println();  // go to next line
5    } // for
```

How can we tell (in line 3) if 10 numbers have been printed on this line? Here's two possibilities: 1) Add a counter; initialize it to 0, and each time we print a number, add one; when we do the `println()`, reset it to 0. Alternatively, 2) Figure out some clever way to discern when 10 numbers have been printed. The former is more code, but more general; the latter is, well, clever, but likely to be hard to generalize (i.e., to use in another context).

Adding Another Counter

With a counter, the pseudocode appears in Listing 8.12.

LISTING 8.12 Pseudocode for printing 10 numbers on each line using a counter.

```
1    for (int count=2; count<=N; count=count+2) {
2        System.out.print(" " + count);
3        wordCount++;       // increment wordCount
4        if (wordCount == 10) {
5            System.out.println();  // go to next line
6            reset wordCount to 0;
7        } // if
8    } // for
```

Of course, the variable `wordCount` must be declared and initialized to 0 before the loop. This produces the output shown in Figure 8.6.

A Clever Trick

If there were some property shared by all the final numbers on a line, the code could check that property instead of keeping a counter to tell when it is time to end the line. Looking at that output, can you see anything unique about the last number on each line? Right, they are all multiples of 20. So, to tell if it is time to end the line we could just check if `count%20==0`, as in Listing 8.13.

```
2  4  6  8  10  12  14  16  18  20
22  24  26  28  30  32  34  36  38  40
42  44  46  48  50  52  54  56  58  60
62  64  66  68  70  72  74  76  78  80
82  84  86  88  90  92  94  96  98  100
102  104  106  108  110  112  114  116  118  120
122  124  126  128  130  132  134  136  138  140
```

FIGURE 8.6 Ten even numbers on each line; too bad the alignment is so bad.

LISTING 8.13 Pseudocode for printing 10 numbers on each line using a trick.

```
1    for (int count=2; count<=N; count=count+2) {
2        System.out.print(" " + count);
3        if (count % 20 == 0)
4            System.out.println();  // go to next line
5    } // for
```

This kind of coding trick is fun, but can lead to disaster if later the code must be modified. Nonetheless, it is useful to remember.

The Empty Statement

Here's an unusual statement, the empty statement. BNF 8.5 shows its syntax and semantics. It consists of nothing and does nothing.

BNF 8.5 The Empty Statement

<empty stmt> ::=
Semantics:
Does nothing.

What good is it? It allows the programmer to omit a statement in a place where syntactically a statement must appear and still match the grammar. In other words, it allows the programmer to get around the rigidity of the compiler, which can be a very good thing.

An Infinite for Loop

The format of a for loop makes it difficult to forget to update the control variable, and so, one is less likely to write an infinite for loop. However, sometimes you want to write an infinite for loop (as you will see in the next chapter). Listing 8.14 shows how to send the something() message forever. Note that the {}s are not necessary.

LISTING 8.14   Doing something() forever.

```
1    for (;;) {
2        something();
3    } // for
```

The line something(); is a single message statement, so Listing 8.15 is legal as well.

LISTING 8.15   Listing 8.14 without the {}s.

```
1    for (;;)      // forever!
2        something();
```

The empty statement sometimes causes nasty bugs (yet another example of the fact that most things have two sides). Can you see what is wrong with the code in Listing 8.16?

LISTING 8.16   An infinite loop that doesn't do anything—forever!

```
1    for (;;);     // forever!
2        anything();
```

If you don't see it immediately, try matching the symbols one by one with BNF 8.3. It starts like this: for matches for, (matches (, absolutely nothing matches the empty statement, which is a <statement> which is an <initialization>. Continue this process until you reach the end of <stmt>.

If you ran this code it would never do anything, but unlike the empty statement, which does nothing immediately, it would do nothing, forever!

Strings: A VERY BRIEF INTRODUCTION

The Java String class is used to store literal sequences of characters. Many methods operate on Strings; you can read about them in the documentation. This section will introduce a bare minimum of String methods with the signatures int

length(), char charAt(int), boolean equals(String), and String toUpperCase().
Notice that these four methods return int, char, boolean, and String values, respectively. Then, it will present a better way of breaking lines of even numbers.

A Few String Methods

Here are several String methods that will get you started using Strings.

The int length() Method

As you might guess, if you send length() to a String, it will return its length. So the
code:

```
String s = "hello";
System.out.println("s=" + s + " s.length()=" + s.length());
```

will print s=hello s.length()=5. No surprises.

char charAt(int)

A String is a series of characters. The Java type for characters is char; each char
holds a single character. Character constants have single quotes around them, like
'a' or '$'. The first character in a String is at location 0. That's zero, not one, but
zero. Forgetting this will cause little annoying bugs. Rather like mosquitoes—not
really harmful, but annoying. The reason the first char is at zero is that Strings are
implemented as arrays, which are coming up in a few chapters. Arrays in Java, as in
C++ and C, start at zero. No way around it. Deal with it. Accept it. Remember it!
    With String s="hello"; the following are true:

s.charAt(0) returns 'h'

s.charAt(1) returns 'e'

s.charAt(2) returns 'l'

s.charAt(3) returns 'l'

s.charAt(4) returns 'o'

You could write a loop to produce those five lines. Pseudocode for it is shown
in Listing 8.17.

LISTING 8.17   Pseudocode to print all the chars in a String.

```
1    String s="Howdy!";
2    for (each char in s) {
3        output the next char with suitable description
```

```
4    } // for
```

This is a pattern for many methods that process Strings. If you want to become expert at Java programming, it would be worth committing to memory; both the pseudocode and the code. Your choice.

When you want to access each of the chars in a String from first to last in order, you use the idiom shown in Listing 8.18.

LISTING 8.18 Printing the chars in a String one per line.

```
1    String s="Howdy!";
2    for (int i=0; i<s.length(); i++) {
3        System.out.println("charAt(" + i + ") is: '" + s.charAt(i) +
"'");
4    } // for
```

Notice the various parts of the String parameter sent to System.out.println() that produce the readable output.

Line 2: The generic for loop you write to access the chars in the String, s, sequentially. In the body of the loop, s.charAt(i) is each char, one after another each time around the loop. In pseudocode, s.charAt(i) is "the next char." The output of Listing 8.18 is shown in Figure 8.7.

```
charAt(0) is: 'H'
charAt(1) is: 'o'
charAt(2) is: 'w'
charAt(3) is: 'd'
charAt(4) is: 'y'
charAt(5) is: '!'
```

FIGURE 8.7 Output from code in Listing 8.18.

Notice how the String "charAt(0) is: " is constructed in the println() on line 3 in Listing 8.18. It is inconvenient, but highly informative to output such descriptive text along with the data one is outputting. If you are printing chars, the delimiters can be surprisingly important. The difference between printing nothing and printing an invisible character is important, but invisible. The single quotes bracketing the char let the reader see this difference.

The boolean `equals(String)` Method

You cannot compare `Strings` with `==`. Instead, you must use `equals()`. Worse, if you forget and use `==`, no error message will appear, because Java will compare the memory locations of the two `Strings`. Not what you expected, or wanted. Therefore, if you wanted to know if the same text is in two `TextFields`, you must write code like:

```
String s1 = aTF.getText();
String s2 = bTF.getText();
if (s1.equals(s2))
    "yes! they are the same";
else "no. not equal"
```

String toUpperCase()

This method does what you might expect, it makes an uppercase copy of the `String` it is sent to and returns that. So:

```
String s = "abcDEFghi";
System.out.println(s.toUpperCase());
```

would output `ABCDEFGHI`.

There are many useful methods that you should learn if you are going to do any extensive programming with `Strings`, including `substring()`, `replaceAll()`, and `subSequence()`.

Breaking Lines Using `Strings`

The technique to print 10 even numbers per line in Listing 8.12 worked, but it was rigid and produced somewhat ugly output. This example will do the same job more generally and elegantly. It will count to 1000 by twos and print as many numbers on each line as will fit.

Decoupling the Output

An important step to writing elegant, general code is to decouple the logic and the output. This is true of all code. Input and output are inherently messy and idiosyncratic. A standard technique is to consolidate output in a method called `emit()`, as shown in Listing 8.19.

LISTING 8.19   Using `emit()` to decouple the output.

```
1    static void countTo_N_Improved() {
2        for (int count=2; count<=N; count=count+2) {
3            emit(" " + count);
4        } // for
5    }
```

Each `String` to be output is sent to `emit()`, which handles the formatting and output. This way, the logic of the loop is kept simple and whatever needs to be done with output `String`s happens in one place, `emit()`.

Buffers

An area of working storage is called a *buffer*. There is a built-in Java class called `String-Buffer`, which some people would argue should be used here. However, that would be one more class to learn, and your task now is to understand the basics of `String`s. If you are going to be doing extensive work with buffering `String`s, definitely look up `String-Buffer`!

The job of `emit()` here is to put as many output `String`s on each line as will fit. It will accomplish this with an output buffer. The buffer will start empty. Whenever a `String` is sent to `emit()`, if it fits in the buffer, it will be concatenated onto the end. If it overfills the buffer, two things will happen: first, the buffer will be output (or flushed, as is sometimes said); second, the `String` will be added to the now empty buffer as the first thing on the next line. Pseudocode for `emit()` appears in Listing 8.20.

LISTING 8.20   Pseudocode for `emit()`—first try.

```
1    static void emit(String nextChunk) {
2        if (nextChunk would overfill the buffer) {
3            flush buffer
4            add nextChunk to the buffer
5        }
6        else add nextChunk to the buffer
7    }
```

Notice that lines 4 and 6 are identical. When the same thing is done at the end of both the `if` and `else` parts of an `if-else`, you can do what is called *bottom factoring*.

Bottom Factoring

Since either the `if` part or the `else` part of an `if-else` is bound to execute, when the last thing in both is the same, it is always the last thing done before the next statement. Thus, it can be moved after the `if-else`. This is illustrated in Listing 8.21.

LISTING 8.21 Pseudocode for `emit()`—after bottom factoring.

```
1    static void emit(String nextChunk) {
2        if (nextChunk would overfill the buffer)
3            flush buffer
4        add nextChunk to the buffer
5    }
```

Since the next chunk is always added to the buffer, this code does the same thing as Listing 8.20. It is simpler and easier to read.

Having thought through the logic and written detailed pseudocode, it is fairly easy to write the actual code; see Listing 8.22.

LISTING 8.22 Breaking lines at 70 `chars`—a complete program.

```
1    public class TestIteration {
2
3        public static void main(String[] args) {
4            countTo_N_Improved();
5        }
6
7         private final static int MAX_LINE_LENGTH=70;
8         private static String buffer = "";
9         private static void emit(String nextChunk) {
10            if (buffer.length() + nextChunk.length() > MAX_LINE_LENGTH) {
11                System.out.println(buffer);
12                buffer = "";  // empty the buffer
13            }
14            buffer += nextChunk;
15        }
16
17         private static final int N=1000;
18         private static void countTo_N_Improved() {
19            for (int count=2; count<=N; count=count+2) {
20                emit(" " + count);
21            } // for
22        }
23    }
```

Line 8: Declares and initializes the buffer.

Line 9: Method heading for `emit()`. Notice that this method is `static`, like `countTo_N_Improved()`. These methods are not instance methods, but class methods. Thus, they cannot access instance variables (and there are none in this class). They also cannot be invoked unless messages are sent to the `TestIteration` class.

Line 10: Checks if adding this next chunk would overfill it. If so, it must be flushed.

Line 11: Outputs it.

Line 12: Empties the buffer.

Line 14: Always adds the new output to the end of the buffer.

Make sure you understand how this listing implements the pseudocode; these are standard techniques you will need to know.

The reason why static methods are appropriate there is that there will never be multiple instances of a `TestIteration`; thus, it is simpler to make them class methods. The output using this line-breaking scheme is shown in Figure 8.8. It is much better balanced and adaptable than the original. This technique could be easily adapted to a word processing application.

```
2 4 6 8 10 12 14 16 18 20 22 24 26 28 30 32 34 36 38 40 42 44 46 48
50 52 54 56 58 60 62 64 66 68 70 72 74 76 78 80 82 84 86 88 90 92 94
96 98 100 102 104 106 108 110 112 114 116 118 120 122 124 126 128 130
132 134 136 138 140 142 144 146 148 150 152 154 156 158 160 162 164
166 168 170 172 174 176 178 180 182 184 186 188 190 192 194 196 198
```

FIGURE 8.8 Output from code in Listing 8.18.

Palindromes

A palindrome is a word that is the same backward and forward, like "noon" or "race-car." This section will develop a program that inputs a `String` and reports whether it is palindromic. Palindromic, here, means a `String` would be a palindrome if we neglected case, spaces, and punctuation. A famous palindromic sentence is "A man, a plan, a canal—Panama!" This and many others are at various Web sites, including: *www.jps.at/palindromes/english/EA.html*

Design: Two Approaches

There is usually more than one way to approach a problem. Sometimes, the first approach you think of is the best way to handle a problem, but other times a fresh perspective will yield better results. If you conceptualize two different approaches before beginning to implement either, you reduce the likelihood of frustrating missteps; and if you do start on a path that turns out to be rocky, you have an alternative in the wings. To illustrate this, two approaches to this problem will be presented.

Approach Number One: Converging Pointers

Formulating an algorithm to decide if a `String` is palindromic is not entirely trivial. There may be spaces, punctuation, and lower- or uppercase letters at any position in it. Therefore, it makes sense to solve a subset of the problem.

A simpler version of this problem is deciding if a single word with all lowercase letters is a palindrome. This is a sensible place to start thinking about this problem. Could you solve this simpler problem? If so, you could likely skip ahead to the next section. If not, here's a way to get started.

One technique for designing an algorithm to convert into a program to solve some problem is to solve a simple example of that problem yourself. If you keep track of what you did to solve it, that technique can be cast as pseudocode and then converted to actual code.

Problem Solving Technique: How would you do it without a computer?
If you can't think of an algorithm for a problem, start solving it yourself and then convert the technique you would use into an algorithm.

One way a human might check if a word were a palindrome is to point one finger at the first letter and another at the last letter. If those two letters are the same, move the fingers toward each other; if they are different, the word is not a palindrome, and you stop. Otherwise, continue this procedure until the fingers cross.

Most people point with their first finger; that's why it is called the index finger. Figure 8.9 shows the initial state of the algorithm for the two strings "racecar" and "dogfood."

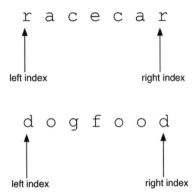

FIGURE 8.9   Initially, the pointers are at the first and last letters.

Since 'r'=='r' and 'd'=='d', both sets of pointers will next move toward each other. At that next step, shown in Figure 8.10, both 'a'=='a', in "racecar" and 'o'=='o' in "dogfood."

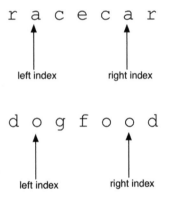

FIGURE 8.10   Since the first and last letters of each word are the same, the pointers move toward each other by one position.

So, again, both words may still be palindromes, and both sets of pointers move toward each other. Then, as shown in Figure 8.11, 'c'=='c', but 'g' != 'o', so we know "dogfood" is not a palindrome.

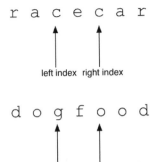

FIGURE 8.11 In "racecar" the pointers still point at identical letters, so it may still be a palindrome, but 'g' is not 'o', so "dogfood" cannot be a palindrome.

Continuing, when the indices are advanced once more in "racecar" (see Figure 8.12), they are both pointed at the 'e' in the middle. Since the fingers have run into each other, "racecar" is judged a palindrome.

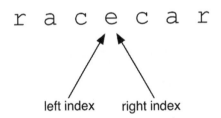

FIGURE 8.12 The two pointers meet without ever pointing to different letters, so, the word must be a palindrome.

Pseudo-Code for isPalindrome(String)

Having thought carefully about the algorithm to decide if a String is a palindrome, we are ready to write pseudocode for it.

```
set leftIndex to the start of the String
set rightIndex to the end of the String

while (pointers not crossed and letters at pointers are ==) {
    move left pointer right 1 letter
    move right pointer left 1 letter
}
```

```
if (pointers are crossed)
    the String is a palindrome
else it is not
```

Java Code for `isPalindrome(String)`

With the pseudocode in hand, the Java code is straightforward to write, assuming you recall several details.

1. You can access a particular character in a `String` using `charAt(int)`.
2. The first character is `charAt(0)` .
3. You can learn the length of a `String` by `length()`.

Thus, the last char is `charAt(length()-1)`, since the first index in a `String` is 0.
You can increment an `int` with `++` and decrement it with `--`.
Methods with non-`void` return types must return values.
When you exit a `while` loop, you know the condition is `false`; therefore, the `return` statement returns `true` (meaning it is a palindrome) just in case the pointers have crossed. If they have not, it must be the case that two letters the same distance from the ends of the `String` were `!=`, since otherwise you would still be in the `while` loop.
The code for the `isPalindrome()` method appears in Listing 8.23.

LISTING 8.23   The `isPalindrome()` method.

```
1    boolean isPalindrome(String s) {
2        int leftIndex = 0;
3        int rightIndex = s.length()-1;
4
5        while (leftIndex < rightIndex
6                && s.charAt(leftIndex) == s.charAt(rightIndex)) {
7            leftIndex++;
8            rightIndex--;
9        }
10
11       return leftIndex >= rightIndex;
12   }
```

Adjourn to the screen now, type in this method, and test it. The simplest way is to make an `Applet` with two `TextFields`; one for input, one for output. Remember that if you are trying to learn to program, instead of just transcribing the code, a good technique is to recreate it from memory; this will force you to internalize the various language and logic features. So, study the code in Listing 8.23, and try to type it in without looking. If you have to peek, that's okay, but don't just copy it!

Converting isPalindrome(String) **to** isPalindromic(String)

Having solved the simpler problem, we are ready to adapt that solution to the more difficult problem. One's first idea of how to convert isPalindrome(String) to isPalindromic(String) might be to modify it to handle the more complex case. In other words, the basic structure of the algorithm is the same, but each time around the loop, instead of just incrementing one pointer and decrementing the other, we must move them until they are both pointing to a letter (as opposed to a space, or punctuation).

There is a method in the Character class, isLetter(char), which tells if a char is a letter. Character.isLetter('a') returns true, whereas Character.isLetter('8') returns false.

Thus, the code might be rewritten as in Listing 8.24.

LISTING 8.24 The isPalindromic(String) method: take one.

```
1    boolean isPalindromic(String s) {
2        int leftIndex = 0;
3        int rightIndex = s.length()-1;
4
5        while (leftIndex < rightIndex
6                && s.charAt(leftIndex) == s.charAt(rightIndex)) {
7            leftIndex++;
8            rightIndex--;
9            while (!Character.isLetter(s.charAt(leftIndex)))
10               leftIndex++;
11           while (!Character.isLetter(s.charAt(rightIndex)))
12               rightIndex--;
13       }
14
15   return leftIndex >= rightIndex;
16   }
```

Lines 9–10: Move the leftIndex right one position at a time until it is pointed at a letter.

Lines 11–12: Move the rightIndex left one position at a time until it is pointed at a letter.

This would work, as long as all the letters were either upper- or lowercase, but if you compare 'a' with 'A' they are not equal. The other problem is that there are two `while` loops inside a third. This is not necessarily wrong, but it is rather complicated, and complicated code leads to mysterious bugs.

There is a method to convert all the letters in a `String` to lowercase; `toLowerCase()`. So, if you convert the `String` to lowercase before starting the loop, that problem is avoided. To do this, insert the line:

```
s = s.toLowerCase();
```

as the first line in the method.

Approach Number Two: Filters

There are two ways to reuse classes, inheritance and composition (recall Chapter 6, "Software Reuse"). Similarly, there are two ways to reuse a method. The first way is to modify it (as shown previously); the second is to invoke it in the context of another method. That conversion of the `String` to lowercase is the first step in this second approach to the palindromic algorithm. We already have a simple method that tells if a `String` is a palindrome, assuming it only contains lowercase letters. If we could transform the `String` containing letters of both cases and non-letters (spaces, and punctuation) into one with only lowercase letters, we could then use that method to test the result. The pseudocode looks like:

```
convert to all lowercase
remove all non-letters
use palindrome() to determine if the remaining letters are a palindrome
```

This transduction is shown in Figure 8.13.

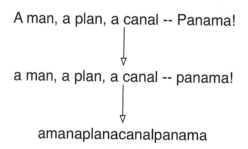

FIGURE 8.13   The filtering method for deciding palindromic.

The only part of that pseudocode that needs explication is `remove all non-letters`. What is required is to look at each `char` in the `String` and filter out everything except the letters. Thus, logically, we must:

```
create a String to hold the filtered input
for each char in s
    if (it is a letter)
        add it to the filtered String
```

As you may recall (see Listing 8.18), there is an idiom for accessing each char in a String, one at a time from first to last. Using that idiom, we obtain Listing 8.25.

LISTING 8.25 isPalindromic() as a filter.

```
1    boolean isPalindromic(String s) {
2        s = s.toLowerCase();
3        String filteredS = "";
4
5        for (int i=0; i<s.length(); i++)
6            if (Character.isLetter(s.charAt(i)))
7                filteredS += s.charAt(i);
8
9        return isPalindrome(filteredS);
10   }
```

Line 2: Convert to lowercase.

Line 3: Create the filtered String.

Lines 5–7: Filter out all non-letters.

Line 5: For each char in s.

Line 6: If it is a letter.

Line 7: Add it to the end of the filtered String.

Line 9: Return whatever isPalindrome() returns for the filtered String.

Which of these two techniques is better? It is difficult to say, but the latter method is certainly simpler; and simplicity is a virtue.

CONCLUSION

This chapter introduced loops and Strings. It also presented the filter method of information processing (which is the hallmark of the famous Unix operating system). Once you are familiar with classes, methods, instances, Strings, chars, conditional and iterative statements, you have the skills to solve a great number of problems.

REVIEW QUESTIONS

8.1 What is the difference between a `while` loop and a `for` loop syntactically?

8.2 What can you do with a `while` loop that you can't do with a `for` loop?

8.3 If `String s="stuff";` what is `s.charAt(1)`?

8.4 What is a buffer?

8.5 What is bottom factoring?

8.6 Hand simulate Listing 8.5.

8.7 Why is it a good idea to come up with two ways to approach a problem before beginning implementation?

Programming Exercises

8.8 Write and run the three methods for counting to 1000 by twos.

8.9 Write a method, `String reverse(String)` that returns its parameter backwards.

8.10 Write a method `int countEs(String)`, that returns the number of `'e'`s in the parameter.

8.11 Write a method `int countVowels(String)` that returns the number of vowels in the parameter.

8.12 Use `reverse()` to write a very simple method, `boolean palindrome(String)`, that returns `true` just if its parameter is the same backwards as forwards. For example, "noon," "madam," and "aha" are palindromes.

8.13 Extend the previous method to handle spaces, punctuation, and capital letters. For example, "A man, a plan, a canal. Panama!" is a palindrome. Hint: use a filtering scheme. First make everything uppercase (`toUpperCase()`), then remove punctuation and spaces (`Character.isLetter(char)`), then use the method used previously.

8.14 Write a method `boolean anagram(String, String)` that returns `true` just if its parameters are anagrams. Hint: this is not simple! It will take careful design. You might want to ask your instructor how to go about it.

9 Simulation and Animation

INTRODUCTION

This chapter presents a program that implements a discrete-time simulation and animation of a ball being dropped and bouncing. Perhaps that sounds daunting, but it is relatively simple once you know how. The only new programming construct required for simulation and animation is threads. The only new concept is discrete time simulation, which may turn out to be more familiar than you expect.

AN INTRODUCTION TO Threads

As discussed throughout, information processing is accomplished by sending messages to objects. A message invokes a method; first, the parameter linkage is performed, and then the method body is executed. When a method body is executed, first the first statement is executed, then the second, and so on, until the last statement finishes execution. Then, the method returns control to wherever the message that invoked it was sent.

Imagine the path of execution through a program over time. It includes the sequential execution of statements in method bodies and the transfer of control from one method to another by sending messages.

At any one time, one particular statement is being executed. If it is a message statement, it invokes a method, which executes until it reaches the end of its block statement. For example, in the Eye Applet, when the user pushes the shrink Button, the runtime system invokes its ActionPerformed() method (see Listing 9.1), which sends a shrinkPupil() message to first the leftEye, and then the rightEye, and then finally sends a repaint() message to itself (since repaint() is changed to this. repaint() by the compiler).

LISTING 9.1   shrinkButtonActionPerformed() from EyeApplet.

```
1    private void shrinkButtonActionPerformed(
             java.awt.event.ActionEvent evt) {
2        leftEye.shrinkPupil();
3        rightEye.shrinkPupil();
4        repaint();
5    }
```

The shrinkPupil() method in the Eye class (see Listing 9.2) sends a setRadius() message to the pupil object, which is a FilledCircle. However, to do the parameter linkage, first it must evaluate the parameter pupil.getRadius() - 2.

LISTING 9.2   shrinkPupil() from the Eye class.

```
1    public void shrinkPupil() {
2        pupil.setRadius(pupil.getRadius() - 2);
3    }
```

To do so, it first sends the getRadius() message to the pupil object, and then subtracts 2 from whatever value that returns. Both getRadius() and setRadius(), although sent to a FilledCircle, end up in Circle (as FilledCircle inherits them from Circle).

Therefore, the sequence of messages sent (and methods executed) is:

```
EyeApplet:actionPerformed()
    Eye:shrinkPupil()
        Circle:getRadius()
        Circle:setRadius()
    Eye:shrinkPupil()
        Circle:getRadius()
        Circle:setRadius()
    EyeApplet:repaint()
```

This sequence of statements is executed in order; each statement has control while it is executing. If you were to print the entire program, tape all the sheets together, and draw a line from the first statement executed to the second, on to the third, and through the eighth, you would have a record of the path of execution when the shrinkButton is pushed. The path would lead from one method to another across various classes, and would look a bit like a thread running through fabric. By following this path, you can see which statements in the program are executing in which order. This imaginary line, this path through the program, is referred to as the or thread of control for short.

Each program you have seen thus far has had a single explicit thread, but to implement animation, a second thread is needed. Fortunately, Java has a built-in Thread class you can extend. Here's how.

Simplest Threaded Animation

The simplest threaded animation is an animated counter. It has two classes, a Frame and a Thread. An application with a Frame is used because with JDK1.5 and later, Applets cannot create threads using the standard SecurityManager. The Frame creates and kicks off a Thread that repeatedly increments a counter (in the Frame) and has the Frame display its current value. To begin implementation of this example, create a GUI Frame named ThreadedFrame. Next, create a Controller class and copy the code from Listing 9.3.

LISTING 9.3 Threaded Controller class.

```
1    public class Controller extends Thread {
2        private ThreadedFrame theFrame;
3
4        /** Creates a new instance of Controller */
5        public Controller(ThreadedFrame theFrame) {
6            this.theFrame= theFrame;
7        }
8
9        public void run() {
```

```
10                  for(;;) {
11                      step();
12                      pause();
13                  }
14          }
15
16          private void step() {
17              theFrame.incCounter();
18              theFrame.repaint();
19          }
20
21          private void pause() {
22              try {
23                  Thread.sleep(50);
24              } catch (Exception e) {}
25          }
26      }
```

The Controller class has a single instance variable named theFrame, which is used to both increment the counter in the Frame and to send the repaint() message to it (in the step() method).

Controller(ThreadedFrame)

The initializing constructor takes a single parameter, of type ThreadedFrame, and simply stores it in the theFrame instance variable. This is a standard technique to establish a two-way linkage between objects; the Frame object has a Controller variable that points to the Controller object, and the Controller object has a ThreadedFrame variable that points back to the Frame. It is common to need a reference back to the object that created another object, and that is how it is done.

The run() Method

When the start() message is sent to the Controller from the Frame, because Controller extends Thread, it first *spawns* a new thread of control, and then sends the Controller in that Thread the run() message. This new Thread exists until the run() method returns. The run() method here is an infinite loop (see the section, "An Infinite for Loop," in Chapter 8, "Iterative Statements and Strings"). It runs forever (or until the user closes the Frame), and it does just two things—step() and pause()—over and over.

The step() Method

The step() method sends first incCounter(), and then repaint() to the Frame. The pause method does only one thing; it sleeps for 50 milliseconds, but it looks rather complicated because the sleep() method, which is sent to the Thread class, throws an exception, which must be caught (see the section "Exceptions" in Appendix B). The simplest thing to do right now is any time you need a program to pause, simply copy and invoke this method. The Thread:sleep() method takes an int parameter and sleeps for that many milliseconds.

Add the bold lines in Listing 9.4 to your Frame.

LISTING 9.4   Changes to the ThreadedFrame class.

```
1    public class ThreadedFrame extends java.awt.Frame {
2
3        private Controller theController;
4        private int counter;
5        public void incCounter() {counter++;}
6        Thread aThread;
7
8        /** Creates a new instance of ThreadedFrame */
9        public ThreadedFrame() {
10           initComponents();
11           theController = new Controller(this);
12           theController.start();
13           show();
14           setBounds(10,10,200,200);
15       }
16
17       public void paint(java.awt.Graphics g) {
18           g.drawString(""+counter, 100, 100);
19       }
```

Line 3: A variable of type Controller; this is the new Thread.

Line 4: A counter; will start by default as 0.

Line 5: A method to increment (add 1 to) the counter; the Controller will use this.

Line 11: Create and store the Controller. Notice this as a parameter; this is the ThreadedFrame.

Line 12: Start the controller; in other words, spawn a new Controller thread and send the run() message to it.

Line 13: Show the Frame; forget this and you will not see anything when it runs!

Line 14: Set the bounds of the Frame; forget this and it will be very small in the upper left corner of the screen.

Lines 17–19: The paint() method; draws the counter value in the Frame.

That's all it takes! Run it, and if you've made no mistakes, you should see a counter counting...forever. Close the Frame to make it stop.

To make it seem more animated, modify paint() as in Listing 9.5.

LISTING 9.5   Addition to the ThreadedFrame:paint() to draw a circle.

```
1   public void paint(java.awt.Graphics g) {
2       g.drawString(""+counter, 100,100);
3       g.drawOval(counter%200, counter%200, counter%177, counter%177);
4   }
```

Alternatively, if you'd like the circle to stay the same size, use a constant (e.g., 20) for the third and fourth parameters. Do you see why this does what it does? Recall that the % operator gives the remainder after integer division (see the section "Arithmetic Operators" in Chapter 5, "Toward Consistent Classes"), so the first two parameters range from 0–199. When counter is 200, 400, or any even multiple of 200, counter%200 is zero, which is why the circle goes back to the upper left periodically.

THE PROGRAMMING TASK

Your task for this chapter is to implement and animate a user-controlled simulation of a ball falling under the influence of gravity and bouncing until it stops. Let the user start and stop the simulation by pressing a button. Make the radius of the ball 20 pixels and its color red. Assume the elasticity of the collision with the floor is 90 percent; thus, if the downward velocity of the ball were 100 when it hit the floor, its subsequent upward velocity would be 90.

Design

As always, before starting to write code, you should do enough design work to avoid wasting many frustrating hours going down blind alleys. Never start programming before you have a clear idea of what you are trying to accomplish and how you will approach the problem. To design this program, in addition to sketching the GUI and deciding which classes to use, you must also have some idea of what discrete time simulation is. These three are discussed in the next three subsections.

GUI

The problem description says there must be a Button to start and stop the simulation, so you will need a Button (or two). It also says that the ball should bounce when it hits the floor; thus, drawing a line for the floor or perhaps a box around the ball would make it less mysterious for the user when the ball changes direction.

How big should the Frame be? The bigger it is, the farther the ball will be able to fall before it hits the floor, but the particular size is not critical.

Discrete Time Simulation

Models are built to learn about systems of interest. A model allows you to practice and/or experiment with a system safely and inexpensively. A simulation of a jetliner allows pilots to train without risking lives and expensive equipment. A simulation of an economy allows planners to try different measures without disrupting the actual economy. A simulation of the interaction of greenhouse gases, temperature, and glaciation allows scientists to make predictions about the likely effect of various levels of greenhouse gas emissions. A model is always simpler than what it models (and so, no model is perfect). Simulation is the implementation of a model in software; thus, the essence of simulation is simplification.

A discrete time simulation is so named because time moves in discrete steps. The size of the step is up to the modeler; a simulation of a computer might have a time step of a nanosecond, whereas one of continental drift might use a time step of a century or a millennium. In the real world, time is entirely beyond our understanding or control. In a simulation, the modeler has complete control over time; it is whatever time the time variable says it is. Welcome to cyberspace!

A simulation has some set of simulated objects. The state of each simulated object is completely specified by its state variables. Similarly, the state of a simulation is completely specified by the values of all its state variables. To move from one time step to the next, the modeler provides a transition function. Given the values of all the state variables at one time step, it calculates their values at the next time step. This transition function may be simple or extremely complex depending on the application.

In the SnowPerson program, each time the user pushed the button, the SnowPerson melted some and the puddle under it grew some. If you think of that as a simulation of a snowman melting, the state variables for a SnowPerson were x, y, size, and the size of the puddle. The transition function decreased the size by 10 percent and increased the size of the puddle by 10 pixels. The location of the SnowPerson never changed (unless you made it move), and there was no interaction between the SnowPersons. In a more complicated simulation—for instance, one implementing a model of planetary motion around the sun—the various elements of the simulation affect each other.

A dropped ball bouncing straight up and down under the effect of gravity will need two state variables; one for its height from the floor and one for its velocity (up or down). Given a position, velocity, and a gravitational constant, its position and velocity at the next time step can be computed using equations from elementary physics. Using standard physics notation, s stands for position, v for velocity, and a for acceleration. As you might guess, v_t is the velocity at time t, and v_{t+1} is the velocity at the next time step. Thus, the transition function may be written as two equations:

$$s_{t+1} = s_t + v_t$$
$$v_{t+1} = v_t + a_t$$

Therefore, the ball's height at the next time step is just its current height plus its current velocity; its velocity at the next time step is just its current velocity plus the acceleration due to gravity.

If you have not studied physics, those equations may seem a bit mysterious; but they are quite simple once you understand them. If a ball is traveling at 10 pixels/step and is currently at location 100, after the next step it will be at 110. In symbols, $s_t = 100$, $v_t = 10$, $s_{t+1} = s_t + v_t = 100 + 10 = 110$. Velocity is updated similarly.

Classes

The only thing in this program is the bouncing ball, so an obvious choice for a class is Ball. If Ball extends FilledCircle, the position and color variables are already defined, and paint() code is already written. The only additional variable needed is velocity in the y direction. The only additional method needed is step(), which implements the transition function from one time step to the next.

Implementation

Given your experience with the counter animation, you have seen code that does almost everything the code for this program must do. You only need to create three classes: the Frame, Controller, and Ball (although you will need to copy FilledCircle and Circle from your previous project).

The Frame

The Frame needed for this program is almost identical with Listing 9.4. Create a GUI AWT Frame, name it BallFrame, and copy the code from Listing 9.6. As you can verify, this is very similar to Listing 9.4, except the import (line 1) has been added, the counter has been removed, and lines 4 and 19 have been added.

LISTING 9.6   Initial `BallFrame`.

```
1    import java.awt.*;
2
3    public class BallFrame extends Frame {
4        public static final int HT = 700;
5
6        private Controller theController;
7        Thread aThread;
8
9        /** Creates a new instance of ThreadedFrame */
10       public BallFrame() {
11           initComponents();
12           theController = new Controller(this);
13           theController.start();
14           show();
15           setBounds(10,10,500,800);
16       }
17
18       public void paint(Graphics g) {
19           g.drawRect(30,30, 300, HT-30);
20           theController.paint(g);
21       }
```

Line 1: Makes for fewer keystrokes in lines 3 and 18.

Line 4: A constant for the distance from the top of the screen to the bottom of the box. This will be used in `Ball` to decide when to bounce.

Line 19: Draw a rectangle for the `Ball` to bounce in. The height is 700, so that with a `Frame` height of 800, the bottom of the rectangle still shows.

Alternatively, since you just typed most of this code for the previous program, simply copy it from there, delete the counter code, and add the `drawRect()` message (line 19). Notice that this draws a rectangle 670 pixels high; you could choose another size if you wanted.

The `Controller` Class

The `Controller` class is very much like the `Controller` in Listing 9.5. Copying, pasting, and then editing it would be the most efficient, but feel free to retype it if doing so will help you remember it better. The code you need is in Listing 9.7 with the changes from the previous `Controller` indicated in **bold**.

LISTING 9.7 `Controller` for the `BallFrame`.

```
1    import java.awt.*;
2
3
4    public class Controller extends Thread {
5        private Frame theFrame;
6        private Ball theBall;
7
8        /** Creates a new instance of Controller */
9        public Controller(Frame theFrame) {
10           this.theFrame = theFrame;
11           theBall = new Ball(100,100,20,Color.RED);
12       }
13
14       public void run() {
15           for(;;) {
16               step();
17               pause();
18           }
19       }
20
21       public void paint(Graphics g) {
22           theBall.paint(g);
23       }
24
25       private void step() {
26           theBall.step();
27           theFrame.repaint();
28       }
29
30       private void pause() {
31           try {
32               Thread.sleep(50);
33           } catch (Exception e) {}
34       }
35   }
```

As you can see, this `Controller` is very similar to the one in Listing 9.5, with the addition of the `Ball` and the `paint()` method.

Line 11: The `Ball` will initially be centered at (100,100).

As you can see, you must declare a `Ball` variable (line 6), instantiate it in the constructor (line 11), and send it the `step()` method when the `Controller` steps (line 26). In addition, you must `paint()` it when the `Controller` is painted. That's all. What remains is writing the `Ball` class.

Be sure you are familiar with the `Controller` code. Read each method, line by line. Think about how they interact (i.e., which invokes which, and when). Next, read the following descriptions. Pay special attention if there are any surprises—surprises are clues for what to focus on.

Controller(Frame)

The constructor stores the reference to the `Frame` in the variable named `theFrame`. Then, it instantiates a red `Ball` of radius 20, centered at (100,100), and stores it in the variable named `theBall`.

The *run()* Method

The `run()` method is an infinite for loop with two statements. Each *iteration*, it steps and then pauses (for 50 msecs).

paint(Graphics)

Sends `paint(Graphics)` to `theBall`. The only thing in the simulation is the `Ball`, so that's all that needs to be painted.

The *step()* Method

The `step()` method ends `step()` to `theBall`, and then repaints the `Frame` so the `Ball`'s new position will be displayed.

The Ball Class

The `Ball` class extends `FilledCircle`. It needs a variable for the *y* velocity (say, vy), an initializing constructor, and a `step()` method. The constructor can just use `FilledCircle`'s initializing constructor (i.e., it is one line: `super(x,y,r,c);`). The `step()` method has just two lines; one to update the position (`y = y + vy;`), and one to update the velocity (`vy = vy + GRAVITY;`). Recall that constants by convention are all uppercase (see the section "Case Conventions" in Chapter 5), and gravity is definitely constant!

Gravity is constant, but what value should it have? That decision is entirely arbitrary unless you assign some correspondence between pixels and distances in the world. That would be possible, but not necessary in this case. Let the acceleration due to gravity be one pixel per time step. By the way, the unit of velocity is also pixels/time step.

Given that description, you can write the `Ball` class. If some part of that still seems mysterious, feel free to look at Listing 9.8.

LISTING 9.8 The `Ball` class.

```
1    import java.awt.*;
2
3    public class Ball extends FilledCircle {
4        public int GRAVITY=1;
5        private int vy;
6
7        public Ball(int x, int y, int r, Color c) {
8            super(x,y,r,c);
9        }
10
11       public void step() {
12           y += vy;
13           vy += GRAVITY;
14
15           System.out.println("v=" + vy);
16       }
17   }
```

Line 4: Defines acceleration due to gravity as one pixel per time step.

Line 12: Updates the *y*-coordinate.

Line 13: Updates the *y*-velocity.

Line 15: Prints the velocity so you can get an idea of how it changes.

However, if you want to learn to program, instead of copying that example, keystroke for keystroke, take the time/spend the effort to study and understand it; then, go to the screen and type it in without peeking (if you have to peek once or twice, that's okay).

Testing

With those three classes written, there's enough code to test. Make the `Frame` taller, so you can see the `Ball` hit the bottom of the rectangle (change the fourth parameter in `setBounds()`).

Once you fix all the syntax errors, you should see the `Ball` falling faster and faster and disappearing off the bottom of the screen. If you look at the output, you will see that it is going one unit faster each time step. Now it's time to add the bouncing off the floor code.

Making the `Ball` Bounce–Design

There are two steps to making the `Ball` bounce when it hits the floor: 1) detecting that it hits the floor, and 2) reversing its direction. The latter is simple; just set the y-velocity to its opposite (i.e., vy = -vy;). Note that the minus sign is unary minus; it only has one operand. The former is a bit more complicated.

Logically, when the ball hits the floor, it should reverse direction. In the real world, physics takes care of that; in the simulation, the programmer must decide how to simulate the physics. Here's an idea. On each time step, after updating the position, if the `Ball` has hit the floor, reverse its direction. Looking at Figure 9.1 you can see that the distance from the bottom of the `Ball` to the floor is $750 - (y + radius)$, since y is the y-coordinate of the center of the `Ball`.

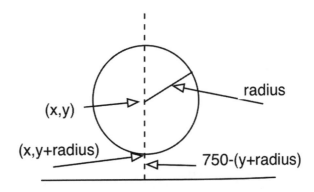

FIGURE 9.1   Calculating the distance to the floor.

Thus, the `Ball` has hit the floor if $750 - (y + radius) < 0$, or equivalently if $(y + radius) > 750$. In that case, you want to reverse its direction.

Making the `Ball` Bounce–Implementation

The `step()` method from Listing 9.8 can be modified to reverse directions when the `Ball` hits the wall as shown in Listing 9.9.

LISTING 9.9   The `Ball:STEP()` method with bounce code.

```
1    public void step() {
2        y += vy;
3        vy += GRAVITY;
4
5        if (y+radius > BallFrame.HT) // if it hit the wall
            vy = -vy;        // reverse direction
6    }
```

Lines 5–6: If the bottom of the Ball is through the floor, reverse the direction. BallFrame.HT is the variable in the BallFrame that controls where the bottom of the box is drawn.

Add the if statement and run the simulation again.

If your machine works as ours does (and it might not, exactly), you see the Ball bounce, but it goes part way into the floor and gradually bounces higher and higher (another possibility is that it appears to bounce, initially, at some height from the floor). This is a bit surprising, and not at all like a real ball! What's gone wrong? There are actually two different, interacting causes. One of them stems from using ints, which can only represent whole numbers; the other from a flaw in our simulation methodology.

First, we will confront a shortcoming of discrete time simulations. Assume the Ball is traveling 10 pixels/step, and before the time step, it is 3 pixels from the floor. After the time step, if it moves 10 pixels down, it will be 7 pixels into the floor before we check. However, let's ignore that for now until we get the bouncing higher problem solved.

Consider carefully what happens when the step() method in Listing 9.9 is executed with vy = 17, and y = 721. The first line changes y to 738, and the second changes vy to 18. The if compares (738 + 30) to 750; since 758 > 750, it evaluates to true and so changes vy to −18. Therefore, the Ball goes 8 pixels into the floor, and the velocity *increases*! Perhaps you should only increase the velocity if the Ball does not change directions as in Listing 9.10.

LISTING 9.10 A Ball:step() method that only accelerates if no bounce.

```
1    public void step() {
2        x += vx;
3        y += vy;
4
5        if (y+radius > BallFrame.HT) { // if it hit the wall
6            vy = -vy;        // reverse direction
7            System.out.println("vy=" + vy + " y=" + y);
8        }
9        else vy += GRAVITY;  // no bounce? accelerate
10   }
```

Line 5–9: If the bottom of the Ball is through the floor, reverse the direction; otherwise, add the influence of gravity to the velocity.

Try this version. If your machine works as ours does, the ball always bounces the same height (although it continues to go into the floor a bit).

The problem description said the elasticity of the ball/floor collision was 90 percent, so when it changes direction, you should reduce the speed by 10 percent as in Listing 9.11.

LISTING 9.11   The `Ball:step()` method with 90-percent elasticity.

```
1    public void step() {
2        x += vx;
3        y += vy;
4
5        if (y+radius > 750) { // if it hit the wall
6            vy = -vy*9/10;        // reverse direction and reduce 10%
7            System.out.println("vy=" + vy + " y=" + y);
8        }
9        else vy += GRAVITY;  // no bounce? accelerate
10   }
```

Line 6: The collision between the ball and the floor has 90-percent elasticity, so reduce magnitude by 10-percent when changing direction.

Try this. It comes to a stop for us, but into the floor by 8 pixels. Some code to fix the problem is shown in Listing 9.12.

LISTING 9.12   The `Ball:step()` method improved?

```
1    public void step() {
2        x += vx;
3
4        int bottomY = BallFrame.HT-(radius+y);
5        if (vy >= bottomY) {
6            //System.out.println("vy=" + vy + " y=" + y);
7            int bounceHt = vy - bottomY;    // how high it bounces
                                                  this step
8            y = BallFrame.HT- (radius + bounceHt); // y after this
                                                         step
9            vy = -(vy-1)*9/10;
10       }
11       else {
12           y += vy;
13           vy += GRAVITY;
14       }
15   }
```

Line 7: Calculate how far it will travel up after bouncing.

Line 8: From that, calculate the new *y*-coordinate of the center.

Line 9: Reverse vy and subtract 1 to avoid endless small bounces.

This code is a bit complicated, and it's okay if you don't understand it. If you want to figure it out, draw a picture. This code causes the Ball to eventually come to rest exactly touching the floor. Without the –1 in vy-1 on line 9, it got caught in a loop and never stopped bouncing because of the way int arithmetic works. This is by no means a perfect simulation, but it's close enough for now.

Starting and Stopping with Two Buttons

The last task remaining is to allow the user to start and stop the simulation by pressing a button. This will be done first with two Buttons, and then with one. The former is easier to understand; the latter is less cluttered and illustrates a useful technique.

Assume the two Buttons are named stopButton (which sends a stop() message to the Controller) and goButton (which sends a go() message). The question is, how to implement stop() and go()? Recall that the Conroller:run() method (shown in Listing 9.13) is running in a separate Thread. It is an infinite loop that does step(), and then pause(), over and over.

LISTING 9.13 Controller:run() from Listing 9.3.

```
1    public void run() {
2        for(;;) {
3            step();
4            pause();
5        }
6    }
```

How can you arrange that stop() will stop the simulation and go() will resume it? If stop() has been executed since go(), the loop should just pause() and not step(); otherwise, it should do both. Do you know what programming construct to use?

Whenever you want to do something or not, you use an if statement. You would like to modify run() as shown in Listing 9.14, so the step() message is only sent if the last button pushed was go.

LISTING 9.14 An if statement to make step() conditional.

```
1    public void run() {
2        for(;;) {
```

```
3              if (last button pushed was go)
4                  step();
5              pause();
6          }
7      }
```

Lines 3–4: `step()` will only happen if the last button pushed was the `goButton`.

How do you write that in Java? You use a `boolean` variable, called, perhaps, `running`. The type `boolean` is used when you only need to represent two values, `true` and `false` (see the section "Details II—Types, Operators, and Expressions" in Chapter 5). This situation is perfect for a `boolean` variable, because the simulation is either running or paused. When the `Controller` gets the `stop()` message, it should set `running` to `false`; when it gets the `go()` message, it should set it to `true`; and the expression guarding the `step()` message should just be the `boolean` variable named `running`. This is illustrated in Listing 9.15.

LISTING 9.15   Modifications to make the `run()` method stoppable.

```
1      private boolean running=true;
2
3      public void go() {
4          running = true;
5      }
6
7      public void userStop() {
8          running = false;
9      }
10
11     public void run() {
12         for(;;) {
13             if (running)
14                 step();
15             pause();
16         }
17     }
```

Line 1: Declares a `boolean` variable named `running` whose initial value is `true` (so the simulation will start when `run()` starts).

Lines 3–5: The `go()` method sets `running` to `true`.

Lines 7–9: The userStop() method sets running to false. Java would not allow a method named stop() in a Thread (since there already was one declared final).

Line 13: Guards the step() message; it is only sent if running is true.

Notice that the stop() method has been renamed to userStop(). This was because when it was named stop(), the compiler complained that:

```
Controller.java [29:1] stop() in Controller cannot override stop() in
java.lang.Thread; overridden method is final
```

What this means is that the Thread class already has a method with that signature (i.e., public void stop()), and it is declared final, so it *cannot* be overridden. You will never have to declare any methods final (in the context of introductory programming), so you may safely ignore this, but you do need to learn how to cope when you bump into this type of error message. The rule is, when an error message says "...cannot override...," or "...access type...," you have stumbled on a method declared in a superclass. The simplest solution is to rename your method.

That's all you need to know to make it start and stop. Do that now. Then, return here to learn how to accomplish it with only one Button.

Starting and Stopping with Only One Button

Using one Button to stop the simulation and another to restart it works, but it is not very elegant. You can unclutter your GUI by writing code to make your Button a *toggle* switch. Light switches are sometimes push-button toggles; if the light is on, pushing the switch turns it off, and if it is off, pushing the switch turns it on. Here's how to do that in Java.

The Button must do one of two things: make the Controller stop if it is going, or make it go if it is stopped. The construct in Java that does either one thing or the other is if-else. So, logically, the actionPerformed() method might be as in Listing 9.16; if the simulation is currently running, send the Controller the userStop() message, otherwise send go().

LISTING 9.16 Logic of actionPerformed() for a toggle Button.

```
1    private void toggleButtonActionPerformed(
          java.awt.event.Action
     Event evt) {
2        if (the simulation is running)
3            theController.userStop();
4        else theController.go();
5
6        change the label on the Button to say what it does now
7    }
```

Your first idea might be to add a `boolean` variable in the `Frame` to keep track of whether the `Controller` is currently running, and set it to the same value as the `running` variable in the `Controller`. This is a natural mistake. The problem is that having two different variables keeping track of the same information creates an unnecessary situation in which bugs can occur. There will be plenty of bugs no matter what, so there's no reason to encourage them!

The `Controller` already knows whether the simulation is running. The job of the `Frame` is to manage the GUI and pass along information to the `Controller`. When it needs to know if the `Controller` is running, it should ask it (and then set the `toggleButton`'s label appropriately). The logic of changing the state of the `Controller` belongs in the `Controller`. Thus, when the `toggleButton` is pushed, it should send a `toggle()` message to the `Controller` to change the label on the toggle `Button` to reflect what action will be performed if it is pushed. See Listing 9.17 for how to do these two things.

LISTING 9.17   Making a toggle `Button`.

```
1    private void toggleButtonActionPerformed(
             java.awt.event.ActionEvent evt) {
2        theController.toggleRunning();
3
4        if (theController.getRunning())
5            toggleButton.setLabel("stop");
6        else toggleButton.setLabel("go");
7    }
```

Line 2: Toggle the running variable in the `Controller`.

Lines 4–6: An `if-else`. Notice that both the `if` and `else` parts have only one statement, so they do not need to be enclosed in {}s.

Lines 5: Sets the `Button` label to `"stop"`, since `theController` is running.

Lines 6: Sets the `Button` label to `"go"`.

Notice that there are no {}s around the statements after the `if` and `else` parts. If you wanted to do two (or more) things in either the `if` or `else` parts, you must put {}s around them to make the two statements into one, syntactically.

The `Controller` class must be modified to add these two new methods, but you can eliminate two methods at the same time. See Listing 9.18 for the changes.

LISTING 9.18 Controller modifications to support the toggle Button.

```
1    private boolean running=true;
2
3    public boolean getRunning() {return running;}
4
5    public void toggleRunning() {
6        running = !running;
7    }
8
9    public void run() {
10       for(;;) {
11           if (running)
12               step();
13           pause();
14       }
15   }
```

Line 3: The accessor for running.

Lines 5–7: The toggleRunning() method replaces go() and userStop().

Lines 6: Set the value of running to the opposite of what it was before. The ! operator is called, not "Not true is false, not false is true."

Compare Listing 9.18 to Listing 9.15, which it replaces.

RECAPITULATION

To do animation in Java, you must spawn a separate Thread. To do so, you must create a class that extends Thread, create an instance of it, and send it the start() message. The Thread:start() method spawns the new Thread and then sends run() to your object; the new Thread exists until run() returns.

Discrete time simulation advances time by some fixed amount each step. Each modeled object has a set of state variables that completely determine its state in the context of the simulation. A transition function calculates the next state of each thing in the simulation from its previous state variables (and possibly those of other things in the simulation).

Boolean variables are used to store information when the only possible values are true and false. Boolean expressions are used to determine whether to execute the if part of if statements.

CONCLUSION

This chapter introduced two powerful techniques: simulation and animation. It also introduced Java Threads. Simple animations can greatly improve your GUIs. Simple simulations can provide interesting demonstrations. It also presented a Java toggle switch to allow the user to control the simulation.

Review Questions

9.1 What are boolean variables used for?

9.2 Where do boolean expressions appear in Java?

9.3 What is Thread short for?

9.4 If your program has two Threads and is executing on a single CPU machine, since only one instruction can be executed at a time, how can both Threads be running at the same time?

9.5 What is the job of the transition function in a discrete time simulation?

9.6 What are the two unary operators?

Programming Exercises

9.7 Experiment with Buttons; setLabel() looks exactly like an accessor; try getLabel().

9.8 A Button is a Component (like an Applet or a Frame). Any component can be resized. Send setBounds(10,10,100,100) to a Button. What happens?

9.9 Modify your code so that the Ball can be thrown to start the simulation. All that is needed is an additional initializing constructor that takes two additional parameters: x-velocity and y-velocity.

```
public Ball(int x, int y, int r, Color c, int vx, int vy) {
    this(x,y,r,c);
    this.vx = vx;
    this.vy = vy;
}
```

Then, you can initialize the ball in the Controller with:

```
theBall = new Ball(10,100,20,Color.RED, 2, -20);
```

For this to work, you must update the x-coordinate in Ball:step().

9.10 Add code to keep the Ball in the box. It's just like the bounce code, except you must check for hitting the other sides of the box.

9.11 Add another Ball (or two) going in a different initial direction. Add five!

9.12 Modify your code so it creates a pattern. All this requires is adding an update(Graphics g) method to the Frame that simply sends paint(g), as shown in Listing 9.19.

LISTING 9.19   BallFrame:update(Graphics).

```
1    public void update(Graphics g) {
2        paint(g);
3    }
```

Add this method to prevent update() from filling a rectangle the size of the drawable area in the background color before sending paint(). An explanation can be found in Appendix B in the section "repaint(), paint(), and update()."

10 Reading and Writing Files

In This Chapter

- Isolating the I/O Using `java.util.StringTokenizer`
- Putting It All Together

INTRODUCTION

Almost every sophisticated program reads and writes files. Toy programs can run without file input or output, but without *file I/O*, your programs cannot permanently store information, or access information stored on disk. Until you can do file I/O, you don't really know how to program.

Input and output (I/O) are always idiosyncratic, and are always a messy, fiddly, aspect of programming. Folklore has it that fully half the code in a major project is for the GUI. File I/O is simpler, but requires careful thinking and can be incredibly frustrating until it works. This chapter will introduce file I/O and a very helpful class for parsing input, `java.util.StringTokenizer`.

The `Model-View-Controller` **Pattern**

A common (and useful) technique in any complex program is to collect all the I/O into one place. This makes it easier to find and change; and if the program is ever transported to a new context, all the I/O changes can be made at once. This technique is also part of the Model-View-Controller pattern in *Design Patterns* (a groundbreaking book by Gamma, et al., which identified a number of patterns that occur over and over in software—it is highly recommended if you intend to go on in computing). The View is what the user interacts with, the GUI in many cases. The Model is the program and its data; in a database application, the database itself is the model. The Controller is the interface between the two.

On Ignorance, Stupidity, and Utilities

Language evolves constantly. People are born without language, and learn whatever language is spoken around them. They associate words they hear with concepts in their experience; and often make mistakes doing so. New words enter the language, new usages of old words appear; that's why this text is not written in Latin, or Italian—the Roman culture spread and regional dialects turned into French, Spanish, and even English.

Intelligence is the ability to learn, and to be able to flexibly apply what you've learned in novel situations. Knowledge is the stuff you've learned. They are completely different in the same way that algorithms and data are different; just as method bodies and values of variables are different. Everyone is born entirely ignorant, but ignorance can be cured. It is normal, of course, to not know something you have never studied. On the other hand, intelligence is genetic; you get what you get. Slugs can never be frustrated, or bored, or learn to program, or write poetry, or fall in love; they just don't have enough brain cells for it.

How people understand the world, or language, depends on what experiences they have had. No one knows everything, and everyone believes many things that are false. For instance, imagine that you played Monopoly® as a child, and learned the word *utilities* in that context (Monopoly has two properties called "The Utilities," which are Waterworks, and The Electric Company). You might imagine that *utility* was just an abstract noun, like *animal*. Years later, if you found yourself living in a remote cabin without any utilities, and you chopped wood for fire and carried water from the spring, you might discover that it took the whole day just to feed yourself. Then you might realize that utilities are really, really useful—they *have* utility.

Java has a package, `java.util.*`; that has some very useful utilities. Several will be presented here. You have a choice: you can learn to use them, or you can spend the whole day chopping wood, tending the fire, and carrying water. Don't feel bad about lacunae in your knowledge structure; everyone has them—you can fill them in if you choose.

The Programming Task

Your task for this chapter is to write a Java program to copy one file to another, deleting all the words with less than four letters. The user should be able to select the input and output files. Put as many words on each line of the output file as will fit without making any line longer than 80 characters. Ignore punctuation (i.e., treat punctuation as letters).

This task requires knowing how to do four things: 1) input from a file (of the user's choice), 2) output to a file, 3) break lines from a file into individual words, and 4) determine the length of a `String`. The last is easy: `aString.length()`; the other three will be addressed directly.

ISOLATING THE I/O USING `java.util.StringTokenizer`

You saw in the section "Decoupling the Output" in Chapter 8, "Iterative Statements and `String`s," the technique of sending each `String` to be output to a method called `emit()`. This technique makes it simple to redirect the output; instead of finding and changing every `System.out.println`, you simply change `emit()`.

To similarly simplify input, one thinks of the input as a stream of tokens. A *token* is the smallest meaningful unit of input. What is meaningful depends, as always, on the context. It might be letters, or words, or numbers, or something else. A tokenizer converts the input into a stream of tokens that are then used by the next component in the program.

There are a number of classes in `java.util` that are very useful (that's why they are called "utilities"), including `Vector`, `Iterator`, `Hashtable`, and `StringTokenizer`. The first three will be introduced in the next two chapters; the last, immediately. To break up a `String` into a series of smaller `String`s (tokens), `StringTokenizer` is the class to use.

Simple Example

Listing 10.1 is a simple example of how to use a `StringTokenizer`.

LISTING 10.1   Simplest use of a StringTokenizer.

```
StringTokenizer st = new StringTokenizer("this is only a test...");
while (st.hasMoreTokens()) {
    System.out.println(st.nextToken());
}
```

this will print the output:

```
this
is
only
a
test...
```

This is mostly self-explanatory, assuming you are familiar with constructors and while loops, and realize what the StringTokenizer methods do. The constructor, new StringTokenizer(String), creates a StringTokenizer that will separate the String it is passed into a number of tokens. It breaks the input String at each space, so if there are no spaces it will only return a single token (the entire input String). Each time you send the tokenizer nextToken(), it will return the next token, as long as there is one (if you send nextToken(); to a StringTokenizer that is out of tokens, it will throw an Exception). To check if there are more tokens to be had, use has-MoreTokens(); it returns true just if the tokenizer has more tokens. These two methods are well named and once you understand what they do, StringTokenizer is very easy to use.

Sample Exam Question

Here is the kind of question you might expect on an exam in a CS1 class.

Write a method that is passed a String and prints each word in it on a separate line. Assume words are separated by spaces.

Could you answer such a question? If the answer is "yes," feel free to skip this next section.

Making Progress without Thinking Very Hard—or, Syntax Is Your Friend!

When writing a method, a number of things can be done even if you have no idea what the logic of the method will be. A method body contains the algorithm that the method implements; it may require careful, creative thinking. The heading, by contrast, is mostly syntactic and so can be written mostly by rote, once you understand the syntax.

The question says the method is passed a String and outputs to System.out, so you can write the heading with almost no thought, as shown in Listing 10.2.

LISTING 10.2   Using syntax to your advantage.

```
1    void printOneWordPerLine(String input) {
2
3    }
```

Knowing that the method is passed a `String` and returns nothing, you can write this much with minimal thought. On an exam, that would get you lots more points than an empty space, and while you were writing it you could be thinking about how to implement it.

Writing the Body of the Method

Logically, the method will output a line for each word in the input, so there will be a `System.out.println()` in a loop with initialization at the top. Listing 10.2 does almost exactly what is needed and can be copied almost verbatim, as in Listing 10.3.

LISTING 10.3   The complete method.

```
1    void printOneWordPerLine(String input) {
2        StringTokenizer st = new StringTokenizer(input);
3        while (st.hasMoreTokens()) {
4            System.out.println(st.nextToken());
5        }
6    }
```

The only change needed from Listing 10.1 is to use the parameter being sent into the method as the parameter to the `StringTokenizer` constructor. This is a fine solution, but there are many other ways you could write this method. It could also be written as a `for` loop, as shown in Listing 10.4.

LISTING 10.4   An equivalent (if peculiar) `for` loop.

```
1    void printOneWordPerLine(String input) {
2        for (StringTokenizer st = new StringTokenizer(input);
3            st.hasMoreTokens();
4            System.out.println(st.nextToken())); // empty loop body
5    }
```

This does the same thing, but is rather peculiar. Recall that a `for` loop heading has three parts. Here, the initialization instantiates the `StringTokenizer`; the continuation condition is exactly the same as in the `while` loop; and the update does the output. The loop body is an empty statement. See the next example for a more readable version.

Make sure you understand how this `for` loop works, it's a bit of a trick (see the section "The `For` Loop" in Chapter 8 if you need to refresh your memory on the syntax of a `for` loop). Sometimes, programmers do things like this, because they can. For a more ordinary usage, see Listing 10.5.

LISTING 10.5   An equivalent, ordinary `for` loop.

```
1    void printOneWordPerLine(String input) {
2        for (StringTokenizer st = new StringTokenizer(input);
                                      st.hasMoreTokens(); )
3            System.out.println(st.nextToken());
4    }
```

This does the same thing in a more usual form. Here, the initialization and the continuation condition are exactly the same; and the update does nothing. The loop body does the output, as you might expect.

The Other `StringTokenizer` Constructors

Sometimes you want to use other characters besides just spaces to delimit tokens.

Delimiters beside Spaces

For instance, if a user typed in:

```
John,Mary,Frank,Sue
```

and you used the default constructor, you would only get one token, namely the `String`:

```
"John,Mary,Frank,Sue"
```

when what you wanted was four tokens: `"John"`, `"Mary"`, `"Frank"`, and `"Sue"`. Fortunately, `StringTokenizer` includes another constructor that will give you just that.
The line:

```
StringTokenizer st = new StringTokenizer("John,Mary,Frank,Sue");
```

using the one argument constructor, is functionally equivalent to using the two argument constructor:

```
StringTokenizer st = new StringTokenizer("John,Mary,Frank,Sue", " ");
```

The second parameter is a `String` containing all the characters that you want the `StringTokenizer` to use as delimiters. In this case, it is simply the space character. The one argument constructor very likely is implemented by invoking the two-argument constructor, using just a space for the second argument; as shown in Listing 10.6.

LISTING 10.6 Implementation of `StringTokenizer(String)`.

```
1    public StringTokenizer(String input) {
2        this(input, " ");
3    }
```

Line 2: Invoke the two-argument constructor with a space as the second argument.

This is a standard technique to make coding and maintenance simple (see the section "`this`" in Chapter 5, "Toward Consistent Classes").

So, if you say:

```
StringTokenizer st = new StringTokenizer("John,Mary,Frank,Sue", ",");
```

(i.e., with just a comma in double quotes as the second argument), the tokenizer will return the tokens `"John"`, `"Mary"`, `"Frank"`, and finally, `"Sue"`. Unfortunately, if the input were `"John Mary Frank Sue"`, the tokenizer will return just one token `"John Mary Frank Sue"`. This can be solved by passing both a space and a comma inside the quotes, `" ,"`, as the second parameter:

```
StringTokenizer st = new StringTokenizer("John,Mary,Frank,Sue", " ,");
```

That would work with either input.

Delimiters as Tokens

Using either of those constructors, you never see the delimiters, but sometimes you want to. For instance, say you were reading input and wanted to replace certain abbreviations with what they stood for and preserve the punctuation. Then you would need to know what the delimiters had been (so you could output them). The third constructor does this with a third parameter, a `boolean`; if it is `true`, it will return the delimiters as tokens. So:

```
StringTokenizer st = new StringTokenizer("A,B, C,DEF.", " .,", true);
```

would return the sequence of tokens: `{"A", ",", "B", " ", "C", ",", "DEF", "."}`. Chances are the two-parameter constructor is implemented as shown in Listing 10.7.

LISTING 10.7 Implementation of `StringTokenizer(String, boolean)`.

```
1    public StringTokenizer(String input, String delimiters) {
2        this(input, delimiters, false);
3    }
```

Line 2: Invoke the three-argument constructor with `false` as the third argument.

This two-argument constructor is implemented by invoking the three-argument constructor, using `false` for the third argument.

`StringTokenizer` is a very handy class, but it only does simple tokenizing. For complicated tokenizing you should use a `StreamTokenizer`; but not today.

THE `MyReader` CLASS

Many classes in Java do I/O—too many for beginners. The Java I/O class structure is remarkable. It was designed to handle I/O from just about anywhere: the Web, the keyboard, or files (compressed or uncompressed). It is worthy of the time to learn; but not here. For now, you just want to input files one line at a time, with a minimum of effort. Here is a class called `MyReader` to read files easily without having to catch exceptions. (`Exceptions` are Java's mechanism to handle runtime errors elegantly. They are important to understand, but, one thing at a time! If you want to read about `Exceptions` and I/O, here is a link to the Sun Tutorial on `Exceptions` during compilation of file input code:

http://java.sun.com/docs/books/tutorial/essential/exceptions/firstencounter.html

By using `MyReader`, you can avoid `Exceptions` for now.) `MyReader` can read either from wherever the user specifies on the local machine (if it runs from an `Application`), or from the directory an `Applet` loaded from.

Echoing a User-Specified File

The first thing to do when you are trying to process the information in a file is to make sure you can read it. The easiest way to do that is to read it in and display it on the screen; this is referred to as *echoing the file*. Listing 10.8 shows how to echo a file with a `MyReader`.

LISTING 10.8 Echoing a file with `MyReader`.

```
1    MyReader mr = new MyReader();
2
3    while (mr.hasMoreData()) {
4        System.out.println(mr.giveMeTheNextLine());
5    }
6
7    mr.close();
```

Lines 1–7: Reads each line from whatever file the user specifies, and echoes each to System.out.

That's all there is to it. You might want to adjourn to the keyboard and try that, to convince yourself that it works and that you understand how to use it. Don't forget that you must be running an Application to read from files (see the section "Creating a GUI Application" in Appendix A). Now to the internals of MyReader.

MyReader **Internals**

The MyReader class is essentially a wrapper for the BufferedReader class, along with a method that uses a FileDialog to allow a user to select a file at runtime. A *wrapper* is a class that exists to hold a class or a data item without adding much functionality. Wrappers are written to make working with a class or data simpler for the user and/or the programmer.

MyReader: **Constructors, Imports, and the Wrapped Variable**

Listing 10.9 is the beginning of MyReader.

LISTING 10.9   Beginning of MyReader.

```
1    import java.io.*;
2    import java.awt.*;
3    import java.net.*;
4    import java.applet.*;
5
6    public class MyReader {
7
8        private BufferedReader br;
9
10       public MyReader() {
11           openIt(getFileName());
12       }
13
14       public MyReader(String filename) {
15           openIt(filename);
16       }
17
18       public MyReader(String filename, Applet theApplet) {
19           try {
20               URL theURL = new URL(theApplet.getDocumentBase(), file
                     name);
21               InputStreamReader isr
```

```
                                         = new
                                     InputStreamReader(theURL.openStream());
22                  br = new BufferedReader(isr);
23              } catch (Exception e) {
24                  System.out.println("MyReader -- bad file from net" + e);
25              }
26          }
```

There is just one variable, the BufferedReader that MyReader is the wrapper for. The imports are needed for: BufferedReader, FileDialog, URL, and Applet, respectively.

Notice that it has just one variable, a BufferedReader (a class in java.io), called br (for the first letters of the two words in BufferedReader). It is declared private for two reasons: to make it clear that it is only used from within this class, and to prevent any other code from modifying or accessing it. A MyReader is essentially a more convenient form of a BufferedReader. There are three constructors. The default constructor opens whatever file the user wants (see the next section, "Opening the File"). If you pass a file name as a String, it will open that. From an Applet, pass a filename and this, and it will read from the directory the Applet byte code is in. Recall that Applets can *only* read from there.

Opening the File

Listing 10.10 shows the two methods that are used by the constructors to open the file.

LISTING 10.10   MyReader:openIt(String) and getFileName().

```
28      private void openIt (String filename) {
29          try {
30              br = new BufferedReader(new FileReader(filename));
31          } catch (Exception e) {
32              System.out.println("MyReader:can't open " + filename + "!" + e);
33          }
34      }
35
36      private String getFileName() {
37          FileDialog fd = new FileDialog(new Frame(), "Select Input File");
38          fd.setFile("input");
39          fd.show();
40          return fd.getDirectory()+fd.getFile();   // return the complete path
41      }
42
```

Lines 28–34: openIt(String) has the magic that creates a BufferedReader to read a file one line at a time.

Lines 36–41: getFileName() uses a FileDialog to get a filename from the user at runtime.

The getFileName() method is very useful if you ever want to prompt a user for a file to read; feel free to copy it. It is amazing the first time you use a FileDialog; it is so easy! If you omit line 39, the FileDialog will be invisible. Line 39 is a bit unusual in that it does not finish execution until the user closes the FileDialog. The Dialog box the FileDialog opens is modal, so like many Panels it seizes control of the Thread and refuses to relinquish it (until closed). Notice that there are two parts to a complete pathname (line 40); the directory and the filename.

The openIt(String) method has the incantation to open a file for reading. Notice the nested constructor on line 30 (this line does all the work of this method). This is a good example of how constructors are used in object programming (see the section "Constructors" in Chapter 5).

Reading and Closing the File

Listing 10.11 has the three methods that show MyReader to be a wrapper.

LISTING 10.11 MyReader:giveMeTheNextLine(), hasMoreData() and close().

```
40    public String giveMeTheNextLine() {
41        try {
42            return br.readLine();
43        } catch (Exception e) {
44            System.out.println("MyReader -- eof?!" + e);
45        }
46        return "";
47    }
48
49    public boolean hasMoreData() {
50        try {
51            return br.ready();
52        } catch (Exception e) {System.out.println("MyReader:no data!" + e);}
53        return false;
54    }
55
56    public void close() {
57        try {
58            br.close();
59        } catch (Exception e) {
60        System.out.println("MyReader: can't close!" + e);
61    }
```

Lines 40–61: These methods just send `readline()`, `ready()`, and `close()` to the `BufferedReader`. They bracket them with `try-catch` blocks, as required. This way, the programmer does not have to use `try-catch` in the code that uses the `MyReader`.

Line 46: Is required; since if the `readLine()` throws an `Exception`, *something* needs to be returned.

Line 53: Same thing.

Notice that inside the `try-catch` blocks, `close()` just sends `close()` to the `BufferedReader`; `hasMoreData()` simply returns `br.ready()`; and `giveMeTheNextLine()` returns `br.readLine()`. The advantage of using `MyReader` is that you don't have to worry about the `try-catch` blocks around those three methods (which are annoying). Notice also that `MyReader` has `hasMoreData()` and `giveMeTheNextLine()`, whereas `StringTokenizer` has `hasNext()` and `nextToken()`. Perhaps it would be easier to remember the method names in `MyReader` if they were more like those in `StringTokenizer`. You could just change the names in `MyReader`, but if you had old code that used the old names, it would break (not that you couldn't change all the names in the old code, it's just time consuming). Another solution is to write wrappers for the methods with new names, as shown in Listing 10.12.

LISTING 10.12 `MyReader:nextLine()`, and `hasNext()` **wrappers.**

```
60    public String nextLine() {
61        return giveMeTheNextLine();
62    }
63
64    public boolean hasNext() {
65        return hasMoreData();
66    }
```

These methods don't add any functionality; they just wrap other methods with different names. You might do this if you wanted to use the shorter, more familiar names.

Emitting the Tokens One per Line

Now that you understand `StringTokenizer` and `MyReader`, it should be simple to modify the file echo code (Listing 10.8) to output one word on each line. Do that now. You can find the `MyReader` class at:

www.willamette.edu/~levenick/SimplyJava/io/

After you solve the problem, look at Listing 10.13 to see how the author did it. No fair peeking! It really does help you to learn if you actually type in, compile, and execute little sample programs. At least if you're like most people; if you just read code, it doesn't stick—but, if you run it and modify it and wrestle with it a bit, you can remember it later. Okay, here's the code to solve that little problem. It turns out, with the `printOneWordPerLine()` method to be, well, trivial.

LISTING 10.13   Printing the words in a file one on each line.

```
1    MyReader mr = new MyReader();
2
3    while (mr.hasMoreData()) {
4        printOneWordPerLine(mr.giveMeTheNextLine());
5    }
6
7    mr.close();
```

The `printOneWordPerLine()` method from Listing 10.3 does just what we need. Isn't software reuse great?

Writing to a File

It is simple to write to a file if you use the `MyWriter` class (it is simple enough without it as well). Listing 10.14 shows how to write two lines into whatever file the user selects.

LISTING 10.14   Writing to a file using a `MyWriter`.

```
1    mw = new MyWriter();
2
3    mw.println("Hello...");
4    mw.println("Here's the second line of a file");
5
6    mw.close();
7
```

The `MyWriter` class (which is in the directory with `MyReader`) has only three methods: `println(String)`, `print(String)`, and `close()`. It is important to close files after you finish working with them; otherwise, sometimes the data in them cannot be read correctly (although sometimes it makes no difference).

The `MyWriter` class is shown in Listing 10.15.

LISTING 10.15 MyWriter.

```
1    import java.awt.*;
2    public class MyWriter {
3        protected PrintWriter pw;
4
5        public MyWriter() {
6            openIt(getFileName());     }
7
8        public MyWriter(String filename) {
9            openIt(filename);     }
10
11       private void openIt (String filename) {
12           try {
13               pw = new PrintWriter(new FileWriter(filename));
14           } catch (Exception e) {
             System.out.println("Can't open " + filename + "!" + e);}
15       }
16
17       public void print(String s) {
18           pw.print(s);     }
19
20       public void println(String s) {
21           print(s+"\n");     }
22
23       public void close() {
24           pw.close();     }
25
26       private String getFileName() {
27           FileDialog fd = new FileDialog(new Frame(),
                             "Output File", FileDialog.SAVE);
28           fd.setFile("output");
29           fd.show();
30           return fd.getDirectory()+fd.getFile();   // return the complete
                                                        path
31       }
32   }
```

You probably don't need to know how this works, but making sure you do will be good review of the various Java constructs.

Like MyReader there are constructors with and without a filename specified as a parameter. The openIt() method has the magic nested constructor to open a file for writing. The print() and println() methods do what they do in System.out, which, by the way, is a `PrintStream`. Notice on line 27 that there is a third parameter in the `FileDialog` constructor; this allows you to enter a filename that does not yet exist.

PUTTING IT ALL TOGETHER

You have all the pieces to accomplish the task. You must still decide where to filter out the short words. There are several place you might do this:

- As soon as you get the tokens from the `StringTokenizer`
- In `emit()` (assuming you are using `emit()`—you can leverage the code from Listing 8.22 with one minor alteration).
- In a filter that sits in front of `emit()`.

Here's how that last choice might be implemented. In the loop where you are reading tokens from the input file and writing them to the output file, instead of sending `emit(nextToken)`, you might send `emitIf(nextToken)` where `emitIf()` is as in Listing 10.16.

LISTING 10.16   `emitIf(String)`.

```
1    public void emitIf(String s) {
2        if (s.length() > 4)
3            emit(s);
4    }
```

By encapsulating the print criteria in a method, it is easy to find and change later, plus there's no need to alter `emit(String)`.

This has two advantages: 1) The `emit()` method may be left untouched. That way, its logic does not need to be cluttered up with deciding whether to emit the word, it just does what its name says, emits. 2) If you want to implement some other filtering scheme (like only printing words that begin with `'x'`, or whatever), you can make the changes in `emitIf()` and not have to look anywhere else.

Still, maybe it would be easier to put that `if` statement in the method where you are getting the tokens. Perhaps. It could be argued, though, that writing an `emitIf()` method is cleaner and easier to understand and modify later. In addition, mixing the filtering criteria with the input violates the principle of having I/O code do nothing but I/O.

CONCLUSION

This chapter introduced file I/O, the StringTokenizer class, and two convenience classes, MyReader and MyWriter. They simplify reading and writing files, by 1) wrapping up the Exception laden BufferedReader and PrintWriter classes from the java.io package, and 2) using a FileDialog to prompt the user for input and output files.

REVIEW QUESTIONS

10.1   What is a token?

10.2   What are the two StringTokenizer methods?

10.3   What are the three StringTokenizer constructors?

10.4   What is a wrapper?

10.5   When might you wrap a method?

10.6   What is a FileDialog used for?

Programming Exercises

10.7   Write a small test Application to experiment with a FileDialog. Print the Strings that come back from getDirectory() and getFile().

10.8   Comment out the imports in MyReader, one at a time, and see what compiler error you get.

10.9   Write a fourth constructor of MyReader, namely MyReader(Applet), which prompts the users and opens whatever file they choose. Hint: the body is a single line of code.

10.10   Imagine you are using the code in Listing 10.13, but something is going wrong with the input. Modify that code to echo each line input (with descriptive text, like "And the next line is: ==>   <== tokens follow:".

10.11   Maybe you're tired of typing System.out.println all the time, and would rather just type out.println. You can do this by declaring an instance variable of type java.io.PrintStream called out. Do that in a class and test it out.

10.12   Maybe you're tired of typing System.out.println("whatever") all the time, and would rather just type emit("whatever"). You can do this by declaring an emit(String) method. Do that in a class and test it out.

10.13   Maybe you're tired of typing System.out.println("whatever") all the time, and don't want to have to declare emit(String) in every class, but would rather just declare it once. Create a class, called, say, MyUtils, and make `emit()` a class method in it (see the section "Class Methods" in Chapter 5 if you've forgotten how). Then you can just say `MyUtils.emit("whatever")` in any class. Do that.

10.14 Write an `Application` that creates 10 files named junk0, junk1, junk2,..., junk9. The file junk0 should have just one line with a "0" on it; junk1 should have the lines

```
0
1
```

and junk9 should have the lines

```
0
1
2
3
4
5
6
7
8
9
```

10.15 Don't forget to close those files! Close your program and open those files in the NetBeans editor. Hint: you must specify a directory (see `getFilename()` in `MyWriter`. One way to learn the directory you are reading/writing from would be to modify the `getFilename()` code to send the directory out to `System.out` when you select a file in the current directory. Then you could copy that back into the program.

The following refer to the file copy program.

10.17 Modify the file copy program to ignore punctuation in determining whether a word is long enough. As the program stands it would copy "this," because, with the quotes it has length 6.

10.18 Add a GUI control so if the user chooses, the program will remember that last file read and read from it every time the user pushes the Read button. Hint: you will need to store the file name/path and use the `MyReader(String)` constructor if the user wants to reread.

10.19 Add a `Choice` to allow the user to select the minimum word length to copy; allow them to output only words with five letters or more, or eight.

11 Data Structures

INTRODUCTION

Up until now, we have been declaring variables one at a time. However, sometimes you want 10, or 1000 variables. If you were implementing software for a real bank, it might have thousands of accounts. If you wanted to program an army of 100 snowpeople, it would be hopeless to write 100 statements for each action you wanted them to perform. A big advantage of computing is that the machine doesn't mind doing the same thing thousands of times. Data structures allow you to declare and store as many variables as you need with a minimum of effort. This chapter will show you how to use two similar data structures: array and Vector.

ARRAYS

Arrays are part of most programming languages. An array is a list of variables, all with the same type and name, but distinguished by an index. The declaration:

```
int [] anArray = new int[100];
```

declares 100 variables of type int, all named anArray[something], where something is an int between 0 and 99. Thus, the first int variable is named anArray[0], the next, anArray[1], and the hundredth, anArray[99]. Each acts exactly like an int variable, because each *is* an int variable. The value in the square brackets is called the *index*. It may be a constant, but usually it is a variable.

Simplest Examples

Listing 11.1 declares an array of five ints and then displays them to System.out.

LISTING 11.1   Declaring and printing an array of five ints: code and output.

```
1    int [] list = new int[5];
2
3    for (int index=0; index<5; index++) {
4        System.out.println("index=" + index + " list[index]=" +
         list[index]);
5    }

index=0 list[index]=0
index=1 list[index]=0
index=2 list[index]=0
index=3 list[index]=0
index=4 list[index]=0
```

Line 1: Declares an array, called list, of five ints.

Line 2: A for loop to iterate over the five elements of the list

The loop on lines 3–5 is a standard method of accessing the elements of an array one at a time; it is said to "iterate over the elements of the array." As you can see (by the output), they are auto initialized to zero when the array is declared.

If you want values besides zero in the array elements, you must put them there, as shown in Listing 11.2.

LISTING 11.2   The same array with `list[0]` set to 7 and `list[3]` to 33: code and output.

```
1    int [] list = new int[5];
2    list[0] = 7;
3    list[3] = 33;
4
5    for (int index=0; index<5; index++) {
6        System.out.println("index=" + index + " list[index]="
                    + list[index]);
7    }

index=0 list[index]=7
index=1 list[index]=0
index=2 list[index]=0
index=3 list[index]=33
index=4 list[index]=0
```

Line 2: Assign the value 7 to the first element of the array

Line 3: ...and 33 to the fourth.

Listing 11.3 illustrates setting the values of the array in a loop. It uses the current value of the index squared as the value stored in each element.

LISTING 11.3   The same array with each element set to the square of its index.

```
1    int [] list = new int[5];
2    for (int i=0; i<5; i++) {
3        list[i] = i*i;
4    }
5
6    for (int i=0; i<5; i++) {
7        System.out.println("i=" + i + " list[i]=" + list[i]);
8    }

i=0 list[i]=0
i=1 list[i]=1
i=2 list[i]=4
i=3 list[i]=9
i=4 list[i]=16
```

Line 3: Assign each element the value of the square of its index

Notice that "i" stands for "index."

Printing a String Backward

Arrays may be of any type: primitive, built in, or user defined. An array of chars could be used to print a String backward as shown in Listing 11.4.

LISTING 11.4 Printing a String forward and backward, one char per line.

```
1    char [] letters = new char[100];
2    String s = "pals";
3    for (int i=0; i<s.length(); i++) {
4        letters[i] = s.charAt(i);
5    }
6
7    System.out.println("frontwards, it's: ");
8    for (int i=0; i<s.length(); i++) {
9        System.out.println("i=" + i + " letters[i]=" + letters[i]);
10   }
11
12   System.out.println("backwards, that's: ");
13   for (int i=s.length()-1; i>=0; i--) {
14       System.out.println("i=" + i + " letters[i]=" + letters[i]);
15   }
```

```
frontwards, it's:
i=0 letters[i]=p
i=1 letters[i]=a
i=2 letters[i]=l
i=3 letters[i]=s
backwards, that's:
i=3 letters[i]=s
i=2 letters[i]=l
i=1 letters[i]=a
i=0 letters[i]=p
```

Lines 3–5: Assign each char in the String to an element of the array.

Lines 7–10: Print them forward.

If length() and charAt() seem unfamiliar, you might review the section "A Few String Methods" in Chapter 8, "Iterative Statements and Strings."

To print the String frontward and backward, all on the same line, just change the printlns to prints and remove some of the text, as in Listing 11.5.

LISTING 11.5   Printing a `String` forward and backward, all on one line.

```
1    char [] letters = new char[100];
2    String s = "pals";
3    for (int i=0; i<s.length(); i++) {
4        letters[i] = s.charAt(i);
5    }
6
7    System.out.print("the word ");
8    for (int i=0; i<s.length(); i++) {
9        System.out.print(letters[i]);
10   }
11
12   System.out.print(" backwards, is ");
13   for (int i=s.length()-1; i>=0; i--) {
14       System.out.print(letters[i]);
15   }
```

```
the word pals backwards, is slap
```

Lines 3–5: Assign each char in the `String` to an element of the array.

Lines 7–10: Print them forward.

Lines 12–15: ...and backward.

An Array of Accounts

If you were writing a bank simulation with 1000 `Accounts`, you could declare an array like this:

```
Account[] accountList = new Account[1000];
```

This will give you 1000 `Account` variables, each initialized to zero, which, when the variable is a reference (as any `Object` variable is), is interpreted as `null`. Thus, if you wish to have 1000 `Accounts` in those 1000 `Account` variables, you must do the second step of instantiating them all; like this:

```
for (int i=0; i<1000; i++)
    accountList[i] = new Account();
```

If you forget to do this (and, everyone does when they start working with arrays of `Objects`), you will be confronted with `NullPointerExceptions` the first time you send a message to one of them; and if you're not paying attention, it could be very confusing. Don't forget!

Although this could work, it is often better to use Vectors for lists of Objects.

Vector **AND** Iterator

Java provides the Vector class to keep track of lists of objects. A Vector stores a list of variables of type Object. Thus, it can store any type of object, since every object is an instance of some class and every class extends Object (directly or indirectly). This is very convenient, but has a downside. When you get objects back out of the list, the complier considers them to be of type Object. Therefore, it will only allow messages that are defined in Object to be sent to them. To pacify it, you must cast the Object to whatever type it actually is, as will be shown directly.

Vector has a number of useful methods, but to start we will focus on just two: add(Object) and iterator(). That will be enough to demonstrate that we can add things to the list and access them in order.

The add(Object) Method

To add an object, any object at all, to a Vector, use add(Object); simply send the list the add() message with that object as a parameter. The object will be added to the end of the list. For example, to make a list containing three Accounts, you could say:

```
java.util.Vector theList = new java.util.Vector();
theList.add(new Account("xena", 1234567));
theList.add(new Account("abe", 100));
theList.add(new Account("bea", 10000000));
```

Then, the first Account would be xena's, the last bea's.

The iterator() Method

Iterators have only two methods that you will need to use: hasNext() and next(). The former tells if there are any more items, the latter hands back the next one; it works just like StringTokenizer (odds are StringTokenizer is a wrapper for an Iterator initialized by its constructor).

To access each item in a Vector, from first to last in order, use an Iterator, like this:

```
1    for (Iterator theIterator=theList.iterator(); theIterator.hasNext();)
{

2        Account nextAccount = (Account) theIterator.next();
3        System.out.println("\n\nnext account..." + nextAccount);
4    }
```

The form of this loop is always the same; it is an idiom. The initialization declares a variable, theIterator, of type Iterator and initializes it to all the items in theList, by sending theList the iterator() message and storing what it returns (the for loop is described in the section "The for Loop" in Chapter 8). The loop continues as long as the Iterator has any more Objects.

Line 2 in the preceding code:

```
Account nextAccount = (Account) theIterator.next();
```

illustrates a generic technique used when iterating over a set of Objects. Each time around the loop, it gets the next Object from the Iterator, casts it as an Account, and stores it in an Account variable named nextAccount. Once there, you can send it any message Account defines. If the Object returned from the Iterator is not an Account, it will throw a ClassCastException—the exception thrown when an Object is cast as a class, Foo, but is not compatible with that class.

In English, this loop iterates over the Vector called theList; each time around the loop it stores the next Account from the list in the nextAccount variable, and then (implicitly) sends it toString(); whatever toString() returns is then the parameter to System.out.println().

Simplest Test Program

As usual, to convince yourself that a programming technique works and, more importantly, to become familiar with it before trying to use it for anything difficult, you should write a tiny test program. There are many ways one might do this, but here it is done with an Application, as shown in Listing 11.6.

LISTING 11.6 Simplest use of a Vector.

```
1    import java.util.*;
2
3    public class VectorTest {
4
5        Vector theList;
6
7        /** Creates a new instance of VectorTest */
```

```
 8        public VectorTest() {
 9            theList = new Vector();
10            theList.add(new Account("xena", 12345));
11            theList.add(new Account("abe", 100));
12            theList.add(new Account("bea", 10000000));
13
14            for (Iterator it=theList.iterator(); it.hasNext();) {
15                Account nextAccount = (Account) it.next();
16                System.out.println("\n\nnext account..." + nextAccount);
17            }
18        }
19
20        /**
21         * @param args the command line arguments
22         */
23        public static void main(String[] args) {
24            new VectorTest();
25        }
26    }
```

Lines 10–17: Add three Accounts to a Vector and print them.

Line 24: Create a VectorTest that will invoke the default constructor and so run the test code in lines 8–18.

Adjourn to the keyboard, and input and run this program. It will require that there is an Account class in that directory (you could use the ClassMaker to generate one, or look around and find the one you used before).

That's all you need to know to use a Vector. The next example will use a Vector as the database for a bank simulation.

A SIMPLE Bank DATABASE

According to *dictionary.com*, *database* means, "A collection of data arranged for ease and speed of search and retrieval." Thus, a database management system, or DBMS, is software that manages a collection of data easily and quickly. Somehow, that's not as impressive sounding as "database management system." So it goes.

The Database

In the simple Bank program in Chapter 3, "Class Design and Implementation," the database consisted of three Account variables. There were always exactly three Accounts and the only thing a user could do was select the current account and withdraw money from it. It was hardly a database at all. The bank database here will have a variable number of Accounts. The bank administrator will be able to add, delete, or edit accounts, and then save the changes to disk. The data structure used will be a list of all the Accounts in the Bank. A Vector is suitable to implement this list.

Inputting the Database: Load

Assuming there were hundreds or thousands of accounts in a bank, they should not have to be input by hand each time you start the program. Even for a small test bank DBMS, you would not want to type in all the data every time you run the program. Instead, account information should be stored on disk, in files. Program initialization would include inputting the database. An obvious place to input the database would be in the Bank constructor.

File Format

The code to read the data from the file will expect it in a particular order and format. There are many ways to write files, but if they are human readable, they are easy to maintain (since you can simply edit them). Thus, MyReader and MyWriter from Chapter 10, "Reading and Writing Files," are well suited for this job.

It doesn't really matter what format the data is stored in, but you must decide what that format will be. For simplicity, let's store the data for each Account on one line; first the name of the person, then his or her balance, with spaces in between. Therefore, if there were four Accounts, the file might look like:

```
Amy    17
Zoe    9898
Joe    98
Bea    1000000
```

If there were more data fields—like an account number, or social security number, address, phone number, ATM number and password—they could be appended. Two fields are enough for illustrative purposes.

Encapsulation! Input in the Account Constructor

The code to open the file and build the database belongs in the Bank class (since that Bank will be working with the database). Conceptually, it will look something like Listing 11.7.

LISTING 11.7 Pseudocode for reading and building the database.

```
1   while (more data in the input file) {
```

```
2        read the data for the next account
3        create and store the new account
```

Your first idea might be to write the inside of the loop as shown in Listing 11.8.

LISTING 11.8 First idea for inputting and creating the Accounts in that loop.

```
// read the data for the next account
StringTokenizer st = new StringTokenizer(mr.giveMeTheNextLine());
String name = st.nextToken();
int balance = Integer.parseInt(st.nextToken());

// create and store the new account
theList.add(new Account(name, balance));
```

Listing 11.8 is the inside of the loop from Listing 11.7 (the details of lines 2 and 3) with the pseudocode made into comments and the actual code written beneath it. The use of pseudocode as comments for the actual code is good form; you can type the pseudocode right into the class and then comment it out as you implement it. That way, the compiler will remind you if you haven't implemented everything (since the pseudocode will generate compiler errors), and the comments will remind you what you were thinking when you wrote it.

Logically, Listing 11.8 is impeccable (assuming mr is a MyReader and has been properly initialized). However, it violates the principle of encapsulation. What if later, more fields are added to the Account class? Then it would be necessary to edit the Bank class as well. It would decouple Bank and Account better, and be simpler for the programmer adding the fields to Account, if all the changes could be made in Account.

The standard technique to accomplish this is to write a constructor that is passed the input stream, and that reads the data it needs from that, as shown in Listing 11.9.

LISTING 11.9 Account(MyReader) constructor.

```
1   Account(MyReader mr){    //empty default constructor
2       StringTokenizer st = new StringTokenizer(mr.giveMeTheNextLine());
3       name = st.nextToken();
4       balance = Integer.parseInt(st.nextToken());
5   }
```

This reads and stores information for one Account from the parameter. By doing the I/O for Account in Account, encapsulation is increased and the programmer's job is simplified.

To test this code (stepwise implementation), use the Bank class in Listing 11.10.

LISTING 11.10   Testing the Account constructor that inputs.

```
1    import java.util.*;
2
3    public class Bank {
4        private Vector accountList;
5
6        /** Creates a new instance of Bank */
7        public Bank() {
8            accountList = new Vector();
9            inputAccounts();
10       }
11
12       private void inputAccounts() {
13           MyReader mr = new MyReader();
14           while (mr.hasMoreData())    // read and store database
15               accountList.add(new Account(mr));
16
17           displayAccounts();
18       }
19
20       private void displayAccounts() {
21           for (Iterator it=accountList.iterator(); it.hasNext(); )
22               System.out.println(it.next());
23       }
24   }
```

Line 15: Reads in the entire file and stores it in the database.

This code reads, stores, and displays a database from a user-selected file. It is written simply to test input, storage and retrieval of a database of Accounts. Notice the displayAccounts() method. It is written as a method (instead of just a loop) so it can be reused; and uses the idiom to iterate over a Vector. Line 15 would also be good to focus on; this is the line where the database is constructed—oddly enough. It adds one new Account to the list, by invoking the Account(MyReader) constructor (which reads the information for this Account from the file associated with the MyReader, mr). Since it is in a while loop, it will read all the account information, one Account at a time, and store them all in the list, in the same order as they were in the file. That's a lot of functionality for one line, and elegantly done (although, likely aesthetics are personal).

Outputting the Database: Save

To test the save() method (once we have written it), one line can be added, as shown in Listing 11.11.

LISTING 11.11   Testing the Bank: save() method.

```
1    public BankDBMS() {
2         initComponents();
3         setBounds(100,100,500,500);
4         theBank = new Bank();
5         theBank.save();
6    }
```

Line 5: Will output the database to a file of the user's choice.

Can you tell which class this method goes in? If you don't know, answer this question; "What type does the BankDBMS() method return?" It is not specified. Ordinary methods must specify a return type, or void if there is none (see the section "Return Types" in Chapter 5, "Toward Consistent Classes"). Since there is no return type, this must be a constructor, and the name of a constructor is the name of the class in which it appears.

Bank:save()

Save seems a good name for a method that saves the database to a file. The Bank must iterate over the Vector that is the internal database and write each Account to the disk file. A MyWriter will do the job perfectly; see Listing 11.12.

LISTING 11.12   Bank:save().

```
1    public void save() {
2        MyWriter mw = new MyWriter();
3
4        for (Iterator it=accountList.iterator(); it.hasNext(); ) {
5            Account nextAccount = (Account) it.next();
6            nextAccount.save(mw);
7        }
8
9        mw.close();
10    }
```

Line 2: Creates and saves the MyWriter.

Lines 4–7: This iterates over the account list, sending each `Account` the `save(MyWriter)` message.

Line 9: Don't forget to close the file when you are finished with it!

File Format

The file format is entirely arbitrary, but it must be compatible with the input method. The input method expects first the name and then the balance on one line separated by at least one space.

A common pitfall is to write into the same file you are reading from before the `save()` code is completely debugged. Then, the next time you try to read the data, your program crashes. You can ameliorate this by writing to a different file, or making a backup of the input file (*before* trashing it!).

Encapsulation: Output in the `Account` Class

Just as input is best done within the class, so is output. Listing 11.13 is the `save()` method—tough work, eh?

LISTING 11.13   `Account:save(MyWriter)`.

```
1    public void save(MyWriter mw) {
2        mw.println(name + " " + balance);
3    }
```

Not much to it. Simply print the name and balance with a space between them.

This looks (and is) simple, but if a careless programmer wrote it as `mw.println(name + balance);`, what would go wrong? Attention to detail while programming will save hours of frustration.

Enhancing the DBMS

We now have a DBMS that loads and saves a list of `Accounts`. Its only usefulness is to demonstrate that we can do that. There are many things you might do to enhance such a database. The most obvious are to allow the user to select an account and withdraw or deposit funds. Other functions include adding and deleting `Accounts`, changing information in an `Account`, and transferring funds between `Accounts`.

Adding a `java.awt.Choice`

Back in Chapter 3, you selected the current `Account` by pushing one of three buttons. If there are dozens or hundreds of `Accounts`, that would make a very

cluttered GUI. A `Choice` would be a better choice. As the name implies, it is a `Com-`
`ponent` for allowing the user to make a choice from a number of options. Follow the
instructions in the section "Adding and Using a `Choice`" in Appendix A to add one
to your `Application`.

Following those instructions will give you a `Choice` with "this," "that," and "the
other thing" in it. What you want in it for the `Bank` database is the names from all
the `Accounts`. The easiest place to add them is when you read in the `Accounts`, in
`Bank:input()`; that means you will need access to the `Choice` there. The easiest way
to have a reference to it there is to pass it as a parameter with the `Bank` constructor
(see Listing 11.14). Remember, the `Bank` class will not know what `Choice` is unless
`import java.awt.*;` is added. Notice that the reference to the `Choice` is passed along
as a parameter to `inputAccounts()`.

Selecting an `Account` Given a Name

As in the Chapter 3 example, `Bank` will have a `withdraw(int)` method that withdraws
the amount passed in the parameter from the current account. This will require a
variable containing a reference to the current `Account`, so it must be declared and
initialized. It cannot be initialized until after the database is read in, so the logical
spot to do that is right after input; see Listing 11.14.

LISTING 11.14   Initializing `theChoice` and `currentAccount`.

```
1     import java.util.*;
2     import java.awt.*;
3
4     public class Bank {
5         private Vector accountList;
6         private Account currentAccount;
7
8         /** Creates a new instance of Bank */
9         public Bank(Choice theChoice) {
10            accountList = new Vector();
11            inputAccounts(theChoice);
12            currentAccount = (Account) accountList.elementAt(0);
13        }
14
15        private void inputAccounts(Choice theChoice) {
16            MyReader mr = new MyReader();
17            while (mr.hasMoreData()) {
18                Account newAccount = new Account(mr);
19                accountList.add(newAccount);
20                theChoice.addItem(newAccount.getName());
21            }
```

```
22              mr.close();
23          }
24
25          public void withdraw(int withdrawalAmt) {
26              currentAccount.withdraw(withdrawalAmt);
27          }
28      }
```

Line 11: Fills the list with Accounts and initializes theChoice (see line 20).

Line 12: Initializes currentAccount to the first thing in the Vector. Note the cast; remember why?

The elementAt(int) method returns the Object at the ith position in the Vector, where i is the value of the parameter. The first position in the Vector is 0, just like an array. The cast is required for the assignment on line 12, since you cannot assign an Object to an Account. The (Account) persuades the compiler that it should do the assignment; see "The iterator() Method" (earlier in this chapter) if this seems unfamiliar.

When the user selects a new name from the Choice, presumably the code looks something like Listing 11.15.

LISTING 11.15   itemSelected handler for theChoice.

```
1       private void newChoice(java.awt.event.ItemEvent evt) {
2           String item = theChoice.getSelectedItem();
3           System.out.println("new choice from the choice: " + item);
4           theBank.setCurrentAccount(item);
5           displayCurrentBalance();
6       }
```

Line 2: Get the selected item from theChoice.

Line 3: Diagnostic; delete when the code works.

Line 4: The point of this example; set the currentAccount variable in theBank.

Line 5: So the user can always see the balance of the current Account.

Notice that the type of item is String, so on the Bank side the setCurrentAccount() method will have a String parameter and will have to search through all the Accounts looking for one with that name. As always, to iterate through a Vector, copy and paste the Iterator loop; see Listing 11.16.

LISTING 11.16 `Bank:setCurrentAccount(String)`.

```
1    public void setCurrentAccount(String name) {
2        for (Iterator it=accountList.iterator(); it.hasNext(); ) {
3            Account nextAccount = (Account) it.next();
4            if (nextAccount.getName().equals(name))
5                currentAccount = nextAccount;
6        }
7    }
```

Lines 2–6: Iterate over the `Accounts`, and if one is found with the parameter as its name, set `currentAccount` to it.

Line 4: Note that you cannot compare `Strings` with `==`. You must use `equals()`.

This code will work, but could be improved in two ways. First, the loop will continue through the entire list even if it finds the name in the first `Account`, so it will waste fewer cycles if it exits the loop as soon as it finds the name (although, since searching the entire list takes less than a millisecond, this hardly matters). Second, if it never finds the name, that's a bug, and it would be good to report the problem, instead of blithely ignoring it. Listing 11.17 fixes both of these by returning when the name is found and complaining if control falls out the bottom of the loop without having found the name. This loop with an internal return is an idiom that is worthwhile remembering; you will see it again (assuming you continue in computing).

LISTING 11.17 `Bank:setCurrentAccount(String)` **improved.**

```
1    public void setCurrentAccount(String name) {
2        for (Iterator it=accountList.iterator(); it.hasNext(); ) {
3            Account nextAccount = (Account) it.next();
4            if (nextAccount.getName().equals(name)) {
5                currentAccount = nextAccount; // found it
6                return;                       // exit the method NOW!
7            } // if
8        } // for
9
10       System.out.println("Error! Name not found! name=" + name);
11   }
```

Lines 4–7: If the name is found, set `currentAccount` and exit the method.

Line 10: Complain about not finding it; realize it will only get here if line 6 never executes.

Editing an `Account`

Part of database management is the ability to modify the data, both to correct errors and simply to update changing information. This may be done by the software (like updating the balance when money is withdrawn) or by hand (like changing a misspelled name). Conceptually, here's what to do to allow editing.

1. Add an Edit `button` (its action is to tell the `Bank` to edit).
2. Open a new window to edit the current account.
3. Reflect changes the user makes in the edit window in the database.

Step 1 is easy, you know how to add and connect a `Button`. The other two steps need some explaining.

Opening a New Window

Opening a new window is very useful when you want to present or input information under certain circumstances, but don't want to clutter up the GUI. Displaying a new `Frame` is described in the section "Adding a Pop-Up `Frame`" in Appendix A.

Editing from the New Window

Once you have created a GUI `Frame` Form, you can use the `FormEditor` to add `TextFields` for each field in the `Account` to be edited; as of now that would just be name and `balance`. Rename those `TextFields` and connect them so that you get control when the user presses Enter in either.

NetBeans will write the shell of the event handling code, but you must write the code to do the editing. When the user enters a change in the name `TextField`, you would like to simply set the name of the current account to what the user entered, as shown in Listing 11.18.

LISTING 11.8   Editing the name field.

```
1    private void nameTFActionPerformed(java.awt.event.ActionEvent evt) {
2        theAccount.setName(nameTF.getText());
3    }
```

Line 2: Change the value of the name in `theAccount`.

But, how to access the `currentAccount` back in the `Bank` from the `EditFrame`? If you simply type this code, the compiler will inform you that it cannot resolve the symbol "`theAccount`," and for good reason; it is not declared in this class! You could declare it as an instance variable (`Account theAccount;`), and then it would compile; unfortunately at runtime, this alone would generate a `NullPointerException`—

again for good reason, since you have never changed the default null. Some people find themselves stuck at this point.

The solution is obvious if you think carefully, or perhaps draw a picture? Figure 11.1 depicts the data structure after the program has read in those four Accounts from before and the user has selected "Zoe" with the Choice and pressed the Edit Button.

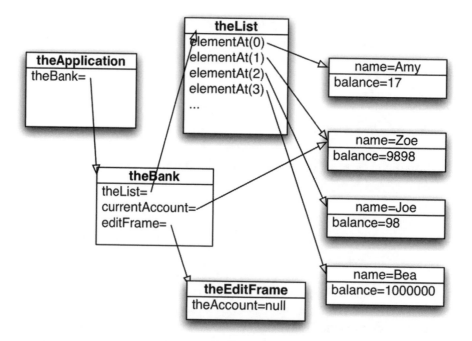

FIGURE 11.1   The state of the program when the user presses Edit. The Application has a variable named theBank, which contains a database of Accounts, a current account, and an EditFrame. When the user pushes the Edit Button, an EditFrame is opened; but how can the EditFrame get access to the current Account?

The problem is that theAccount in theEditFrame is null. It should have been set to point to Zoe's Account, which is the currentAccount back in theBank. How could this information be passed from theBank to theEditFrame? You already know, right? Either with an accessor, or as a parameter to the constructor. It's that easy.

Once we have access to the current account from the edit window, Listing 11.18 will work perfectly. The code to update the balance is similar, except that the String from the TextField must be converted to an int (see the section "String to int" in Chapter 5 if it has slipped your mind).

The code in the preceding section assumes that the user will type a legal `int` into the `balanceTF` in the `EditFrame`. What if the user accidentally types some letters? Try it. It throws an `Exception`. It would be good to catch that `Exception`. It would also be nice to read the values from both `TextFields` whenever the user presses Enter (imagine how annoying it would be to type a new name and balance, press Enter, and only update the balance). However, that is deferred to the exercises; it's just details.

Molecules IN A BOX

In Chapter 9, "Simulation and Animation," a single ball bouncing under the influence of gravity was simulated. The task for this section is to simulate a number of molecules in a box. Most of the code from the ball program from Chapter 9 can be leveraged for this new task.

The Molecule Class

The `Ball` class checked for bouncing on the floor, but not on the ceiling or the two side walls. Thus, the `Molecule` class will need to check for those other three cases as well. Perhaps you are ready to write that code now; in that case, do it, and when you're done, go on to "Changes to the `Controller`" later in this chapter. Otherwise, read on.

Designing the Bounce Code

The code to check whether a `Molecule` will collide with any of the four walls on this time step is a bit complicated. Whenever you are writing code that is not simple, it is important to think clearly before starting; otherwise, you can waste many frustrating hours debugging, sometimes with nothing to show for it when you are done.

First, you need a clear conception of the problem. Second, you need to formulate a simple way to solve the problem. Start with a simple approach that you understand, or writing and debugging the code is likely to be a disaster.

Two problem-solving techniques spring to mind here: Draw a Picture, and Analysis by Cases; if those don't seem familiar, you might want to review them before continuing (see "Problem-Solving Technique: Draw a Picture" in Chapter 4, "Graphics and Inheritance," or "Analysis by Cases (ABC)" in Chapter 7, "Conditional Statements"). Then, using the picture for the bottom as a model (see Figure 9.1), draw the pictures for the top, right, and left.

Applying the Analysis by Cases Technique

Recall the steps in the ABC technique; first you must decide what the cases are, then how to distinguish between them, and finally, what to do in each case.

Step 1: Distinguishing the Cases

Use the pictures you have drawn for the first step. Once you have decided how to determine which of the five cases is applicable, you can decide what to do in each case. Only then should you start writing code.

Are there really five cases? At least. The molecule may bounce on any of the four walls this time step, or none. That makes five cases. Perhaps there are four more cases: bouncing off the left and top, the left and bottom, right and top, and right and bottom. It is possible to check the four bounce cases to handle all eight cases; nevertheless, it is something to keep in mind.

Step 2: Deciding on Actions for Each Case

The action required in each case is similar. If the molecule would hit the wall this time step, reverse its velocity (x or y, depending) and calculate its position after the bounce. This is not quite right, but will do for now.

Writing the Code

You could write the code from scratch, but it would be much faster and easier to adapt the code you already have.

Adapting the Ball Bounce Code

You already have code for the floor bounce (see Listing 11.19).

LISTING 11.19   The `Ball:step()` improved? (Copied from Listing 9.12.)

```
1    public void step() {
2        x += vx;
3
4        int bottomY = 750-(radius+y);
5        if (vy >= bottomY) {
6            //System.out.println("vy=" + vy + " y=" + y);
7            int bounceHt = vy - bottomY;    // how high it bounces this
             step
8            y = 750 - (radius + bounceHt);  // y-coord after this step
9            vy = -(vy-1)*9/10;
10       }
11       else {
12           y += vy;
```

```
13              vy += GRAVITY;
14          }
15      }
```

Line 7: Calculate how far it will travel up after bouncing.

Line 8: From that, calculate the new *y*-coordinate of the center.

Line 9: Reverse vy and subtract 1 to avoid endless small bounces.

Odds are you can adapt this code for the other three cases. Take a minute to review this code and get it in your head so you'll know how to modify it. Okay. Give it one more try. Huh. Maybe you can't make heads or tails of that code. Not good. Too much tricky code. Sorry about that. Perhaps the way to make sense of it is by using stepwise refinement (see "Stepwise Refinement" in Chapter 3).

Stepwise Refining the Bounce Code

Let's start with the step() method for Molecule without worrying about whether the Molecule will hit the wall. It simply updates the *x* and *y*-coordinates and the *y* velocity of the Molecule, as shown in Listing 11.20.

LISTING 11.20   Molecule:step() without considering bounces.

```
1    public void step() {
2        x += vx;
3        y += vy;
4        vy += g;
5    }
```

Line 2: Add the *x*-velocity, vx, to the *x*-position, x; this moves the simulated ball the distance in one time step that it would move in the world.

Line 3: The same for the *y*-position.

Line 4: Adjust the *y*-velocity by the acceleration, g.

One of the reasons step() in the previous example is complicated is that the code for step() and bounce() is intertwined. These two parts can be separated as shown in Listing 11.21.

LISTING 11.21   Molecule:step() considering bounces.

```
1    public void step() {
2        if (!willHitWall()) {
3            x += vx;
```

```
4              y += vy;
5              vy += GRAVITY;
6          }
7          else bounce();
8      }
```

Here the use of methods with descriptive names makes the logic clear. The downside is that now the willHitWall() and bounce() methods must be written. Listing 11.22 shows those two methods.

LISTING 11.22 willHitWall() and bounce().

```
1      private boolean willHitWall() {
2          return willHitSide() || willHitTopOrBottom();
3      }
4
5      private void bounce() {
6          if (willHitTopOrBottom())
7              handleYBounce();
8          if (willHitSide())
9              handleXBounce();
10     }
```

Lines 1–3: willHitWall() returns true just if willHitSide() or willHitTopOrBottom is true.

Lines 5–10: Handles a *y*-bounce, or an *x*-bounce, or both.

Notice that both of them depend on willHitSide() and willHitTopOrBottom(). The Molecule will hit a wall just if it hits a side wall or the top or bottom; thus willHitWall() returns that. The bounce() method may have to handle a bounce in the *y*-direction or the *x*- direction, or both. If it were written as an if-else, it would fail in the cases where the Molecule was going to hit two walls on the same time step.

There are now four more methods that need to be written (stepwise refinement tends to generate a number of methods). They are shown in the next two listings. Listing 11.23 has the two methods that detect upcoming bounces.

LISTING 11.23 Checking for upcoming bounces.

```
1      private boolean willHitTopOrBottom() {
2          if (vy > 0) {
3              return vy > distanceToBottom();
4          }
5          else {
```

```
 6              return -vy > distanceToTop();
 7          }
 8      }
 9
10      private boolean willHitSide() {
11          if (vx > 0) {
12              return vx > distanceToRightWall();
13          }
14          else {
15              return -vx > distanceToLeftWall();
16          }
17      }
```

The logic is the same for both, so only the first four will be explained. If the y-component of velocity is downward (i.e., if vy > 0, see line 2), then it would hit the bottom in the next time step just if the distance it will move in the y direction (vy) is more than the distance to the bottom (line 3). The distances are calculated by the methods in Listing 11.24.

LISTING 11.24   Calculating the distance to the wall the Molecule is headed toward.

```
 1      private int distanceToBottom() {
 2          return HT-(radius+y);
 3      }
 4
 5      private int distanceToTop() {
 6          return y-radius;
 7      }
 8
 9      private int distanceToRightWall() {
10          return WIDTH - (x+radius);
11      }
12
13      private int distanceToLeftWall() {
14          return x-radius;
15      }
```

These four methods implement the four cases of distance to walls.

Refer to your pictures to make sure these make sense. You will notice the use of WIDTH and HT in these methods. You no doubt recall that identifiers in all caps are constants (see the section "Case Conventions" in Chapter 5). It is better to define variables for values like this to avoid embedding numbers like 750 in the code (as was carelessly done in the first version of step() in Ball). The reason is, if you change the size of the display, it will be done automatically (instead of having to search for the numbers that represent the size of the display in various classes). This is accomplished as shown in Listing 11.25.

LISTING 11.25 Setting and accessing the display dimensions.

```
1    // from MoleculeApplet.java
2    public class MoleculeApplet extends java.applet.Applet {
3        Controller theController;
4        public static final int WIDTH=900;
5        public static final int HT=900;
6    }
7
8    // from Molecule.java...
9        public class Molecule extends FilledCircle {
10       private int HT=MoleculeApplet.HT;
11       private int WIDTH=MoleculeApplet.WIDTH;
12       private double ELASTICITY=1.0;
13   }
```

Lines 10–11: WIDTH and HT are declared static and public in MoleculeApplet, so they are accessible from everywhere, including the Molecule class.

The only remaining methods are handleXBounce() and handleYBounce(). The logic of these two methods is a little tricky. The author got it wrong twice and spent more hours than he wants to admit to get it right. There are still four cases to consider (two in each method). The logic for calculating the new values for x and y is shown in Listing 11.26.

LISTING 11.26 Pseudocode for handling bounces.

```
1    handleYBounce() {
2        case 1: bottom -- y = HT - reboundDistance() - radius;
3        case 2: top     -- y =      reboundDistance() + radius;
4    }
5    handleXBounce() {
6        case 3: right -- x = WIDTH - reboundDistance() - radius;
7        case 4: left  -- x =        reboundDistance() + radius;
8    }
```

Logically, if it hits the top or the left, the new position is just the distance it rebounds plus the radius. In the other two cases, the rebound distance and the radius must be subtracted from the wall position.

The only remaining question is how to calculate the distance the Molecule rebounds on this time step. If you care about that detail, it is included in Listing 11.27.

LISTING 11.27 HandleyBounce() and HandlexBounce().

```
1     private void handleYBounce() {
2         if (vy >= distanceToBottom()) {
3             y = HT - (vy - distanceToBottom()) - radius;
4             vy = - (vy-1)*9/10;
5         }
6         else { // top
7             y = -vy -(distanceToTop() - radius) + radius;
8             vy = -vy * 9/10;
9         }
10    }
11
12    private void handleXBounce() {
13        if (vx > 0) // right wall
14            x = WIDTH - (vx - (WIDTH - x - radius)) - radius;
15        else x = -vx - (x-radius) + radius;
16
17        vx = -vx * 9/10;
18    }
```

This is the detailed code to handle bounces; finally, the stepwise refinement bottoms out!. To understand this code, draw a careful picture. Or ignore it, it's hardly pivotal to understanding computing.

The 9/10s should be ELASTICITY, but if it is declared as:

```
int ELASTICITY = 9/10;
```

something terrible happens. Do you know what? See Listing 5.16 for a clue. And if it is declared as

```
double ELASTICITY = 0.9;
```

then it will not compile unless vx * ELASTICITY is cast as an int; like this:

```
vx = (int) (-vx * ELASTICITY);
```

which clutters up the code (although it would be okay to do).

Finally we are done writing Molecule and can turn to testing it.

Changes to the Controller

There are several changes to make to the Controller.

A Single Molecule

To make the Controller from the ball program simulate and animate a single Molecule instead of a Ball is very simple. The changes needed are shown in Listing 11.28.

LISTING 11.28   Modified Controller from the BallApplet.

```
1     import java.awt.*;
2     import java.applet.*;
3
4     public class Controller extends Thread {
5         private Frame theFrame;
6         private Molecule theMolecule;
7         private boolean running=true;
8
9         /** Creates a new instance of Controller */
10        public Controller(Frame theFrame) {
11            this.theFrame = theFrame;
12            theMolecule = new Molecule(10,40,20,Color.RED, 1, -5);
13        }
14
15        public void paint(Graphics g) {
16            theMolecule.paint(g);
17        }
18
19        private void step() {
20            theMolecule.step();
21            theFrame.repaint();
22        }
23    }
```

This Controller is very similar to the one in Listing 9.7; the differences are that every Ball has been replaced by a Molecule.

All that has been done is to replace Ball with Molecule everywhere. The methods that are unaffected are omitted.

Many Molecules

To make the Controller simulate and animate many Molecules is slightly more complicated. Instead of a Molecule variable, it needs a Vector (which will contain all the Molecules). Then, everywhere the original code did something with a Molecule, the new code must iterate over all the Molecules. Three methods need to be changed: the constructor, paint(), and step().

Changes to the Constructor

Listing 11.29 shows the changes needed to create and store NUM_MOLECULES Molecules in a Vector.

LISTING 11.29   Changes to the constructor.

```
1    public Controller(Frame theFrame) {
2        this.theApplet = theApplet;
3        for (int i=0; i<NUM_MOLECULES; i++) {
4            addOneMolecule();
5        }
6    }
7
8    private void addOneMolecule() {
9        theList.add(new Molecule(100,100,20,Color.RED, rand(7), rand(7)));
10    }
```

Line 3: Loop NUM_MOLECULES times (if you have questions about this, see Listing 8.6).

Line 4: Each time around the loop, add one Molecule.

Lines 8–10: The addOneMolecule() method.

Line 9: Create a red Molecule at 100, 100, radius 20, with random vx and vy (between 0 and 6).

Notice that they all start at the same place, are the same color and size, but have random velocities. The use of rand(int) requires that it be defined (see Listing 5.19 for a reminder). You might want to experiment with random sizes and colors once the code is working.

This code assumes that NUM_MOLECULES and theList are defined, and that java.util.* is imported: see Listing 11.30 for the changes needed at the beginning of Controller.

LISTING 11.30   Changes to the beginning of Controller.

```
1    import java.awt.*;
2    import java.applet.*;
3    import java.util.*;
4
```

```
5    public class Controller extends Thread {
6        private final int NUM_MOLECULES=20;
7
8        private Frame theFrame;
9        private Vector theList = new Vector();
10       private boolean running=true;
11   }
```

Line 3: Imports java.util so that Vector and Iterator are defined.

Line 6: Declare the constant NUM_MOLECULES to be 20.

Line 9: Declare and initialize a Vector called theList.

Changes to paint() and step()

The paint() method for the bouncing ball had just one line:

```
theMolecule.paint(g);
```

To make it instead send paint(g) to every Molecule in the list requires an Iterator in a loop, as shown in Listing 11.31.

LISTING 11.31 Modified paint() to paint every Molecule in the list.

```
1    public void paint(Graphics g) {
2        for (Iterator it=theList.iterator(); it.hasNext();) {
3            Molecule nextMolecule = (Molecule) it.next();
4            nextMolecule.paint(g);
5        }
6    }
```

This uses the idiom for iterating over all elements of a list (see "The iterator() Method" earlier in this chapter).

The changes required for step() are very similar; instead of sending step() to the Molecule, it must be sent to every Molecule in the list; see Listing 11.32.

LISTING 11.32 Modified step() to step every Molecule in the list.

```
1    private void step() {
2        for (Iterator it=theList.iterator(); it.hasNext();) {
3            Molecule nextMolecule = (Molecule) it.next();
4            nextMolecule.step();
5        }
6        theApplet.repaint();
7    }
```

As in Listing 11.32, this again uses the idiom for iterating over the elements of a list.

Experimenting with the Program

Having made those changes, the program is ready to run. Experiment with different elasticities, turning off gravity, different delay times, different ranges of velocities, or different numbers of molecules. How many molecules can there be before it stops looking like animation? Note: if you wish, you may access the code at:

www.willamette.edu/~levenick/SimplyJava/code/molecules/

It would be more educational to write it yourself, but if you don't have the time or inclination, experimenting with the code provided is much better than nothing.

CONCLUSION

This chapter introduced Vector and Iterator from java.util, Choice and Frame from java.awt, and techniques to read/write a database from/to disk files. It included a lot of new material and combined most of the material from the previous chapters to make two substantial programs. If you understand both of those examples well, congratulations! If not, condolences; you might consider rereading and working through the chapter again. Alternatively, perhaps, doing the exercises will help solidify your understanding.

REVIEW QUESTIONS

11.1 What are the two methods you use with an Iterator?

11.2 How do you add an Object to the end of the list in a Vector?

11.3 Write the idiom to access every Object in a Vector and send it to System.out.

11.4 How were the nine ways a Molecule could bounce collapsed into five? What are those five?

Programming Exercises

The next exercises refer to the BankDBMS:

11.5 Add a Save button. Save to a file the user specifies. Then (after that works), save to the same file that the database was input from. Hint: save the filename and path when it is input; one String variable will do it.

11.6 Modify the EditFrame code so that both the name and balance fields are input and both the name and balance are updated when the user presses Enter in either. Hint: write an update() method that is invoked from both.

11.7 Add error-checking code so that if the entered balance is not an int, the user is notified in a reasonable manner; perhaps pop up a Panel?

11.8 Add an addAccount button. You could reuse the EditFrame class to get the info for the new Account.

11.9 Add a deleteAccount button. You will find the Vector:remove(Object) method very useful here; as in theAccountList.remove(currentAccount);. Don't forget to also remove the deleted account's name from the Choice. Reading the Sun documentation will help with both of these.

The next exercises refer to the Molecules program:

11.10 Take out the −1 in (vy-1) in handleYBounce() in Listing 11.27. What happens? Explain why. Hint: add debugging printlns to display vy and y at each step.

11.11 Add code to catch mouse clicks, and when the user clicks on a Molecule, make it bigger. See the section "Catching Mouse Clicks" in Appendix A.

11.12 Start with just two large molecules and color them solid red when they are overlapping. Hint: two circles overlap when the distance between their centers is less than the sum of their radii.

11.13 Modify your code to detect overlap in a simulation with *n* Molecules. Hint: you will need a loop that checks every pair of Molecules for every loop.

11.14 Difficult! Modify your code to keep the Molecules from overlapping (it is the same kind of logic as anticipating bounces off the wall). If two Molecules are going to overlap, reverse the signs on their vx and vy variables.

11.15 More difficult! Make the collisions realistic, as if the molecules were billiard balls. If two Molecules hit head on, they should rebound the way they came, but if they hit a glancing blow, their directions change in a more complicated way. Don't forget to conserve momentum! Note: the mass of the Molecules matters—do large Molecules have more mass?

The next exercises refer to a completely new different project:

11.16 Fun! Create a crowd of SnowPersons. Make them all melt each day. The control structure should be just like the Molecules program.

11.17 More fun! Create a crowd of SnowPersons. Then, when the user clicks on a particular SnowPerson, make the rest of the army move to surround that one.

12 Interfaces and Writing a List Class

In This Chapter

- Interfaces
- Designing a List Class
- List Implementation Using an Array: `MyArrayIntList`
- Implementation Using a `Vector`: `MyVectorIntList`
- Testing
- JavaDoc

INTRODUCTION

The previous chapter illustrated the use of arrays and `Vectors` to implement lists. There are many applications where those two generic data structures will do exactly what you want, but there are others when it is more convenient to have a list class that serves your needs more precisely. In that case, writing your own list class makes sense. The next chapter is about sorting lists of `ints`. It will be convenient to have a familiar list class with elements of type `int` to use there.

This chapter presents interfaces, and two different list classes, one based on an array, the other based on a `Vector`. The Java interface construct can be used to specify a set of methods a class must implement. Your job will be to decide which list you like better; they will both implement the same interface, and so will be easy to interchange.

The style of this chapter is rather more terse than the earlier chapters, and assumes rather more sophistication of the reader. You are encouraged to code and test all of the methods as you go along, if you actually want to understand them. Or perhaps how they work will be so obvious that you won't need to. We will turn to designing and implementing the list classes after introducing interfaces.

INTERFACES

Java includes a rather abstract construct called interface, which allows you to specify a set of method signatures. A class may be specified to implement one or more interfaces. A class that implements an interface must implement a method that matches the signature of each method heading in the interface.

There are numerous uses for interfaces. They can 1) help to coordinate two (or more) programmers collaborating on a project; 2) provide a mechanism to help a single programmer organize the functionality of a large program; 3) enhance the encapsulation in a large project, by hiding the details of the implementation; and 4) allow various data structures or methods to be passed through the same parameter at different times (by declaring the parameter type to be an interface the passed class implements). Like many Java constructs, they are designed for large projects, and are not necessary, or even useful in tiny programs (like those a beginning programmer could be expected to write). However, as your programming expertise grows, you will find they can be extremely useful, so a brief exposure to them here may be beneficial.

Interfaces as a Device to Aid Collaboration

To illustrate how an interface may be used to help two programmers collaborate, imagine that you and a friend decide to work together to implement a bank with multiple accounts (as in earlier chapters). Pretend, for the sake of keeping the example simple, that this task is big enough that it makes sense to split it between two people. You agree that your friend will write the Bank class and you will write the Account class. The first decisions you must make to be able to develop your code independently are what actions the Account class will perform in service of the Bank. For each action, you must then decide three things: 1) the method name, 2) what information will be passed as parameters, and 3) what information will be returned.

Once those decisions are made, you have agreed on the interface (in the English sense) between your classes. Now you and your friend could implement your parts of the code, and then, when you are both done, put the code you've each written together for testing and debugging. This can work, but Java provides a construct that makes such collaboration easier, reduces miscommunication, and simplifies debugging when the two parts are put together. It is called, aptly, `interface`.

Defining the Interface

Assume you agree that an `Account` must perform just two actions: 1) return the account balance, and 2) withdraw funds. The former needs no parameter and returns the balance, the latter needs a parameter for the amount of the withdrawal and returns nothing. Therefore, their signatures are:

```
public int getBalance()
```

and

```
public void withdraw(int amtToWithdraw)
```

These can be made into an interface, named `Accountable`, as:

```
public interface Accountable {
    public int getBalance();
    public void withdraw(int amtToWithdraw);
}
```

Notice that there are semicolons after the headings.

Your friend, who is writing the `Bank` class, will include a copy of the `Accountable` interface in his project; and, instead of writing:

```
Account myAccount;
Account yourAccount;
```

now will write:

```
Accountable myAccount;
Accountable yourAccount;
```

You will also include a copy of the `Accountable` interface in your project and your `Account` class will begin with:

```
public class Account implements Accountable {
```

The compiler will now insist that you have methods in your class with the signatures specified in the interface; otherwise, it will not compile.

Interfaces may not be instantiated, so to compile and test the Bank code before the real Account code is written, your friend will need to create a fake account class for testing purposes. Each method in the interface must be written, but need only do enough that the Bank code can be tested. The fake account class might look something like this:

```java
public class FakeAccount implements Accountable {

    public int getBalance() {
        return 123;
    }

    public void withdraw(int amtToWithdraw) {
        System.out.println("withdrawing $" + amtToWithdraw);
    }
}
```

Then, a FakeAccount object may be stored in the Accountable variable myAccount:

```java
myAccount = new FakeAccount();
```

The assignment will work because instances of a class that implements an interface are assignment compatible with variables of the interface's type.

Now, your friend can write code like:

```java
System.out.println("myAccount balance=" + myAccount.getBalance());
```

and it will compile because myAccount is an Accountable, and the Accountable interface has a method with the signature public int getBalance(), so the compiler knows that whatever object is stored in myAccount at runtime must implement getBalance().

Thus, both programmers can write, test, and debug their code independently. Better, when they put it together, it is very likely to work right away, since the Bank code is only allowed to send messages defined in Accountable, and the compiler will force the Account class to implement all the methods in the Accountable.

Of course, if you do not test all the methods in Account before you put the code together, they may still have errors. Moreover, in practice, in any complex situation, the interface specification typically takes several iterations to get right; it is very easy to overlook something that one class may need from the other. However, defining an interface makes the process much easier.

Interfaces as Organizational Constructs

Interfaces can also be useful in large projects since a design team can specify interfaces and ask programmers to implement them. Just as in the previous example, the programmers writing the implementations can do development and testing independently.

Generic data structures, like JTree, define interfaces that the application programmer must implement in whatever fashion is appropriate for his particular application. This use of an interface makes it possible to provide powerful mechanisms without knowing the details of how they will be used.

Interfaces Aid Flexibility

Interfaces provide a mechanism to begin to establish software's shape; they provide a sketch of the functionality of classes by specifying the signatures of the public methods. By establishing a set of interfaces in a program, instead of just writing classes, programmers implement those interfaces. Then, when changes must be made to the existing software, new classes that implement the same interfaces can simply be substituted for the old ones. If there are no interfaces specified, it is anyone's guess just what methods the classes must include to work with other classes. With interfaces, both sides know what methods can be sent.

Interfaces Support Abstraction

A programmer can work with an interface and never know the mechanisms of the methods being invoked. This allows him to focus on the task at hand without being distracted by extraneous detail. There are a number of interfaces provided in Java. One you have encountered is Iterator, although you probably didn't realize it was an interface. If you check the API documentation, you will see that Iterator is an interface with just three methods.

Often, when you are writing an algorithm, you will need a particular kind of data structure, like a list, that supports some standard set of operations, but you don't really care about the details of its implementation. Defining an interface with the methods you need is perfect in that case, as will be seen in the next chapter after we have created some working lists.

DESIGNING A LIST CLASS

As always, the first question in designing a class is, "What must it do?" Think about what you can do with an ordinary paper list. You can add, delete, or replace elements, and you can read elements from the list. Each of those actions can happen anywhere in the list; you can add (or read, or delete, or replace) an element at any position in the list. If someone asked you how many things were on the list, you could count the elements. The list we write must be able to do those things; additionally, we will need `toString()` for debugging, and a constructor to initialize the list.

Next, we must settle on the signatures of the methods. Every action involves the position of the element in the list, so there will be an index as a parameter. Every element in the list will be of type `int`, so if an element is being passed in, the parameter will be of type `int`. If the value is being returned, the return type will be of type `int` as well. Care must be taken when both an `int` value and an `int` index are passed, not to accidentally exchange the two parameters (since bugs stemming from having the actual parameters in one order and the formal parameters in the other can be very elusive).

The signatures of the methods follow:

```
void addElementAt(int nuElement, int i);
void deleteElementAt(int i);
int elementAt(int i);
void replaceElementAt(int nuElement, int i);
int length();
```

Although it is not strictly necessary, a method that adds an element at the end of the list is also convenient:

```
void addElement(int nuElement);
```

These signatures will be common to the two implementations, and would make sense collected together in an interface, like this:

```
public interface IntList {
    public void addElementAt(int nuElement, int i);
    public void deleteElementAt(int i);
    public int elementAt(int i);
    public void replaceElementAt(int nuElement, int i);
    public int length();
    public void addElement(int nuElement);
}
```

LIST IMPLEMENTATION USING AN ARRAY: `MyArrayIntList`

Since you can add and delete elements, the number of things in the list is variable. An array must be declared as a fixed size. If you declare an array as:

```
int [] list[] = new int[10];
```

you have 10 `int` variables named `list[0]` , `list[1]` , `...` `list[9]`, and no more. The array cannot contain more than 10 `int`s, and if there are less than 10 `int` values to store, the rest of the variables are unused. The array examples in Chapter 11, "Data Structures," sidestepped this issue. Here, it must be confronted.

Managing a Variable Sized List in an Array: Representation

One common technique to manage an array of variable size is to keep all the elements at the beginning of the list and add a variable, named `last`, that keeps track of the index of the last element in the list. If there is only one element in a list, it will be at `list[0]` and `last` will be zero. If there are three elements in the list, they will be at `list[0]`, `list[1]`, and `list[2]`; and `last` will be two. If the list currently contains {8,1,2}, its state will be as in Figure 12.1.

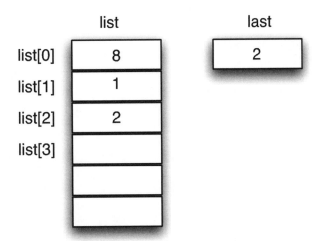

FIGURE 12.1 The list is {8,1,2}. There are three numbers in the list, so `last` is two (the index of the last number).

If 4 is then added to the end of the list, it will be added at `list[3]` and `last` will change to three, as shown in Figure 12.2.

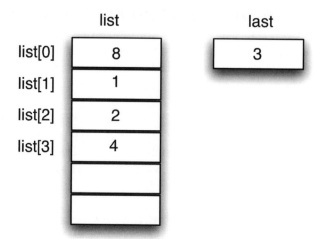

FIGURE 12.2   The list is now {8,1,2,4}. There are four numbers in the list, so `last` is three.

This simple technique allows you to keep track of a variable sized list using an array. Only one variable, `last`, is needed in addition to the array.

Assuming you understand this list representation, it is now time to turn to implementation.

Declarations and Initialization

Two variables must be declared and initialized, the array, named `list`, and the variable that keeps track of the index of the last element in the list, named `last`. To make sure the array will not become full, it is allocated with space for 10,000 elements; see Listing 12.1.

LISTING 12.1   `MyIntArrayList`: declaration and initialization of variables.

```
1    public class MyIntArrayList implements IntList {
2
3        private static final int MAX_ELEMENTS = 10000;
4        private int [] list;
5        private int last;  // where is the last thing in this list
6
7        /** Creates a new instance of List */
8        public MyIntArrayList() {
9            list = new int[MAX_ELEMENTS];
10           last = -1;
11       }
12   }
```

Line 3: Notice the use of the `static final int MAX_ELEMENTS`. You may recall that this is how one defines a constant in Java; `final` means it cannot be assigned a new value. If you wanted to store more than 10,000 values in the list, you would need to increase this constant.

The constructor initializes the two instance variables. You may wonder why `last` is initialized to −1. If so, a moment's thought may yield insight; otherwise, this may help you understand it. When there are three things in the list, `last` is 2; when there are two things in the list, `last` is 1; when there is one thing in the list, `last` is 0. In other words, the value of `last` is always one less than the number of things in the list. This is because the first element in the array is at `list[0]`. See `makeEmpty()` later in the chapter for a dramatic use of this fact.

Adding an Element to the End of the List

To add an element, call it `nuElement`, to the end of the list, its value should be assigned to the variable `list[last+1]`. Since there is now one more thing in the list, `last` should be incremented. So, one might write the code as:

```
list[last+1] = nuElement;
last++;
```

But it would be clearer to increment `last` first, and then use it directly, as in:

```
last++;
list[last] = nuElement;
```

Alternatively, shorthand would be to use the pre-increment, as shown in Listing 12.2.

LISTING 12.2 `MyIntArrayList:addElement()`.

```
1    public void addElement(int nuElement) {
2        list[++last] = nuElement;
3    }
```

Realize the difference between pre-increment and post-increment. The pre-increment, `list[++last]=7;` adds 1 to `last` and then stores 7 at `list[last]`. The post-increment, `list[last++]=7;`, stores 7 at `list[last]` and *then* adds 1 to `last`. They have very different effects!

Adding an Element at a Particular Location

Adding an element at a specific index is a bit more complicated, since first the rest of the list must be shifted down by one (to get it out of the way). Each element below the index where the new element will be inserted must be shifted down by one location. After they have all been shifted, the new element may be inserted. Assuming putHereIndex is the parameter that tells where to insert the new element, every element from last up to putHereIndex must be moved down one space. See Listing 12.3 for how to accomplish that.

LISTING 12.3   MyIntArrayList:addElementAt().

```
1    public void addElementAt(int nuElement, int putHereIndex) {
2        for (int i=last; i>=putHereIndex; i--)
3            list[i+1] = list[i];
4
5        list[putHereIndex] = nuElement;
6        last++;
7    }
```

Line 2: Notice that this does not say for (int i=putHereIndex; i>=last; i++). It is critical to start at last and shift each element from there up to putHereIndex down by one index. Imagine what would happen if it did say that. If it is not immediately clear what goes wrong, hand simulate it.

The toString() Method

The toString() method for a list should display all the elements of the list in order. We have not written an iterator for this list, so Listing 12.4 shows how to do it by hand.

LISTING 12.4   MyIntArrayList:toString().

```
1    public String toString() {
2        String returnMe="{";
3
4        for (int i=0; i<length(); i++)
5            returnMe += "," + list[i];
6
7        return returnMe+"}";
8    }
```

That `for` loop is a generic loop for dealing with a list. In the context of that loop, `list[i]` is thought of as "each element in the list." Notice the use of `{}`s and commas to format the list a bit. This code has a bug in that with the list {8,1,2}, it returns `"{,8,1,2}"`. For now, the extra comma will be ignored, but will be fixed in the exercises.

Deleting an Element

When an element in the middle of the list is deleted, all the elements below it must be shifted up by one position to fill the gap. Listing 12.5 illustrates how this is done. Notice that this loop uses `last` instead of `length()–1`.

LISTING 12.5 `MyIntArrayList:removeElementAt()`.

```
1    public void removeElementAt(int removalIndex) {
2        for (int i=removalIndex; i<last; i++)
3            list[i] = list[i+1];
4        last--;
5    }
```

After deletion (i.e., shifting all the elements after the deletion point up by one), there is one less thing in the list, so `last` must be decremented.

Replacing an Element

Unlike insert, and delete, replace does not require any shifting, so it is just one line, as shown in Listing 12.6.

LISTING 12.6 `MyIntArrayList:replaceElementAt()`.

```
1    public void replaceElementAt(int nuValue, int i) {
2        list[i] = nuValue;
3    }
```

List Length

The length of the list is one more than `last`; thus, length is extremely simple, as shown in Listing 12.7.

LISTING 12.7 `MyIntArrayList:length()`.

```
1    public int length() {
2        return last+1;
3    }
```

Accessing an Element

The accessor for an element at a particular location simply returns that element, as shown in Listing 12.8.

LISTING 12.8 MyIntArrayList:elementAt().

```
1    public int elementAt(int i) {
2        return list[i];
3    }
```

Making the List Empty

Since all operations on the list depend on the value of last, all that is necessary to make the list empty is to set last to –1, as shown in Listing 12.9.

LISTING 12.9 MyIntArrayList:makeEmpty().

```
1    public void makeEmpty() {
2        last = -1;
3    }
```

If this seems mysterious, draw a picture and make sure you understand what all the methods will do when last has the value –1.

IMPLEMENTATION USING A Vector: MyVectorIntList

The Vector class automatically handles lists of variable sizes, so there is no need for our Vector based class to keep track of where the last element is stored and we can eliminate the variable named last. On the other hand, a Vector stores Objects, and int is a primitive type; thus, to store an int in a Vector it must first be wrapped up in an object. When the wrapper is returned from the Vector, the int value must be unwrapped. Fortunately, both those operations are simple, if mildly annoying.

Java has a built-in int wrapper, named Integer. Given an int variable, x, you can create an Integer that contains the value of x, by:

```
new Integer(x);
```

That's all it takes.

The Integer class has a method, intValue(), that returns the int value that is stored inside the Integer.

```
Integer anInteger = new Integer(17);
int x = anInteger.intValue();
System.out.println("x=" + x);
```

will output "x=17".

The MyVectorIntList class is what is called an *adapter class*; it adapts Vector for use with ints. Every method in the following sections, except toString(), has a body with just one line, which sends the appropriate message to the Vector that MyIntVectorList wraps up. You would do well to glance at the documentation for Vector before reading the next section; either at the Sun site or in the IDE.

Declarations and Initialization

Since this class uses a Vector, java.util.* must be imported, but initialization consists only of instantiating the Vector; see Listing 12.10.

LISTING 12.10   MyIntVectorList: declaration and initialization of the Vector variable.

```
1     import java.util.*;
2
3     public class MyIntVectorList implements IntList {
4
5         private Vector list;
6
7         /** Creates a new instance of List */
8         public MyIntVectorList() {
9             list = new Vector();
10        }
11    }
```

Adding an Element to the End of the List

Vector has an addElement(Object) method, so all that has to be done is wrap the int in an Integer, as shown in Listing 12.11.

LISTING 12.11   MyIntVectorList:addElement().

```
1     public void addElement(int nuElement) {
2         list.addElement(new Integer(nuElement));
3     }
```

A beginning programmer might write this as:

```
public void addElement(int nuElement) {
    Integer nuInteger;
    nuInteger = new Integer(nuElement);
    list.addElement(nuInteger);
}
```

This would also work correctly and is perhaps easier to understand. However, there is no need to type those extra lines, so most experienced (and lazy) programmers would write it as in Listing 12.11.

Adding an Element at a Particular Location

Vector has an addElementAt(Object, int) method, so that can be used, once the int is wrapped, as shown in Listing 12.12.

LISTING 12.12 MyIntVectorList:addElementAt().

```
1    public void addElementAt(int nuElement, int putHereIndex) {
2        list.insertElementAt(new Integer(nuElement), putHereIndex);
3    }
```

The toString() Method

The toString() method can use Vector's iterator(), as shown in Listing 12.13.

LISTING 12.13 MyIntVectorList:toString().

```
1    public String toString() {
2        String returnMe="MyIntVectorList: {";
3
4        for (Iterator it=list.iterator(); it.hasNext();)
5            returnMe += "," + it.next().toString();
6
7        return returnMe + "}";
8    }
```

Aside from that, this is identical to Listing 12.4, including the extra leading comma bug.

Notice that there is no need to cast it.next() in line 5 before sending it toString(). Why is this? The type of it.next() is Object; so why does this compile? It is because toString() is defined in Object, so the compiler is willing to accept it.next().toString(). At runtime, the toString() method will be sent to whatever

`Object it.next()` returns, even though its type is unknown at compile time. This is called *polymorphism* and is an important feature of object programming.

Deleting an Element

`Vector` has an `removeElementAt(int)` method, so that can be used, as shown in Listing 12.14.

LISTING 12.14 `MyIntVectorList:removeElementAt()`.

```
1    public void removeElementAt(int removalIndex) {
2        list.removeElementAt(removalIndex);
3    }
```

Replacing an Element

`Vector` has an `replaceElementAt(Object, int)` method, so that can be used once the `int` is wrapped, as shown in Listing 12.15.

LISTING 12.15 `MyIntVectorList:replaceElementAt()`.

```
1    public void replaceElementAt(int nuValue, int i) {
2        list.setElementAt(new Integer(nuValue), i);
3    }
```

List Length

`Vector` has a `size()` method, so this method returns that; see Listing 12.16.

LISTING 12.16 `MyIntVectorList:length()`.

```
1    public int length() {
2        return list.size();
3    }
```

Accessing an Element

`Vector` has an `elementAt(int)` method, so that is returned. But first, the `Integer` must be unwrapped. The `intValue()` method will return the `int` the `Integer` wraps; but `elementAt()` returns an Object, which must first be cast as an `Integer` (recall the section "`iterator()` Method" in Chapter 11); see Listing 12.17.

LISTING 12.17 MyIntVectorList:elementAt().

```
1    public int elementAt(int i) {
2        return ((Integer) list.elementAt(i)).intValue();
3    }
```

Again, this could be written in two lines, as:

```
public int elementAt(int i) {
    Integer anInteger = (Integer) list.elementAt(i);
    return anInteger.intValue();
}
```

if the programmer felt that was clearer.

This is the only method where you must cast the Object returned from Vector, and then unwrap that Integer to obtain an int. If you used a Vector to store ints and did not write an adaptor class like this, you might end up doing it all over your code and get very tired of it.

Making the List Empty

Vector has a removeAllElements() method, which does the job we need done, as shown in Listing 12.18.

LISTING 12.18 MyIntVectorList:makeEmpty().

```
1    public void makeEmpty() {
2        list.removeAllElements();
3    }
```

TESTING

If you were writing this code from scratch (which would be a good idea, if you wanted to internalize it and be ready to use it, or take a test involving it), you would naturally only write one or two methods at a time, and test them before writing more. This would help you avoid making the same mistake repeatedly in every method and having to fix them all after you realized the problem. You would write the constructor, addElement(), and toString() first (since that is the minimum needed for testing); and then add one or two more at a time. However, if you leave implements IntList in the class definition, you must include all the methods in the interface or it will not compile. So, either leave that out during initial testing, or include all the method headings (with null bodies). Remember, all non-void methods *must* return values of the appropriate type (just return –1 if you don't have a real value to return yet).

The testing code might look like Listing 12.19.

LISTING 12.19   Initial testing code.

```
1    void initList() {
2        theList.addElement(8);
3        theList.addElement(3);
4        theList.addElement(2);
5        theList.addElement(1);
6        theList.addElement(4);
7    }
8
9    void testList() {
10       theList = new MyIntVectorList();
11       initList();
12       System.out.println("after initializing, it's:" + theList);
13   }
```

Once this code produces correct output, you know the constructor, addElement(), and toString() work, so it would be time to write and test the other methods. Listing 12.20 shows such a test.

LISTING 12.20   Testing three more methods.

```
1    void testList() {
2        theList = new MyIntVectorList();
3        initList();
4        theList.addElementAt(17,0);
5        theList.addElementAt(177,3);
6        theList.replaceElementAt(222,2);
7        theList.removeElementAt(3);
8        theList.removeElementAt(4);
9
10       System.out.println("{17,8,222,177,4}?" + theList);
11   }
```

Notice that the println() has the correct output as a String constant, so it will be easy to tell if the output is correct.

JAVADOC

Listing 12.21 shows the addElementAt() method with and without JavaDoc comments.

LISTING 12.21 Code with and without comments.

```
1   public void addElementAt(int nuElement, int putHereIndex) {
2       list.insertElementAt(new Integer(nuElement), putHereIndex);
3   }
4
5   /**
6    * Adds an element at a particular index.
7    * Values from there down are first shifted down one.
8    * Last is incremented (since there is one more thing in the list).
9
10   * @param nuElement the new int value to be inserted
11   * @param putHereIndex where to put the value
12   */
13  public void addElementAt(int nuElement, int putHereIndex) {
14      list.insertElementAt(new Integer(nuElement), putHereIndex);
15  }
```

Figure 12.3 is the portion of the formatted documentation these comments produce.

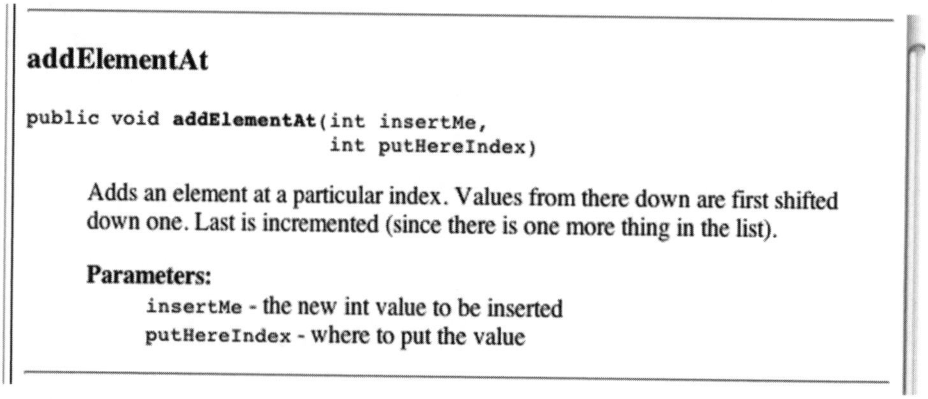

addElementAt

```
public void addElementAt(int insertMe,
                         int putHereIndex)
```

Adds an element at a particular index. Values from there down are first shifted down one. Last is incremented (since there is one more thing in the list).

Parameters:
    insertMe - the new int value to be inserted
    putHereIndex - where to put the value

FIGURE 12.3 JavaDoc output from Listing 12.21.

If your goal is to produce beautifully formatted, professional quality documentation, JavaDoc is a great tool! Its use is described in the section "Adding JavaDoc Comments" in Appendix A.

CONCLUSION

This chapter presented two implementations of interfaces for a list of `ints`. It also introduced JavaDoc for documenting Java programs. Both list classes, one based on an array, the other based on a `Vector`, implemented the `IntList` interface. These will be used in the next chapter as we move on to sorting lists and abstract classes.

REVIEW QUESTIONS

12.1 What is an adapter class?

12.2 How do you get the `int` value into and out of an `Integer` wrapper?

12.3 Which of the two `int` list implements do you prefer? Why?

12.4 Why is it good practice to only write a few methods at a time when implementing a large class using an unfamiliar data structure?

12.5 What's wrong with this code? What exception would it throw?

```
Account [] accountList = new Account[1000];
System.out.println("First Account name is=accountList[0]
    .getName());
```

Programming Exercises

12.6 What would go wrong with the `addElementAt()` method in Listing 12.3 if the loop were rewritten as shown?

```
for (int i=0; i<=last; i++)
    list[i+1] = list[i];
```

12.7 Fix the extra comma bug in the `toString()` method in Listing 12.4. Hint: the problem is that the comma is always added before the element, but it shouldn't be added before the first element. Thus, the action of adding a comma should only be performed under certain conditions.

12.8 Fix the extra comma bug in the `toString()` method in Listing 12.13. Hint: the problem is identical with the previous exercise, but it is not as easy to tell what the condition is. Worst case, you could add a variable to tell you if it is the first time around the loop, but a more elegant solution appends the comma after the `int` (instead of before it) only if there is another `int` coming (you can check `it.hasNext()`).

13

Abstract Classes and Sorting Lists

In This Chapter

- Intuitions for Three Sorts
- Algorithm/Pseudocode
- Implementation
- Making the Sorts More Modular
- Timing the Sorts Using an Abstract Class

INTRODUCTION

There are many reasons why lists need to be sorted. Mailing lists must be sorted by zip code to reduce postage costs. Lists of names are sorted before being displayed to allow a human to find names alphabetically. This chapter will present three simple sorts and then show how to pass them as parameters to a timing method using abstract classes.

Before reading the descriptions of the sorts, take a minute and think of an algorithm to sort a list of `ints`. If nothing comes to mind, use the following.

How would you do it without a computer?
If you can't think of an algorithm for a problem, start solving it yourself and then convert the technique you would use into an algorithm.

So, write down five single-digit numbers in a list and sort them. What did you do? Odds are you used one of the first two techniques that follow.

INTUITIONS FOR THREE SORTS

Sorting algorithms must work on lists of any length, so, speaking abstractly, the length of the list is some fixed number, *n*. For concreteness, assume you have an unsorted list of five `int`s; say, {8,3,2,1,4}. Sorted, this list would be either {1,2,3,4,8} or {8,4,3,2,1}; let's use the former, smallest element first. For insertion and selection sorts it is sometimes easier to create a second list, although traditionally these sorts are done in place. If we create a second list, the original list will be referred to as unsorted and the new list as sorted. Each element from the original list will be added to the sorted list in order (using different techniques in the different sorts).

Insertion Sort

The plan here is to start with an empty list, and repeatedly insert the next element from the unsorted list at the correct location; thus, always keeping the list in order. We start with the unsorted list {8,3,2,1,4} and an empty sorted list, as in Figure 13.1.

unsorted   sorted

| 8 |
| 3 |
| 2 |
| 1 |
| 4 |

FIGURE 13.1 The initial states of the lists.

First, we take the first element, 8, and insert it in the empty sorted list. Thus, we will have a sorted list of length one, {8}, as in Figure 13.2.

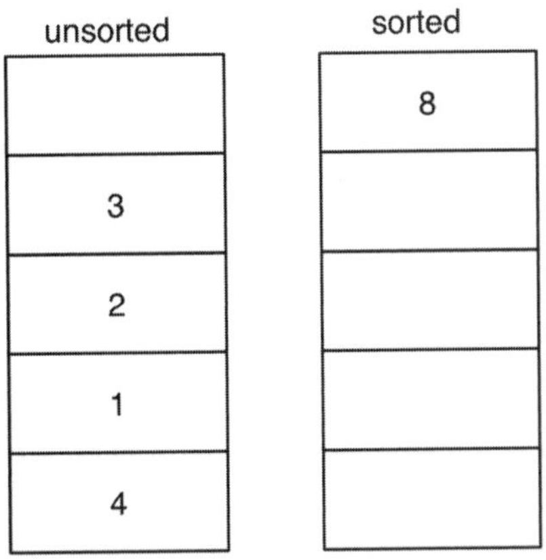

FIGURE 13.2 The lists after one element has been transferred.

Next, taking what was the second element from unsorted, 3, we insert it in order before the 8. We thus have a sorted list of length two, see Figure 13.3.

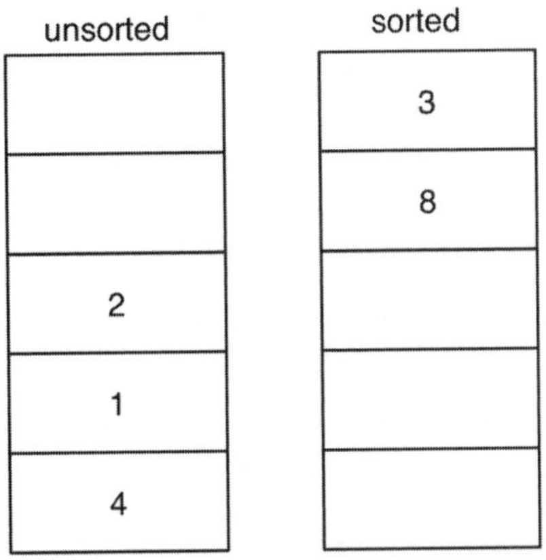

FIGURE 13.3 The lists after two elements have been transferred.

Continuing, the 2 (see Figure 13.4), and the 1 are transferred (see Figure 13.5).

unsorted	sorted
	2
	3
	8
1	
4	

FIGURE 13.4 The lists after three elements have been transferred.

unsorted	sorted
	1
	2
	3
	8
4	

FIGURE 13.5 The lists after four elements have been transferred.

Finally, we have a sorted list of length 5, {1,2,3,4,8} as shown in Figure 13.6.

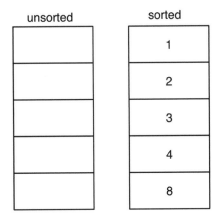

FIGURE 13.6   The lists after all the elements have been transferred.

Before each insertion the sorted list is in order; after each insertion it is still in order and one element longer. The list is always in order; sometimes this fact is referred to as an *invariant*; invariants figure prominently in some styles of programming.

Selection Sort

This is the sort most people invent. The lists begin as shown in Figure 13.7.

unsorted   sorted

| 8 |
| 3 |
| 2 |
| 1 |
| 4 |

FIGURE 13.7   The initial states of the lists for selection sort.

First, select the smallest element in the unsorted list and put it in the empty sorted list, as shown in Figure 13.8.

unsorted	sorted
8	1
3	
2	
4	

FIGURE 13.8 The lists after the smallest element has been transferred.

Next, select the second smallest from unsorted and add it to the end of sorted, as shown in Figure 13.9.

unsorted	sorted
8	1
3	2
4	

FIGURE 13.9 The lists after the two smallest elements have been transferred.

Continuing, locate and transfer the smallest remaining element, the 3 (see Figure 13.10), and then the 4 (see Figure 13.11).

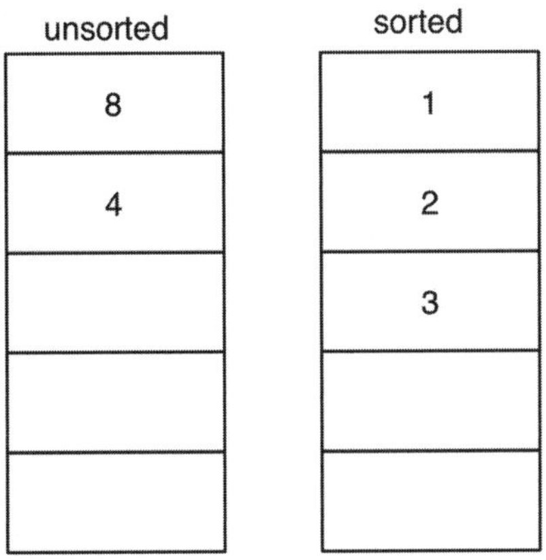

FIGURE 13.10 The lists after the three smallest elements have been selected and transferred.

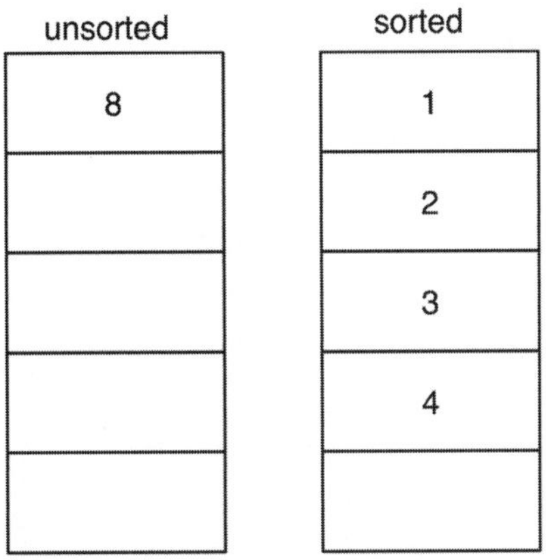

FIGURE 13.11 The lists after the smallest element has been transferred four times.

Finally, take the smallest remaining element (the only one) and add that to sorted. Now the elements are in their proper positions in the sorted list, and the unsorted list is empty, as shown in Figure 13.12.

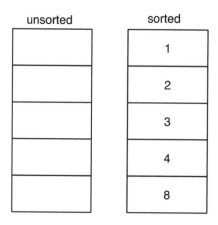

FIGURE 13.12 The lists after all the elements have been transferred.

Bubble Sort

Bubble sort is not a sort people normally invent. However, this much-maligned sort is the simplest to code. It is based on the fact that if every pair of adjacent elements is in the correct order, then the entire list is in order. Thus, a local property produces a global property. The plan is to scan through the list, comparing each pair of adjacent elements and exchanging them if they are out of order. After one pass over the list (from first to last), the largest element is guaranteed to be in the last position. After two passes, the second largest element will be in the second to last position as well. After $n-1$ passes, the entire list will be in order.

Thus, the state of the list during the first pass will be as shown in Figure 13.13 (**bold** elements are about to be compared).

to start	after first swap	after next swap	after third swap	after last swap
8	3	3	3	3
3	8	2	2	2
2	2	8	1	1
1	1	1	8	4
4	4	4	4	8

FIGURE 13.13 The list during the first pass of bubble sort.

Notice that every comparison results in swapping the 8 down (since it is the largest item in the list and started in the first position). The states of the list during the next pass are shown in Figure 13.14.

pass 2 to start	after first swap	after next swap	after third compare	after last compare
3	2	2	2	2
2	3	1	1	1
1	1	3	3	3
4	4	4	4	4
8	8	8	8	8

FIGURE 13.14   The list during the second pass of bubble sort.

On this pass, there are only two swaps as the 3 moves right twice. On the third pass, there is even less movement, only the first two elements are swapped; see Figure 13.15.

pass 3 to start	after first swap	after next compare	after third compare	after last compare
2	1	1	1	1
1	2	2	2	2
3	3	3	3	3
4	4	4	4	4
8	8	8	8	8

FIGURE 13.15   The list during the third pass of bubble sort.

Notice that the list is now in order, after only three passes; in general, *n–1* passes are required, since if the smallest element begins in the last position, it can only move one position up on each pass.

No human would ever sort like this (one would hope), but the machine does the mindless repetition, well, mindlessly, and this algorithm is very easy to code.

ALGORITHM/PSEUDOCODE

The next step, after understanding the mechanics of an algorithm is to write pseudocode describing the operation of the algorithm to carry out that technique. Notice that for this level of description the representation of the list is not specified; it might be an array, a `Vector`, or some other list representation. To understand this pseudocode, you should get a pencil and paper and draw the states of the lists and keep track of the values of the indices as the loops repeat. Just glancing at the pseudocode is not likely to work; if that's what you're going to do, it might be time to put this down and do something constructive.

Insertion Sort Pseudocode

```
create an empty list, called sorted
for each element of unsorted
    find where it goes in sorted*
    insert it there*
```

The asterisks (`*`) indicate that this step requires additional specification. These subalgorithms are candidates for methods when the code is written.

Here is pseudocode for finding the next element goes in the sorted list:

```
:*: find where an element, insertMe, goes in sorted
for each element in sorted (call it current element)
    if insertMe < current element
        return location of current element
return one past the end of the list (since current >= all of them)
```

And, here is pseudocode for inserting an element in a list at location *i*:

```
:*: insert an element at location i
shift the elements from i down, down by 1
store the element at i
```

Selection Sort Pseudocode

```
create an empty list, called sorted
iterate n times (with index, i, moving from first to last in unsorted
    find the location of the smallest item remaining in
    unsorted*
    remove it from unsorted and add it to sorted
```

Finding the minimum element in a list is something that must be done time and again. There are various ways to accomplish this. Here, we need to know where the minimum element is, as opposed to just what it is; otherwise, deleting it from the list will require finding it again. Thus, this algorithm keeps track of the index of the minimum value. Note that minIndex is initially set to the first location.

```
:*: find the smallest item remaining in unsorted
set minIndex to 0
for look=1 to last location of unsorted
    if elementAt(i) < elementAt(minIndex)
        minIndex = i
```

Bubble Sort Pseudocode

```
iterate n times
    do one pass*

:*: do one pass
for each element in the list (except the last)
    if it is > the next element
        exchange them
```

IMPLEMENTATION

All of these sorts can be written as nested loops. They can also be written as single loops that invoke a method or two. The latter is perhaps easier to understand. Which is preferable depends on the context and is a matter of taste.

Bubble Sort Implementation

Listing 13.1 shows a decomposed bubble sort.

LISTING 13.1 Bubble sort decomposed.

```
1    public void bubbleSort() {
2        // iterate n times
3        for (int pass=0; pass<list.length(); pass++) {
4            onePass();
5        }
6    }
7
8    private void onePass() {
9        // for each element in the list (except the last)
10       for (int look=0; look<list.length()-1; look++) {
11           // if it is > the next element
12           if (list.elementAt(look) > list.elementAt(look+1))
13           swap(look, look+1);    // exchange them
14       }
15   }
```

Lines 3–5: Invoke onePass() *n* times (where *n* is the length of the list).

Lines 12–14: Compares adjacent elements (at look and look+1), *n–1* times, and if they are out of order, swaps them

The pseudocode was entered as comments, and the code written around it.

There is no way anyone who understands Java could be confused about what the bubbleSort() method does; it iterates *n* times (*n* being length of the list)—each iteration it does one pass. By contrast, Listing 13.2 presents a nested loop bubble sort implementation.

LISTING 13.2 Bubble sort as a single nested loop.

```
1    public void bubbleSort() {
2        for (int pass=0; pass<list.length(); pass++) {
3            for (int look=0; look<list.length()-1; look++) {
4                if (list.elementAt(look) < list.elementAt(look+1))
6                    swap(look, look+1);
7            }
8        }
9    }
```

This code does what Listing 13.1 did, but using a nested loop. It does exactly the same thing, except the body of onePass() is inserted in the loop in bubbleSort(). Which is better? It depends.

Notice that both alternatives use swap(int, int), illustrated in Listing 13.3.

LISTING 13.3   The swap() method.

```
1    private void swap(int here, int there) {
2        int pocket = list.elementAt(there);
3        list.replaceElement(list.elementAt(here), there);
4        list.replaceElement(pocket, here);
5    }
```

Lines 2–4: Exchange the elements at here and there.

Line 2: Save the element at there in our pocket (so the next line does not clobber it).

Line 3: Replace the element at there with the element at here.

Line 4: Replace the element at here with the element we saved in our pocket.

It swaps the elements at the two indices passed as parameters. Swap is a familiar computing idiom. The use of a temporary variable, pocket, is necessary; what would go wrong with the version in Listing 13.4?

LISTING 13.4   Broken swap() method.

```
1    private void swap(int here, int there) {
2        list.replaceElement(list.elementAt(here), there);
3        list.replaceElement(list.elementAt(there), here);
4    }
```

What's wrong with this code?

This code relies on there being a replaceElement() method in whatever class the list object instantiates (which the IntList interface from Chapter 12, "Interfaces and Writing a List Class" does). It also assumes there is a variable named list in the class in which it exists. In what class should that variable, and the sort methods, be declared? It depends. For testing purposes, they could both be declared in an Applet written simply to do that testing, as shown in Listing 13.5.

LISTING 13.5 `Applet` for testing bubble sort.

```
1   public class SortTest extends java.applet.Applet {
2       IntList list;
3
4       /** Initializes the applet SortTest */
5       public void init() {
6           initComponents();
7           testBubbleSort();
8       }
9
10      private void testBubbleSort() {
11          list = new MyList(8);
12          System.out.println("before bubblesorting, it's:" + list);
13          bubbleSort();
14          System.out.println("after bubblesorting, it's:" + list);
15      }
16  }
```

Line 11: Create and initialize a `MyList` and store it in `list`. Notice that this constructor has an int parameter. This constructor will initialize the list with eight random values (see Listing 13.6).

Line 12: Display the initial state of `list`.

Line 13: Bubble sort `list`.

Line 14: Display the state of `list` after bubble sorting.

Lines 12 and 14: Notice that these assume `list` defines `toString()`.

`MyList` **Implementation**

Since Listing 13.5 uses a `MyList` object, it must be defined. The simplest way to implement it is to extend either `MyIntArrayList` or `MyVectorList` from the previous chapter. The former is used in Listing 13.6.

LISTING 13.6 `MyList` class extends `MyIntArrayList`.

```
1   public class MyList extends MyIntArrayList {
2
3       public MyList(int n, boolean initialize) {
4           super();  // initialize an empty list
5           for (int i=0; i<n; i++) // add n elements
6               addElement(rand(100));  // each between 0-99
```

```
7          }

9          private int rand(int max) {
10             return (int) (Math.random() * max);
11         }
12     } // MyList class
```

Line 4: Invoke the `MyIntArrayList` default constructor. This will create the empty list

Lines 5–7: Add *n* random numbers between 0 and 99. Notice that the object the `addElement` message is sent to is omitted; thus, the compiler inserts `this` so the message is sent to the `MyList` that is being constructed. But, `MyList` does not have an `addElement()` method (as you can plainly see), so the message will go to the superclass, `MyIntArrayList`, which does.

Lines 9–11: The `rand()` method. `Math.random()` returns a `double` in the range [0,1]. That is multiplied by `max` (in this case, 100) to get a `double` in [0,100]. That is cast as an `int`, which truncates anything after the decimal point, yielding a random `int` in [0,99]. The parentheses are necessary since cast has a higher precedence than *.

The `MyList` class only adds the initializing constructor, so some people would prefer to modify the `MyIntArrayList` class. It's a matter of convenience and style; your choice. This way, there is no need to modify `MyIntArrayList`; the other way, there is one less class.

Insertion Sort Implementation

Listing 13.7 presents a decomposed insertion sort.

LISTING 13.7   Insertion sort decomposed.

```
1     public void insertionSort() {
2         //create an empty list, called sorted
3         sorted = new MyList();
4
5         //for each element of unsorted
6         for (int nextI=0; nextI<list.length(); nextI++) {
7             int nextNum = list.elementAt(nextI);
8             //find where it goes in sorted*
9             int putHereIndex = findInsertIndex(nextNum);
10            // insert it there
```

```
11              sorted.addElementAt(nextNum, putHereIndex);
12          }
13
14      list = sorted;
15  }
16
17  public int findInsertIndex(int insertMe) {
18      //for each element in sorted
19      for (int here=0; here<sorted.length(); here++) {
20          //if insertMe < current element
21          if (insertMe < sorted.elementAt(here))
22              //return location of current element
23              return here;
24      }
25      //return one past the end of the list (current >= all of them)
26      return sorted.length();
27  }
```

This sort is rather more complex to code than bubble sort is.

As you can see, the code has been added to the pseudocode (which was first commented out). Look back at the pseudocode to refresh your memory on the plan, before looking closely at the code. In lines 9 and 11, the value returned from findInsertIndex() is stored in a variable, putHereIndex, which is then passed as a parameter to addElementAt(). Thus, these lines could be combined as:

```
sorted.addElementAt(nextNum, findInsertIndex(nextNum);
```

Either technique will work. It is just a question of style.

Notice also that the control idiom from Listing 11.19 is used in findInsertIndex(), which returns as soon as it finds an element in the list that is bigger than the value to be inserted.

The code for selection sort is left to the reader. Realize that if you are stuck, you could type "selection sort java" into a search engine, and it would find numerous implementations. However, of course it will be more educational to write it yourself.

MAKING THE SORTS MORE MODULAR

If you feel it was a bit odd to have the sorts operating on a global variable declared in the applet, your intuition is correct; this was rather peculiar, and not very modular. It would be better to pass the list as a parameter to the sort. This section will show how to do that.

A BubbleSort **Class**

One way to make our bubble sort more modular (and hence reusable) is to define a BubbleSort class, as shown in Listing 13.8.

LISTING 13.8 A BubbleSort class.

```
1     public class BubbleSort {
2
3         private IntList theList;
4
5         public void sort(IntList theList) {
6             this.theList = theList; // store the list
7
8             for (int pass=0; pass<theList.length(); pass++) {
9                 for (int look=0; look<theList.length()-1; look++) {
10                    if (theList.elementAt(look) >
                          theList.elementAt(look+1))
11                        swap(look, look+1);
12                } // inner for
13            }  // outer for
14        }  // sort
15
16        private void swap(int here, int there) {
17            int pocket = theList.elementAt(there);
18            theList.replaceElementAt(theList.elementAt(here), there);
19            theList.replaceElementAt(pocket, here);
20        }
21    }
```

Line 3: The IntList variable is declared private; this is because no other class should ever be able to access it.

Line 16: The swap() method is also declared private, for the same reason.

To use this form of the sort requires instantiating BubbleSort and invoking its sort() method with the IntList you wish to sort. Although Java methods cannot change the values of parameters, they can change the values inside the objects that reference parameters refer to; thus, the list can have its values rearranged by the sort() method.

An InsertionSort **Class**

Similarly, the code for insertion sort can be encapsulated in a class, as shown in Listing 13.9.

LISTING 13.9 An InsertionSort class.

```
1    public class InsertionSort
2
3        private IntList theList;
4
5        public void sort(IntList theList) {
6            this.theList = theList;
7
8            for (int here=0; here<theList.length()-1; here++) {
9                swap(here, findMinIndex(here));
10           }
11       }
12
13       private int findMinIndex(int startingIndex) {
14           int minIndex = startingIndex;
15           for (int look=startingIndex; look<theList.length(); look++)
{
16               if (theList.elementAt(look) < theList.elementAt(minIndex))
17                   minIndex = look;  // where is the biggest so far
18           }
19           return minIndex;
20       }
21
22       private void swap(int here, int there) {
23           int pocket = theList.elementAt(there);
24           theList.replaceElementAt(theList.elementAt(here), there);
25           theList.replaceElementAt(pocket, here);
26       }
27   }
```

Notice the similarities with the BubbleSort class. The theList variable and the swap() method are identical. As always in computing situations, when the exact same code is in two different places, odds are there is some way it could be combined. The next section will show how to do that using an abstract class.

TIMING THE SORTS USING AN ABSTRACT CLASS

Abstract classes can be used to accomplish the organizational function of interfaces. By including abstract methods in a class, every class that extends it will be forced to implement them, just as if their signature were in an interface that class implemented. Additionally, variables and methods that are identical in two (or more) classes can be factored out into an abstract class that those classes extend. This makes the classes smaller, and allows changes to common code to be made just once (and makes it impossible to change the common code in one class and forget to change it in the other). Abstract classes cannot be instantiated; they are used for organizational purposes.

Like interfaces, abstract classes allow you to pass instances of subclasses as parameters with the type of the superclass, as will be seen in the section on the `SortTimer`.

The `AbstractSort` Class

A class is abstract if the reserved word `abstract` precedes `class`. The name of an abstract class may be any legal identifier, but including abstract in the name is a mnemonic.

Factoring Out the Commonalities

The `AbstractSort` class in Listing 13.10 has the method and variable common to `BubbleSort` and `InsertionSort`.

LISTING 13.10   The `AbstractSort` class prototype.

```
1    public abstract class AbstractSort {
2
3        protected IntList theList;
4
5        protected void swap(int here, int there) {
6            int pocket = theList.elementAt(there);
7            theList.replaceElementAt(theList.elementAt(here), there);
8            theList.replaceElementAt(pocket, here);
9        }
10   }
```

Line 1: The reserved word *abstract* makes it an abstract class.

Line 3: The private access has been changed to protected. Having protected access means that subclasses can access `theList`, which is essential if the subclasses are going to work.

Line 5: Again, the private has been changed to protected, for the same reason.

Ensuring that the Subclasses Implement Particular Methods

The timer will send both sorts the `sort()` message and the `toString()` message. To ensure that every subclass of `AbstractSort` implements these methods, they are included as abstract methods. This is shown in Listing 13.11.

LISTING 13.11   The AbstractSort class with abstract methods.

```
1    public abstract class AbstractSort {
2
3        protected IntList theList;
4        public abstract void sort(IntList theList);
5        public abstract String toString();
6
7        protected void swap(int here, int there) {
8            int pocket = theList.elementAt(there);
9            theList.replaceElementAt(theList.elementAt(here), there);
10           theList.replaceElementAt(pocket, here);
11       }
12   }
```

Lines 4 and 5: Abstract methods declared to force subclasses to implement them. This makes it possible to pass subclass instances as parameters of type AbstractSort.

BubbleSort and InsertionSort as Subclasses

Because theList and swap() are defined in AbstractSort, they are inherited and can be omitted from the two subclass sorts, as shown in Listing 13.12 and Listing 13.13.

LISTING 13.12   BubbleSort as a subclass.

```
1    public class BubbleSort extends AbstractSort {
2
3        public void sort(IntList theList) {
4            for (int pass=0; pass<theList.length(); pass++) {
5                for (int look=0; look<theList.length()-1; look++) {
6                    if (theList.elementAt(look) >
                         theList.elementAt(look+1))
7                        swap(look, look+1);
8                }
9            }
10       }
11
12       public String toString() {
13           return "Bubblesort";
14       }
15   }
```

LISTING 13.13 InsertionSort as a subclass.

```
1    public class InsertionSort extends AbstractSort {
2
3        public void sort(IntList theList) {
4            this.theList = theList;
5            for (int here=0; here<theList.length()-1; here++) {
6                swap(here, findMinIndex(here));
7            }
8        }
9
10       private int findMinIndex(int startingIndex) {
11           int minIndex = startingIndex;
12           for (int look=startingIndex; look<theList.length(); look++) {
13               if (theList.elementAt(look) < theList.elementAt(minIndex))
14                   minIndex = look;   // where is the biggest so far
15           }
16           return minIndex;
17       }
18
19       public String toString() {
20           return "Insertion sort";
21       }
22   }
```

Timing the Sorts

Sometimes, people worry about how long an algorithm will take to execute. This makes more sense in some cases than in others. Bubble sort is notoriously slow; the comparison (at line 6 in Listing 13.12) will occur n^2 times (where n is the length of the list). This is because the outer loop will execute n times, and each time the outer loop executes, the inner loop will execute n times as well. For small lists, this doesn't take much time, but if a list with a million elements were sorted this way there would be a trillion comparisons, which would take a while. Who would ever have a list of a million things? Think of the U.S. government, the Census Bureau, or the IRS. Or scientists modeling atmospheric chemistry, or sequencing genomes. In those cases, faster sorts are needed, but they are topics of a more advanced course.

To convince ourselves that the running times of our two sorts are really n^2, we will write a timer class to time them. It will be passed either of them as an AbstractSort. However, how can we tell how long they take to run?

Java includes a method that returns the current time, in a rather odd format. The message: System.currentTimeMillis() will return the number of milliseconds since January 1, 1970, as a long (recall that a long is like an int, but twice as long;

i.e. 64 bits instead of 32, so instead of 2^{32} values, it has 2^{64} values, so it can store values up to 2^{63-1}). Although this is a bizarre format for the current time, it is easy to use it to compute the time some action took. The time to do something can be recorded and output as follows:

```
long startTime = System.currentTimeMillis();
doSomething();
long endTime = System.currentTimeMillis();
long elapsedTime = endTime - startTime;
System.out.println("something took " + elapsedTime);
```

First, record the current time, then do something, then record the current time again; the difference is how long it took.

The SortTimer Class

The SortTimer class is a generic timing algorithm; it can time any AbstractSort sorting any IntList. The constructor is passed the sort and the list, and then time() returns a String with the name of the sort, the length of the list, and the time it took in milliseconds to sort it; as shown in Listing 13.14.

LISTING 13.14   The SortTimer class.

```
1    public class SortTimer {
2
3        AbstractSort theSort;
4        IntList theList;
5
6        /** Creates a new instance of Timer */
7        public SortTimer(AbstractSort theSort, IntList theList) {
8            this.theSort = theSort;
9            this.theList = theList;
10       }
11
12       public String time() {
13           long before = System.currentTimeMillis();
14           theSort.sort(theList) ;
15           long after = System.currentTimeMillis();
16           long elapsedTime = after - before;
17
18           return theSort.toString() + " n=" + theList.length()
                                    + " msec=" + elapsedTime;
19       }
20   }
```

Using the `SortTimer` Class

To run the `SortTimer` requires a main program. One with two buttons (one for each sort) is shown in Listing 13.15.

LISTING 13.15 An application that uses the `SortTimer`.

```
1    public class TimingFrame extends java.awt.Frame {
2
3        /** Creates new form TimingFrame */
4        public TimingFrame() {
5            initComponents();
6            setBounds(10,10,500,400);
7            show();
8        }
9
10       private void initComponents() {//GEN-BEGIN:initComponents
11           theTA = new java.awt.TextArea();
12           bbsortButton = new java.awt.Button();
13           isortButton = new java.awt.Button();
14
15           setLayout(null);
16
17           addWindowListener(new java.awt.event.WindowAdapter() {
18               public void windowClosing(java.awt.event.WindowEvent
                 evt) {
19                   exitForm(evt);
20               }
21           });
22
23           add(theTA);
24           theTA.setBounds(20, 30, 380, 230);
25
26           bbsortButton.setLabel("Bubble");
27           bbsortButton.addActionListener(new java.awt.event.Action
                 Listener() {
28               public void actionPerformed(java.awt.event.ActionEvent
                 evt) {
29                   bbsortButtonActionPerformed(evt);
30               }
31           });
32
33           add(bbsortButton);
34           bbsortButton.setBounds(50, 270, 57, 24);
35
```

```
36            isortButton.setLabel("Insertion");
37            isortButton.addActionListener(new java.awt.event.Action
              Listener() {
38                public void actionPerformed(java.awt.event.ActionEvent
                  evt) {
39                    isortButtonActionPerformed(evt);
40                }
41            });

43            add(isortButton);
44            isortButton.setBounds(250, 270, 64, 24);

46            pack();
47        }//GEN-END:initComponents

49        private void timeEm(AbstractSort theSort) {

51            for (int n=1000; n<10000; n *=2) {
52                SortTimer theTimer = new SortTimer(theSort, new
                  MyList(n));
53                theTA.append(theTimer.time() + "\n");
54            }

56        }

58        private void bbsortButtonActionPerformed(java.awt.event.Action
          Event evt) {//GEN-FIRST:event_bbsortButtonActionPerformed
59            theTA.setText("Bubble sort\n");
60            timeEm(new InsertionSort());
61        }//GEN-LAST:event_bbsortButtonActionPerformed

63        private void isortButtonActionPerformed(java.awt.event.Action
          Event evt) {//GEN-FIRST:event_isortButtonActionPerformed
64            theTA.setText("Insertion sort\n");
65            timeEm(new InsertionSort());
66        }

68        /** Exit the Application */
69        private void exitForm(java.awt.event.WindowEvent evt) {//GEN-
          FIRST:event_exitForm
70            System.exit(0);
71        }//GEN-LAST:event_exitForm

73        // Variables declaration - do not modify//GEN-BEGIN:variables
```

```
74        private java.awt.Button bbsortButton;
75        private java.awt.Button isortButton;
76        private java.awt.TextArea theTA;
77        // End of variables declaration//GEN-END:variables
78
79    }
```

Listing 13.16 is the method that is invoked when the user pushes the InsertSort button (lines 63–66, in Listing 13.15). It is copied because it is much easier to focus on in isolation.

LISTING 13.16 The ActionPerformed() method for the insertion sort button.

```
63   private void isortButtonActionPerformed(java.awt.event.ActionEvent
evt) {
64        theTA.setText("\nInsertion sort\n");
65        timeEm(new InsertionSort());
66   }
```

Line 64: Append the name of the sort, with new lines before and after, to the TextArea.

Line 65: Invoke timeEm() with an InsertionSort instance.

The timeEm() method (reproduced in Listing 13.17) contains a loop. It performs the loop with n=1000, 2000, 4000, and 8000. Each time around the loop, it creates a SortTimer with the AbstractSort passed to it and a list of length n. Then it uses that SortTimer to time whatever sort it was passed, and appends the timing data to the TextArea named theTA.

LISTING 13.17 The code to time insertion sort with n=1000, 2000, 4000, and 8000.

```
49   private void timeEm(AbstractSort theSort) {
50
51        for (int n=1000; n<10000; n *=2) {
52            SortTimer theTimer = new SortTimer(theSort, new MyList(n));
53            theTA.append(theTimer.time() + "\n");
54        }
55
56   }
```

The output from twice invoking `timeEm()` with a `BubbleSort` and then an `InsertionSort` is shown in Listing 13.18.

LISTING 13.18 The output from timing bubble sort, and insertion sort with n=1000, 2000, 4000, and 8000; twice.

```
Bubble sort
Insertion sort n=1000 msec=0
Insertion sort n=2000 msec=110
Insertion sort n=4000 msec=380
Insertion sort n=8000 msec=1430

Insertion sort
Insertion sort n=1000 msec=0
Insertion sort n=2000 msec=110
Insertion sort n=4000 msec=330
Insertion sort n=8000 msec=1490

Bubble sort
Insertion sort n=1000 msec=0
Insertion sort n=2000 msec=50
Insertion sort n=4000 msec=330
Insertion sort n=8000 msec=1480

Insertion sort
Insertion sort n=1000 msec=60
Insertion sort n=2000 msec=50
Insertion sort n=4000 msec=390
Insertion sort n=8000 msec=1480
```

As you can see, for small lists the timing data is meaningless; but as the lists grow larger (i.e., for lengths greater than 2000), they show very clearly that when the length of the list doubles, the running time for both sorts roughly quadruples. Although on different runs, the exact values differ (because the state of the physical machine and the Java virtual machine (JVM) differ unpredictably), this data provides good empirical evidence that the running time of both sorts increases as a function of n^2 as n increases.

CONCLUSION

This chapter presented abstract classes and three simple sorts: insertion, selection, and bubble sort. Insertion and selection sorts mimic the way a human might sort a list, but bubble sort is simpler to code. Sorting is ubiquitous in computing, although perhaps less than titillating.

An abstract class was used to allow various sorts to be passed as parameters to a Timer that timed them. The timer class was used to perform an experiment that demonstrated the running time of both insertion and bubble sort to vary with the square of the length of the list sorted.

The next chapter is the last, and will present a quick overview of all the material in the text.

REVIEW QUESTIONS

13.1 Why is insertion sort called that?

13.2 Why is selection sort called that?

13.3 Why is bubble sort called that?

13.4 Write pseudocode for insertion sort (without copying it).

13.5 Write pseudocode for selection sort.

13.6 Write pseudocode for bubble sort.

13.7 Why are the three sorts presented in this chapter called n^2 sorts? If such a sort takes one second to sort a list of length 1000, how long will it take to sort a list of length 10,000? Length 100,000?

13.8 Compare and contrast interfaces and abstract classes.

13.9 How can you pass sorts (or other algorithms) as parameters?

Programming Exercises

13.10 Write a method, called min(), that returns the minimum of its two int parameters.

13.11 Write a method, called min(), that returns the minimum of its four int parameters.

13.12 Write a method, called min(), that returns the minimum of its eight int parameters.

13.13 Write a method that is passed a list of ints (your choice which kind) and returns the maximum value of those ints.

13.14 Implement and test selection sort.

13.15 Add your selection sort to the TimerFrame program and time it. Which of the three sorts is faster?

13.16 Add a Sort button in your BankDBMS. Sort alphabetically by name. Be sure to rearrange the names in the Choice to be alphabetical as well.

13.17 Add another Sort button that will sort the list by the size of the balance.

14 Lightning Review

In This Chapter

- Once Over, Quickly
- Idioms
- The Process of Programming

ONCE OVER, QUICKLY

This book presented an introduction to Java programming, from scratch. Since the reader was assumed to know no Java at all, the early examples were extremely simple and were explained at length. This chapter will present much of the information in this text in a way that can only be understood by someone who knows something about Java programming and information processing in general. If you have internalized most of the information in the previous chapters, this should all seem simple and obvious. If you have not, it will likely just be words, words, words.

The Basics

Almost all processing in Java is accomplished by sending messages to objects. Every message statement has the syntax:

<object>.<message>(<parameters>)

Objects are instances of classes. Class definitions include variables, and methods; these are both referred to as *members*. There are two types of methods: ordinary methods and constructors. Members may belong to instances, or to classes (the former by default, the latter by the use of the reserved word static).

Methods

A message invokes the method with the matching signature. When a method is invoked, first the parameter linkage is performed, and then the method body is executed. In the body of an instance method, there is a hidden parameter, named this, which is a reference to the object that received the message. If the <object> is omitted before a <message>, Java inserts this as the object (in cases where that would be syntactically correct). This is illustrated on line 10 of Listing 14.1; balance is converted to this.balance implicitly. By contrast, on line 11, this. is typed explicitly.

LISTING 14.1   From Listing 5.7; an example class definition.

```
1    public class Account {
2
3        protected int balance;
4        protected String name;
5
6        public Account(){}    //empty default constructor
7
8        public Account(int nuBal, String name) {  //init'izing constructor
9            this();
10           balance = nuBal;
11           this.name = name;
12       }
13
14       public int getBalance() {return balance;}
15       public String getName() {return name;}
16
17       public void setBalance(int balance) { this.balance = balance;}
18       public void setName(String name) { this.name = name;}
19
20       public String toString() {
```

```
21              String returnMe = "I am a Account: ";
22              returnMe += "\tbalance=" + getBalance();
23              returnMe += "\tname=" + getName();
24              return returnMe;
25          } // toString()
26      }  // Account
```

The syntax of a method definition is [<access>] <type> <name> ([<parameters>]) <body> (see lines 14, 15, 17, 18, and 20 of Listing 14.1), unless the method is a constructor; then its name is the same as the class it is in, and it has no type (lines 6 and 8 of Listing 14.1). A void method returns nothing (lines 17 and 18 of Listing 14.1); a non-void method must end with

```
return <expression>;
```

where <expression> has a type compatible with the return type (lines 14, 15, and 24 of Listing 14.1). Messages invoking non-void methods are, syntactically, expressions of that type (lines 22 and 23 of Listing 14.1).

Variables

Information within a program is stored in variables. There are four types of variables in Java: instance (lines 3 and 4 of Listing 14.1), class, local (line 21 of Listing 14.1), and parameter (lines 8, 17, 18, and 10 of Listing 14.1). They have different scopes (portions of code in which they are defined) and lifetimes; see "Variables II (Varieties and Scope)," in the section "Details II" in Chapter 5, "Toward Consistent Classes" for more detail).

The only way to change the value of a variable is the assignment statement (lines 10 and 11 of Listing 14.1), with one exception; formal parameters are initialized to the values of their corresponding actual parameters when methods are invoked—in a sense, this part of the parameter linkage is an implicit assignment.

Realize that it is possible to declare more than one variable with the same name in the same scope. In that case, the most local variable with a particular name is used. The more local variable hides, or shadows, the less local version. See Listing 14.1, lines 8 and 11 for an example. In that case, you must explicitly add the this. to specify the less local instance variable. Some compilers will catch this error; others will cheerfully ignore it.

Instance Members and Class Members

Variables and methods may be associated either with instances or classes. By default, both are instance members. Instance and class members vary from each other in subtle but important ways.

There are as many copies of each instance variable as there are instances of that class currently instantiated. There is only one copy of each class variable. Thus, information that is peculiar to each instance (like the balance of a bank account) must be stored in instance variables. On the other hand, information that is the same across all instances (like the acceleration due to gravity) can be stored in a class variable.

Static methods do not have access to instance variables, and thus are only useful for implementing actions that do not access instance variables.

There are some very good reasons for advanced students and professional programmers to use class members, but for the most part, beginning programmers can avoid the use of class members unless their instructor feels that they are important to learn early.

Software Reuse

Object-oriented programming allows classes to be reused by two techniques: inheritance and composition.

Inheritance

The ability to extend one class with another is a powerful feature of any object language. Inheritance allows software reuse with a minimum of effort. More importantly, it allows programmers, or teams of programmers, to build enduring class structures. These simplify the tasks of future programmers, who can reuse or extend the extant classes at will. One downside of this is that novice programmers may feel lost until they begin to understand the class hierarchy. Nevertheless, it is possible to use a complex class structure without mastering it.

A good example is `Applet`. If you consult the API documentation at the site:

http://java.sun.com/j2se/1.4.2/docs/api

you will see, at the top, a graphic that looks roughly like Figure 14.1.

java.applet
Class Applet

```
java.lang.Object
   └─java.awt.Component
        └─java.awt.Container
             └─java.awt.Panel
                  └─ java.applet.Applet
```

FIGURE 14.1 The position of `Applet` in the class hierarchy.

This says that `Applet` (which resides in the java.applet package) extends `Panel` (which is in java.awt); `Panel` extends `Container` (again in java.awt); `Container` extends `Component` (from java.awt again); and `Component` extends `Object` (which is part of java.lang). That means that `Applet` inherits all the methods from all those super-classes; about 200 total. What all those methods do is a mystery to an inexperienced Java programmer. However, recalling the very first Java program you ran (see Listing 2.5), even a novice programmer can extend `Applet` to create a working program.

Adding Methods to a Subclass to Add Functionality

Usually when you extend a class, you add functionality by writing additional methods. For example, `FilledCircle` extended `Circle`; it added a color variable and accessors for the color of the `FilledCircle`. See Listing 14.2, lines 4 and 13–16.

LISTING 14.2 A `FilledCircle` class definition.

```
1     import java.awt.*;
2
3     public class FilledCircle extends Circle {
4         protected java.awt.Color myColor;
5         public FilledCircle(){}
6
7         /** Creates a new instance of FilledCircle */
8         public FilledCircle(int x, int y, int r, Color c) {
9             super(x,y,r);
10            setColor(c);
11        }
12
13        public java.awt.Color getColor() {return myColor;}
```

```
14          public void setColor(java.awt.Color c) {
15              myColor = c;
16          }
17
18          public void paint(java.awt.Graphics g) {
19              g.setColor(myColor);
20              g.fillOval(x-radius, y-radius, radius*2, radius*2);
21          }
22      }
```

Overriding Methods to Change Functionality

When you extend a class, some of its methods may do exactly what you want them to, and so not require modifications; they will be invoked automatically from the superclass when their messages are sent to instances of your class. Other methods may need modifications, like paint() in FilledCircle; in that case, a method may be rewritten and thus override the method with the same signature in the superclass (see lines 18–21 in Listing 14.2). Perhaps the most commonly overridden method is toString(). This is because programmers use it for initial testing and debugging, thus it is often among the first methods written when writing a new class.

When overriding a method, the signatures must be identical. If you try to override

```
    public String toString()
```

and leave off the public,

```
    String toString() {...
```

the compiler will say:

```
Game.java [18:1] toString() in Game cannot override toString() in
java.lang.Object; attempting to assign weaker access privileges; was public
```

If you try to make it a class method in the subclass; like this:

```
    public static String toString()
```

the compiler says:

```
Game.java [18:1] toString() in Game cannot override toString() in
java.lang.Object; overriding method is static
```

Accidentally typing `protected`, like this:

```
protected String toString()
```

yields:

```
Game.java [18:1] toString() in Game cannot override toString() in
java.lang.Object; attempting to assign weaker access privileges; was public
```

This is one of the few times that access modifiers are really necessary; most of the time, in small, amateur, one-programmer, one-use programs (like class assignments), they can be omitted without harm (unless, of course, your instructor finds them essential for grading purposes).

Composition

A class can also be reused by including an instance of it in another class. You have seen examples of this in the Eye, SnowPerson, and Bank classes.

Creating Objects (Instances)

Every object must be created by sending new to the appropriate class. If you forget to initialize an object, you will get a null pointer exception if you try to send it a message. Null pointer exceptions are one of the most common bugs, but are always easy to diagnose (at least locally); the problem is always that you are trying to send a message to a null pointer. Sometimes, discerning why the pointer is null is less than trivial, especially if it happened many methods away.

It is especially easy to forget to initialize an object when you have an array of objects. You can initialize the array:

```
Foo[] list = new Foo[100];
```

and forget that if you want to have 100 Foo objects in the list (instead of just 100 null pointers), you must instantiate them all.

When you say new Foo(), it is treated like Foo.Foo(); the Foo() message is sent to the Foo class (classes are, in fact, objects, and constructors are essentially static methods that return a reference to the newly constructed object).

super() and this()

There is a special syntax for invoking one constructor from another. To invoke a constructor in the superclass, use super() (with whatever parameters are appropriate). To invoke another constructor in this class, use this() (again, parameters are allowed; see line 9 of Listing 14.2). Only one of these may appear in a particular constructor and it must come first.

Constructor Chains and Nested Constructors

Object programs often accomplish much of their work in constructors. There are two common techniques; chaining and nesting. When one class extends another, often it is convenient to invoke the superclass' constructor from the subclass' constructor, as illustrated in Listing 14.3.

LISTING 14.3   A constructor chain.

```
1    public class SnowBall extends FilledCircle {
2
3        public SnowBall(int x, int y, int r) {
4            super(x,y,r,java.awt.Color.YELLOW);
5        }
6
7    ...
8
9    public class FilledCircle extends Circle {
10       protected java.awt.Color myColor;
11
12       public FilledCircle(int x, int y, int r, Color c) {
13           super(x,y,r);
14           setColor(c);
15       }
```

The SnowBall constructor invokes the FilledCircle constructor (line 4 of Listing 14.3), which then invokes the Circle constructor (line 13).

Nested constructors, constructors that use the return values of other constructors, are common in methods that do I/O, or use the AWT (see Listing 14.4, lines 30 and 37).

LISTING 14.4   From Listing 10.10 MyReader:openIt(String) and getFileName().

```
28   private void openIt (String filename) {
29       try {
30           br = new BufferedReader(new FileReader(filename));
31       } catch (Exception e) {
32           System.out.println("MyReader:can't open " + filename + "!" +
e);
33       }
34   }
35
```

```
36      private String getFileName() {
37          FileDialog fd = new FileDialog(new Frame(), "Select Input File");
38          fd.setFile("input");
39          fd.show();
40          return fd.getDirectory()+fd.getFile();  // return the complete path
41      }
```

Assignment Compatibility of Objects

Assignment compatibility is an issue in three cases: 1) assignment statements, 2) return statements, and 3) parameter linkage. In the first case, the expression on the right side must be assignment compatible with the variable on the left. In the second case, the returned expression must be compatible with the declared type of the method. In the third case, the actual parameter must be compatible with the corresponding formal parameter.

References to subclasses are always assignment compatible with their superclasses. This is why a Vector can store objects of any type. Every class extends Object, directly or indirectly; thus, objects of any class can be assigned to variables of type Object or returned as return values of type Object. On the other hand, when an instance of some class, say Account, has been stored in a variable of type Object, it can only be sent messages that Objects refer to. This is why objects stored in a Vector, or other generic data structure, must be cast as a particular type when accessed.

IDIOMS

There are a number of idioms that every Java programmer comes to know. Once you have internalized all these, most elementary programming becomes quite simple. Until you become familiar with them, much of programming remains a mystery. If you are trying to learn them, the best way is by typing them in, testing, and experimenting with them. However, only if you want to get good at Java programming.

public static void main(String [] args) {}

Every Java application starts by having its public static void main(String [] args) method invoked. This is a peculiar holdover from C and C++, but we seem to be stuck with it. Although this was initially presented as an incantation, now all its parts have been covered. Now you know that public means it is visible from everywhere; static means it is a class method (i.e., it is sent to the class it appears in, and cannot access instance variables); void means that it does not return anything; and (String [] args) means it has one parameter that is an array of Strings, which is called args locally. The name args is short for arguments; this array can be used to send in command-line (or other) arguments.

Accessors

Accessors are the standard technique for accessing variables in an object. There is a getX() and a setX() method for each variable, x. These are so simple they are written automatically by the ClassMaker, which was introduced in Chapter 5, "Toward Consistent Classes." It takes novice programmers several weeks to internalize enough Java to learn to write accessors, but once they do, they understand a very important part of object programming. Listings 14.1 and 14.2 both contain accessors.

Constructors, Chained and Initializing

It is common for a significant portion of the functionality of a class to be carried out by its constructors, often in concert with other classes' constructors. This was illustrated in Listing 14.3 and Listing 14.4.

toString()

The toString() method is used primarily for testing and debugging. The pattern the ClassMaker follows is to declare a local String returnMe variable, and then concatenate all the instance variables and their values to that.

This technique makes all the toString() methods similar, and so reduces cognitive overhead. The following is from Listing 14.1:

```
20      public String toString() {
21          String returnMe = "I am a Account: ";
22          returnMe += "\tbalance=" + getBalance();
23          returnMe += "\tname=" + getName();
24          return returnMe;
25      } // toString()
26   } // Account
```

Returning Values

There are three idioms related to returning values.

returnMe

When typing a non-void method body, if you make a habit of creating a variable called returnMe, then the last line of the method is always:

```
return returnMe;
```

This helps to avoid forgetting to return anything.

Return to Short Circuit a Loop

Assume you have an array full of ints and want to know if a particular value occurs in the array. You might write a method that returns true just if that value is in the array; as shown here:

```
boolean findAValue(int[] list, int findMe) {
    boolean returnMe = false; // as far as we know

    for (int i=0; i<list.length; i++)
        if (list[i] == findMe)
            returnMe = true; // found it!

    return returnMe;
}
```

This works fine, but there is a slightly more elegant way to do it.

```
boolean findAValue(int[] list, int findMe) {
    for (int i=0; i<list.length; i++)
        if (list[i] == findMe)
            return true; // found it!

    return false; // never found it
}
```

This second technique allows the method to return as soon as if finds the value; the first always searches the entire list.

Returning a boolean Directly

If you had just learned to program and were asked to write a method that returned true just if its parameter was odd, you might write this:

```
boolean odd(int x) {
    boolean returnMe=false;

    if (x % 2 != 0)
        returnMe = true;
    else returnMe = false;

    return returnMe;
}
```

Or perhaps you would realize that returnMe is not doing much, and write this instead:

```
1    boolean odd(int x) {
2        if (x % 2 != 0)
3            return true;
4        else return false;
5    }
```

But, that's all rather silly, since the semantics of that if-else is that if (x % 2 != 0) evaluates to true, then line 3 is executed; otherwise, line 4 is executed. However, the semantics of return true is to evaluate true (which has the value true) and return its value. It's simpler to write:

```
1    boolean odd(int x) {
2        return x % 2 != 0;
3    }
```

Iteration

There are idioms for five different iterative loops.

Over a String by chars

One iterates over a String one char at a time as was shown in Listing 8.18:

```
1    String s="Howdy!";
2    for (int i=0; i<s.length(); i++) {
3        System.out.println("charAt(" + i + ") is: '" + s.charAt(i) + "'");
4    } // for
```

Inside the loop, s.charAt(i) will be each char in order. To perform some other action with each char, simply replace line 3.

Over an Array

Similarly, one iterates over an array, by:

```
void doSomethingWithEachElement(int[] list) {
    for (int i=0; i<list.length; i++)
        something(list[i]);
}
```

Here, in the body of the loop, list[i] is each element of the list, from first to last. Notice that length for an array does not have ()s; life is strange.

Over a Vector

You can iterate over a Vector in two different ways.

Using Iterator

The generic technique to access each element of the Vector in order was shown in Listing 11.6. Here it is:

```
14          for (Iterator it=theList.iterator(); it.hasNext();) {
15              Account nextAccount = (Account) it.next();
16              System.out.println("\n\nnext account..." + nextAccount);
17          }
```

Within the loop, it.next() will return each element in order. The only thing to watch out for is that you must remember to store the element if you need to use it more than once (unlike list[i], it.next() returns a different value each time it is called).

Using an index

You can also iterate over a Vector by hand, like this:

```
for (int i=0; i<theList.size(); i++) {
    Account nextAccount = (Account) theList.elementAt(i);
    System.out.println("\n\nnext account..." + nextAccount);
}
```

This is apropos when you need to access the elements in some way besides just one time through. Notice that instead of `length()` (like a `String`) or `length` (like an array), you must use `size()` for a `Vector`. Sorry, computing is still in its infancy.

Over a File Using `MyReader`

Here is a copy of Listing 10.8:

```
1    MyReader mr = new MyReader();
2
3    while (mr.hasMoreData()) {
4        System.out.println(mr.giveMeTheNextLine());
5    }
6
7    mr.close();
```

In this loop, `mr.giveMeTheNextLine());` returns each line in the file, one by one.

Over a `String` Using `StringTokenizer`

Listing 10.1 showed this simplest use of a `StringTokenizer`:

```
StringTokenizer st = new StringTokenizer("this is only a test...");
while (st.hasMoreTokens()) {
    System.out.println(st.nextToken());
}
```

In this loop, `st.nextToken()` returns portions of the `String` delimited by spaces. For other forms, see "The Other `StringTokenizer` Constructors" in Chapter 10, "Reading and Writing Files."

Wrappers

Sometimes it is useful to write a class that does little more than wrap up another class or some data. Wrapper classes are typically built for convenience, and do not add any functionality past that. A built-in example is `Integer`; another example is `MyReader`.

Integer

You cannot store `int`s in a `Vector` directly since `int` is a primitive type, and not an `Object`. You can get around this by first wrapping the `int` in an `Integer`. To wrap up an `int`, say 17, you write:

```
Integer anInteger = new Integer(17);
```

To unwrap it, simply send it `intValue()`;

```
int x = anInteger.intValue();
```

MyReader

The `MyReader` class in Chapter 10, "Reading and Writing Files," was a wrapper for a `BufferedReader`, which allows you to read files using a `BufferedReader` without dealing with `Exceptions`. The code is long enough that it is not copied here. It may be found in Listings 10.9 through 10.13.

THE PROCESS OF PROGRAMMING

Programming is a process skill. It depends on a number of details, but the skill is in managing the complexity, and developing habits that make debugging easy. There are, roughly speaking, five phases of programming.

Specifying the Problem

Programs are written for reasons. In a programming class, the instructor specifies a problem and assigns students to write solutions for it. In a software company, executives identify demand for a product and direct the management to create it. In a programming class, a student doesn't get much chance to specify the problem to be solved by a program, and can even fail to realize that this is inevitably the first step. If you plan to be an executive instead of a programmer, the question of what software would be useful to people might bear some thought.

Design

Given the specification of a problem, the next step is to design the software to solve that problem. The first step of design is to understand the problem; it is a mistake to solve the wrong problem! Once the problem is understood, a class structure can be developed, and algorithms formulated. After the design is coherent and complete, coding can begin. How much design is necessary depends on how big the program will be, and who is writing it. If the program will only be a few hundred lines, and written by one person, often little design is required. If, by contrast, the program will have millions of lines of code, and be written by hundreds of programmers, considerably more design is in order.

However, big or small, programs that are inadequately designed can be awful to debug. Perhaps you are spending more time, and being more frustrated by, debugging than you would like. Careful design reduces the time and stress of debugging.

Once you reach an intermediate level of sophistication with Java, part of the design process includes specifying interfaces and designing abstract classes. These allow you to conceptualize programs at a higher level of abstraction, which reduces cognitive overhead as the details are abstracted away.

Implementation

Once you have a coherent design, the program can be implemented. Writing code is considered by some novices to be the essence of programming. In a sense it is, but experienced programmers know that design is more important, and that debugging takes much longer.

There are many different styles of programming, even in a particular language. Java is a big language, and code written by different programmers may look completely different. Similarly, different people have different ideas about what constitutes good style. Some people are dogmatic about it, others are more relaxed. There are even courses at the undergraduate and graduate level entitled "Software Engineering."

This text has not harped much on style, but has tried, implicitly, to illustrate and teach the following three principles of software engineering: 1) legibility, 2) flexibility, and 3) robustness.

Legibility

A program is legible (i.e., capable of being read or deciphered) when it 1) is simple, 2) uses meaningful identifiers, and 3) has a consistent style. Defining interfaces and abstract classes can make code much easier to understand; the former as it collects all the public methods into one place, and allows you to completely ignore the details of the implementation, the latter as common code is removed from the subclasses (allowing the programmer to focus on the essentials, and keep down the cognitive overhead).

Flexibility

A program is flexible when it can be modified easily without introducing many new bugs. Object programming tends to increase flexibility, by allowing the programmer to extend a class to do something similar to what the old class did, without modifying the old class. Using constants, like

```
private final static int N=1000;
```

instead of embedding numeric constants like 1000 all over your code makes a program more flexible.

Defining and implementing interfaces helps to make programs flexible, as updated implementations of interfaces can be substituted for old implementations almost effortlessly.

Defining abstract classes and factoring out commonalities from subclasses also makes code simpler and easier to modify.

Robustness

A program is robust if it works on many inputs, not just the one particular set on which it was tested. The use of the Java utilities `StringTokenizer` and `Vector` illustrated generic techniques that improve robustness.

Testing

Part of writing code is testing it. Part of testing code is debugging it when the tests fail. So, this step blurs into the steps before and after it in student programming. In a professional setting, once a programmer completes code, it is submitted to automatic testing protocols; in that case, testing is better delimited.

The importance of testing is that if you test each class as you write it, once you know it works, you can forget about *how* it works. This frees up your cognitive capacity so that you can focus on, and succeed at, the next part of the programming task. A programmer has no more precious resource than cognitive capacity; waste it at your peril!

Debugging

After the various parts of the program are written and tested, they can be assembled. Programs rarely work the first time; finding and fixing the errors is called *debugging*. Debugging can be time consuming, tedious, and frustrating in the extreme. Good design, careful implementation, and thorough testing can combine to reduce the amount and difficulty of debugging. Lack of design, careless implementation, and haphazard testing may result in bugs that can never be found.

CONCLUSION

Programming is not easy. Correctly specifying any non-trivial algorithm to the level of detail that a mindless automaton can perform it is an intellectual feat. Programming expertise is not gained without sustained effort and many hours of practice. If you have persevered and mastered all the concepts in this chapter, congratulations! You have the skills to handle a great number of programming problems. If you started this text not knowing how to program and at least recognize all the concepts in this chapter, you have learned a tremendous amount; good job!

One course, no matter how well constructed, and no matter how talented and dedicated the student or the instructor, cannot provide the level of expertise a professional has. This is true whether the course is in programming, writing, or tennis. Professional-level expertise takes many years to achieve. However, if you have understood the basics of object programming, you know more than most of the people on the planet. May you make good use of your expertise. If you have read this entire book, you have demonstrated amazing patience; programming texts are not quite as riveting as novels—thank you for your attention. Farewell.

Appendix

A NetBeans 4.1 Appendix

GETTING STARTED WITH NETBEANS AND THE GREETINGS PROGRAM

There are four steps to get started with NetBeans. If you (or someone else) have already downloaded and installed the program, you can skip the first step. After that, there are three steps: 1) start up NetBeans, 2) create a project, and 3) modify and execute the main program.

Download and Install NetBeans

If NetBeans is not installed on the machine you are using (lab machines will have it installed already), download and install NetBeans and the current JDK from the Web (*www.netbeans.org*); there are good instructions there.

Start NetBeans

Open the NetBeans Launcher to start the IDE (integrated development environment). On a PC, double-click the icon; on a Mac, single-click.

Create a New Project

1. Create a new project (File/New Project); click on the File menu in the menu bar at the extreme upper left (just under where it says NetBeans IDE 4.0 in the title bar—the bar at the top of each window is called the title bar, and normally contains the name of the window), and then click New Project in the list that opens under it. This will open a New Project window (i.e., the title bar of the new window will say "New Project").
2. In the New Project window:
   a. Under Categories (the left hand white pane), select General.
   b. Under Projects (the right-hand white pane), select Java Application.

    c. Press the Next > button; this will open a New Java Application window

3. In the New Java Application window:

    a. In the Project Name: text field, type the name you want for your Application. You may type any legal name (confine yourself to letters, numbers and underscores to be safe), but on this first try, just type Test.

    b. In the Project Location: text field, type the directory you wish to store all the files for this project in; or use the Browse button to navigate to it. It does not matter what you name it, or where it is exactly, but it will be simpler in the long run if you keep your files in directories under a directory called "programming," or some such. Browse will take you to the Explorer in a PC environment, or the Finder in a Mac environment where you can create a new directory (also called a *folder*).

    c. Press the Finish button. After a short delay, the new project will appear. There will be a file in the right-hand pane, in a tab with the name "Main.java" that looks like Listing A.1.

LISTING A.1   Simplest Application created with NetBeans.

```
1    /*
2     * Main.java
3     *
4     * Created on February 22, 2005, 7:11 PM
5     */
6    package test;
7    /**
8     *
9     * @author levenick
10    */
11   public class Main {
12       /** Creates a new instance of Main */
13       public Main() {
14       }
15       /**
16        * @param args the command line arguments
17        */
18       public static void main(String[] args) {
19           // TODO code application logic here
20       }
21   }
```

This is what NetBeans writes for you when you create an Application.

Modify and Execute the Main Program

1. Replace `//TODO code application logic here` with `System.out.println("greetings");` in the main method (line 19). There is a shortcut for this; simply type `sout` followed by a space. When you wish to display something from inside your program, you will often want to use `System.out.println("something");`.

   The NetBeans authors put in a shortcut, `sout` space, for your convenience.

2. Execute the program (Run/Run Main Project); if you made no typing mistakes, some lines like

   ```
   init:
   ```

   and

   ```
   run:
   ```

   Then

   ```
   greetings
   ```

   should appear in the output window (the output window is the window at the bottom that says "Output" in the title bar). If you would like to set your program's output off with blank lines to make it easier to see, add a newline before and after greetings—newline is `\n`, called backslash-n. This is not the front slash, `/`, but the backslash. So, the new line 19 would be `System.out.println("\ngreetings\n");`.

CREATING THE SIMPLEST Applet IN NETBEANS

Creating an `Applet` is slightly different from creating an `Application`, but consists of almost the same three steps: 1) start up NetBeans, 2) create a project, and 3) modify and execute the code NetBeans writes automatically. This may seem complicated and confusing now, but in a few weeks this will seem simple; honest, it's just a question of doing it enough times to become familiar with the process.

Start NetBeans

As done previously, open the NetBeans Launcher to start the IDE. On a PC, double-click the icon; on a Mac, single-click.

Create a New Project

1. Just as for an Application, create a new project (File/New Project); click on the File menu in the menu bar at the extreme upper left (just under where it says NetBeans IDE 4.0 in the title bar—the bar at the top of each window is called the "title bar," and normally contains the name of the window), and then click New Project in the list that opens under it. This will open a New Project window (i.e., the title bar of the new window will say "New project").

2. Just as for an Application, in the New Project window:
   a. Under Categories: (the left-hand white pane) select General.
   b. Under Projects: (the right-hand white pane) select Java Application.
   c. Press the Next > button; this will open a New Java Application window.

3. Just as for an Application, in the New Java Application window:
   a. In the Project Name: text field, type the name you want for your Application. You may type any legal name (confine yourself to letters, numbers and underscores to be safe), but on this first try, just type TestApplet.
   b. In the Project Location: text field, type the directory you wish to store all the files for this project in; or use the Browse button to navigate to it.
   c. Press the Finish button. After a short delay, the new project will appear. There will be a file in the right-hand pane, in a tab with the name "Main.java" that looks like Listing A.2.

LISTING A.2 Main.java created with NetBeans.

```
1    /*
2     * Main.java
3     *
4     * Created on February 22, 2005, 7:11 PM
5     */
6    package testapplet;
7    /**
8     *
9     * @author levenick
10    */
11   public class Main {
12       /** Creates a new instance of Main */
13       public Main() {
14       }
```

```
15        /**
16         * @param args the command line arguments
17         */
18        public static void main(String[] args) {
19            // TODO code application logic here
20        }
21    }
```

This is the same thing that NetBeans writes for you when you create an `Application`. The only difference between this and Listing A.1 is that line 6 says `testapplet` instead of `test`.

Create, Modify, and Execute the `Applet`

1. To create an `Applet`, choose File/New File; this will open a New File window.
2. In the New File window:
   a. Under Categories:, select Java Classes.
   b. Under File Types:, select Applet.
   c. Press the Next > button; this will open the New Applet window.
3. In the New Applet window:
   a. In the Class Name: text field, type the name of the `Applet` class, for the first one type `TestApplet`.
   b. Press the Finish button. This will generate the code shown in Listing A.3.

LISTING A.3   `TestApplet.java` created with NetBeans.

```
1     /*
2      * TestApplet.java
3      *
4      * Created on February 22, 2005, 7:56 PM
5      */
6     package testapplet;
7     /**
8      *
9      * @author levenick
10     */
11    public class TestApplet extends java.applet.Applet {
12        /** Initialization method that will be called after the applet
          is loaded
13         *   into the browser.
14         */
15        public void init() {
```

```
16                  // TODO start asynchronous download of heavy resources
17          }
18          // TODO overwrite start(), stop() and destroy() methods
19      }
```

4. Replace line 16 with `System.out.println("I wrote an Applet!");`.
5. Execute the `Applet`:
   a. In the left-hand pane, under the Projects tab, there should be the name of your project (`testApplet` if you followed the previous instructions) to the right of a coffee cup icon. Expand it by clicking the small + button to the left of it. This should show two folders: Source Packages and Test Packages.
   b. Expand Source Packages (the + button). This should show one line, again called `testApplet` with a package icon.
   c. Expand the `testApplet` package (again, the + button). This should show two files: Main.java, and TestApplet.java.
   d. Right-click TestApplet.java (i.e., click with the right mouse button); this will open a menu.
   e. Select Run File. You should see some output in the Output window, including `I wrote an Applet!`, and a small window should open in the upper left of the screen, with the title Applet Viewer: testapplet/TestApplet.class—this is the running Applet. It doesn't do much, but try resizing it and selecting Clone... from the `Applet` menu.

CREATING A GUI `Applet`

Creating a GUI `Applet` is very much like creating an non-GUI `Applet`.

Follow the instructions in the previous section to 1) Start up NetBeans, and 2) Create a project (call your project `testGUIApplet` in step 3). Then, follow the instructions following to create, modify, and execute the GUI `Applet`.

Create a GUI `Applet`

1. To create an `Applet`, choose File/New File, this will open a New File window.
2. In the New File window:
   a. Under Categories:, expand Java GUI Forms (click the + button).
   b. Select AWT Forms.
   c. Under File Types: select Applet Form.
   d. Press the Next > button; this will open the New Applet window.

3. In the New Applet window:
   a. In the Class Name: text field, type the name of the `Applet` class, for this one type `GUIApplet`.
   b. Press the Finish button. This will generate the code for the skeleton of an `Applet`, and open the visual editor in the center of the screen. The `Applet` displays as the outline of a blue rectangle.
   c. Look around at the various parts of the screen. Think of it as a new environment you have never seen before, but that you are likely to be spending considerable time in. As in a real environment, the first thing to do is get oriented. What's where? Sometimes, people make the mistake in a computing environment of not taking the time to look around, to orient themselves, to become familiar. They feel like there is something they need to accomplish, and just want to know which button to push. That is not the way to become an expert in a computing (or any) environment.
4. There are five distinct regions displayed in this mode. At some point, you will need to become familiar with most of them. Is this the best time to learn them? Here are brief descriptions—feel free to learn them now, or later; your choice.
   a. At the top of the screen, right under the title bar (which says NetBeans IDE...) is the menu bar (with File, Edit, View...Help), and under that is a tool bar. If you hover the cursor over items in the tool bar, they will display their function. Notice that the two leftmost icons are New File and New Project, so if you would prefer to push the New File button instead of clicking File/New, you can. Notice also that along with New File, hovering displays (Ctrl+N); that means holding down the control key and pressing n is the keyboard equivalent of pushing that button (this is sometimes written as ctrl-n and other times as ^n).
   b. At the bottom of the screen is the Output window (notice that its title is "Output").
   c. On the left is a pane that has three tabs, labeled Projects, Files, and Runtime. Click each to select it. The only one you need right now is Projects. It is important to realize that there are tabs there; if Files is selected instead of Projects, and you click in the left pane, expecting it to work like Projects (and it looks rather like it), you may be disappointed. Dismiss the Files and Runtime tabs (by clicking the little x in the upper left); that way, there's no chance of making that mistake. How to get them back? In the menu bar, click Window/Files, or Window/Runtime. Try out the little arrow-box icon right next to the x. Notice that the tab moves over to the left margin. You can restore it by clicking that icon and then the little dot (where the arrow-box used to

be).

d.   The center portion is the editor; it is another tabbed pane, and contains the files that are open. This is an ordinary text editor; and can be used to view and change any text file. There should be two tabs (assuming you closed your old projects before creating the GUI Applet project; if you did not, they are all still open in the Project tab, and the source files are still open in the editor—you can close them with the little x in the corner of the tab) labeled Main.java and TestGUIApplet. The latter is selected (and so is bluish). Select the Main.java tab and you will see the code from Listing A.2. Now select the TestGUIApplet tab. Just under the tabs are two buttons labeled "Source" and "Design." The latter (which is depressed) selects the visual editor mode for a GUI Component. Press the Source button to go to the text editor and you will see the code for your GUI Applet, as shown in Listing A.4. Notice that the right-hand portion of the screen disappears when in Source mode. Click Design to go back to the visual editor.

e.   The right side of the screen has three panels labeled Palette, Inspector, and Other Components—Properties. These are used in adding and modifying elements to your GUI, as will be described shortly.

LISTING A.4   `TestGUIApplet.java` **created with NetBeans.**

```
1    /*
2     * TestGUIApplet.java
3     *
4     * Created on February 23, 2005, 11:16 AM
5     */
6
7    package testguiapplet;
8
9    /**
10    *
11    * @author   levenick
12    */
13   public class TestGUIApplet extends java.applet.Applet {
14
15       /** Initializes the applet TestGUIApplet */
16       public void init() {
17           try {
18               java.awt.EventQueue.invokeAndWait(new Runnable() {
19                   public void run() {
20                       initComponents();
21                   }
```

```
22                });
23            } catch (Exception ex) {
24                ex.printStackTrace();
25            }
26        }
27
28        /** This method is called from within the init() method to
29         * initialize the form.
30         * WARNING: Do NOT modify this code. The content of this method
is
31         * always regenerated by the Form Editor.
32         */
33        private void initComponents() {
34
35            setLayout(new java.awt.BorderLayout());
36
37        }
38
39
40        // Variables declaration - do not modify
41        // End of variables declaration
42
43    }
```

That is a lot of code (and comments); everything between /* and */ are comments, and anything on a line after // are comments. Comments are for people to read, Java does not see them; the part of Listing A.4 that is actually Java code is shown in Listing A.5.

LISTING A.5 `TestGUIApplet.java` created with NetBeans with comments deleted.

```
7     package testguiapplet;
8
13    public class TestGUIApplet extends java.applet.Applet {
14
16        public void init() {
17            try {
18                java.awt.EventQueue.invokeAndWait(new Runnable() {
19                    public void run() {
20                        initComponents();
21                    }
22                });
23            } catch (Exception ex) {
24                ex.printStackTrace();
```

```
25              }
26          }
27
33          private void initComponents() {
34
35              setLayout(new java.awt.BorderLayout());
36
37          }
43      }
```

But, do not delete the comments in your code, or the visual editor will become confused.

Set the Layout to Null

The last thing you should do when you create a GUI `Applet` is to set the layout to null. If you omit this, and add a button, it will fill the entire Applet. Here's how:

1. Select the TestGUIApplet tab in the editor (the center portion of the screen).
2. Select Design mode, if it is not already selected (it will display an empty rectangle).
3. Expand the [Applet] on the Inspector pane (on the right, second pane from the top) by clicking the + button.
4. Right-click BorderLayout, select SetLayout, and then select Null Layout.

Continue with the next section, "Adding, Connecting and Testing a `Button`," to add a `Button`.

ADDING, CONNECTING, AND TESTING A `Button`

Continuing from the previous section, "Set the Layout to Null," or anytime you have the visual Editor open (select the `ATM_Applet` tab and the Design button in the top bar to open it) and the Layout set to Null Layout already (you can check by expanding the [Applet] in the Inspector—to set it if it is not set, right-click BorderLayout, select SetLayout, then select Null Layout).

Add an AWT `Button`

1. Select (click) the AWT tab in the Palette pane (on the right, at the top). Click on the `Button` icon (top row, second from left, with the OK on it, just right of the big A).
2. Click in the `Applet` pane (the colored rectangle). A `Button` should appear where you clicked, with the label button1.

Connect It to Your Program

Double-click the button. You will be taken to the text editor, with the cursor positioned in the `private void button1ActionPerformed(...)` method; line 51 in Listing A.6 (which was copied from NetBeans).

LISTING A.6   `Applet` GUI with a single `Button`—first pass.

```
1      /*
2       * TestGUIApplet.java
3       *
4       * Created on February 23, 2005, 11:16 AM
5       */
6
7      package testguiapplet;
8
9      /**
10      *
11      * @author   levenick
12      */
13     public class TestGUIApplet extends java.applet.Applet {
14
15         /** Initializes the applet TestGUIApplet */
16         public void init() {
17             try {
18                 java.awt.EventQueue.invokeAndWait(new Runnable() {
19                     public void run() {
20                         initComponents();
21                     }
22                 });
23             } catch (Exception ex) {
24                 ex.printStackTrace();
25             }
26         }
```

```
27
28      /** This method is called from within the init() method to
29       * initialize the form.
30       * WARNING: Do NOT modify this code. The content of this method
is
31       * always regenerated by the Form Editor.
32       */
33      private void initComponents() {
34          button1 = new java.awt.Button();
35
36          setLayout(null);
37
38          button1.setLabel("button1");
39          button1.addActionListener(new java.awt.event.ActionListener() {
40              public void actionPerformed(java.awt.event.ActionEvent
evt) {
41                  button1ActionPerformed(evt);
42              }
43          });
44
45          add(button1);
46          button1.setBounds(190, 150, 57, 24);
47
48      }
49
50      private void button1ActionPerformed(java.awt.event.ActionEvent
        evt) {
51          // TODO add your handling code here:
52      }
53
54
55      // Variables declaration - do not modify
56      private java.awt.Button button1;
57      // End of variables declaration
58
59  }
```

Line 51 reads:

```
// TODO add your handling code here:
```

Anything on a line after a // is a comment and is only visible to the programmer; the compiler ignores it.

Because you double-clicked the Button in the visual Editor, NetBeans wrote code that will be executed when you push the Button (when the Applet is running). In particular, the private void button1ActionPerformed(...) method will be executed each time the button is pushed. To test that that actually happens, replace

//TODO add your handling code here: in line 51

with System.out.println("button was pushed"); or some similar message.

Test It

As before, compile and execute your Applet, by:

1. In the left-hand pane, under the Projects tab, there should be the name of your project (testApplet if you followed the previous instructions), to the right of a coffee cup icon. Expand it by clicking the small + button to the left of it. This should show two folders: Source Packages and Test Packages.
2. Expand Source Packages (the + button). This should show one line, again called testGUIApplet with a package icon.
3. Expand the testGUIApplet package (again, the + button). This should show two files: Main.java and TestApplet.java.
4. Right-click TestGUIApplet.java (i.e., click with the right mouse button); this will open a menu. Select Run File.
5. Press the Button and it should output your message to the output window. Push the Button several times. Assuming you see the message repeated each time you push the Button, it's working!

CREATING A GUI Application

This is almost identical to creating a GUI Applet. The only difference is that you must choose Frame Form instead of Applet Form, and you must add a setBounds() message in init(). Once that's done, you can use the visual editor to add components.

Follow the instructions in the previous section to 1) start up NetBeans, and 2) create a project (call your project testGUIApplet in step 3). Then, follow the instructions following to create, modify, and execute the GUI Applet.

Create a Frame Form

1. To create an Application, choose File/New File, this will open a New File window.
2. In the New File window:

     a. Under Categories:, expand Java GUI Forms if it is not already expanded (click the + button).
     b. Select AWT Forms.
     c. Under File Types:, select Frame Form.
     d. Press the Next > button; this will open the New Frame Form window.
3. In the New Frame Form window:
     a. In the Class Name: text field, type the name of the Frame class; for this one, type `TestFrame`.
     b. Press the Finish button. This will generate the code for the skeleton of the Frame, and open the visual editor in the center of the screen. The Frame displays as the outline of a blue rectangle.

Set the Layout to Null

Again, there are three steps:

1. Select the TestFrame tab in the editor (the center portion of the screen).
2. Select Design mode, if it is not already selected (it will display an empty rectangle).
3. In the Inspector pane (on the right, second pane from the top), right-click the [Frame] and select Set Layout; then click Null Layout.

Making the `Frame` Bigger

Unless you add a `setBounds()` method in the constructor, the `Frame` will be very small. Line 18 in Listing A.7 shows how to fix this; the four parameters are the usual for a rectangle, (`x`, `y`, `width`, `ht`).

LISTING A.7   Making the `Frame` bigger.

```
1    /*
2     * TestFrame.java
3     *
4     * Created on February 23, 2005, 3:10 PM
5     */
6
7    package testframe;
8
9    /**
10    *
11    * @author  levenick
12    */
```

```
13    public class TestFrame extends java.awt.Frame {
14
15        /** Creates new form TestFrame */
16        public TestFrame() {
17            initComponents();
18            setBounds(100,100,400,400);
19        }
20
```

Line 18: NetBeans does not write this line for you, and if you forget it, your Frame will be very small and in the upper left corner. You can move it by clicking and dragging the title bar, and make it bigger by clicking and dragging the lower right corner; but the right way to fix it is by adding line 18.

ADDING A POP-UP Frame

Sometimes, you want a frame to display something, or interact with the user, but you only want it to appear when necessary. This can be done using a Frame Form, just as in "Creating a GUI Application," with the following changes.

1. Delete the main() method (this is not an Application and no one will ever send it a main() message).
2. Change System.exit(1); to setVisible(false); in exitForm() on line 41 of Listing A.8.

LISTING A.8 Expanding the Frame, and avoiding ending the program when it closes.

```
1     /*
2      * TestFrame.java
3      *
4      * Created on February 23, 2005, 3:10 PM
5      */
6
7     package testguiapplet;
8
9     /**
10     *
11     * @author   levenick
12     */
13    public class TestFrame extends java.awt.Frame {
14
```

```
15        /** Creates new form TestFrame */
16        public TestFrame() {
17            initComponents();
18            setBounds(100,100,400,400);
19        }
20
21        /** This method is called from within the constructor to
22         * initialize the form.
23         * WARNING: Do NOT modify this code. The content of this method
   is
24         * always regenerated by the Form Editor.
25         */
26        private void initComponents() {
27
28            setLayout(null);
29
30            addWindowListener(new java.awt.event.WindowAdapter() {
31                public void windowClosing(java.awt.event.WindowEvent
    evt) {
32                    exitForm(evt);
33                }
34            });
35
36            pack();
37        }
38
39        /** Exit the Application */
40        private void exitForm(java.awt.event.WindowEvent evt) {
41            setVisible(false);
42        }
```

Line 18: Resizing your `Frame`.

Line 41: `exitForm()` is sent when the user closes the `Frame`; NetBeans writes it to send `System.exit()`, which exits the program. This way, the `Frame` is simply rendered invisible, and the program continues.

ADDING, CONNECTING, AND TESTING A `TextField`

This is just like adding the `Button` (see the earlier section "Adding, Connecting, and Testing a `Button`"). Open the visual editor (you can do this by selecting the pane with the GUI `Frame`, or `Applet` you wish to add the `TextField` to). Make sure the

AWT tab is selected in the Palette pane. Click the TextField icon (just to the right of the Button icon), and then click in the form rectangle (as the upper left corner of where you want it to appear (you can move it by clicking and dragging it). A TextField should appear. Double-click it. You will be switched to the text editor, ready to add code that will be executed when the user presses Enter in the TextField; see Listing A.9.

LISTING A.9 Applet fragment with a Button and a TextField.

```
1    private void textField1ActionPerformed(java.awt.event.ActionEvent
     evt) {
2        // TODO add your handling code here:
3    }
4
5    private void button1ActionPerformed(java.awt.event.ActionEvent evt)
{
6        System.out.println("they pushed the button!!");
7    }
```

Listing A.6 is what NetBeans writes for you when you add a TextField and Button and double-click both in the visual editor.

Replace the comment at line 2 with the code:

```
System.out.println("TextField contains: " + textField1.getText());
```

Execute the Applet or Frame; try typing in the TextField and then pressing Enter.

ADDING A TextArea

Adding a TextArea is exactly like adding any other Component. Click the TextArea icon (fourth from the left—hover over the icons to see their names), in the AWT pane of Palette window in the visual editor view of the Applet. Then, click where you want it, resize it, and rename it. If you always call your TextAreas the same thing, like theTA, you won't have to remember what they are called later when you want to access them.

ADDING AND USING A `Choice`

As with other AWT `Components`, choose the AWT pane of the Palette window in the visual editor view, click on the Choice icon (sixth from the left—hover over the icons to see their names), and then in the visual editor (yes, choose Null Layout to get control of the size). Now:

1. Change its name (maybe to `theChoice`).
2. Select Events in the Properties pane (`theChoice` must be selected for this to work).
3. Select `ItemStateChanged` and click the ellipses box; a "Handlers for Item-StateChanged" window will open; click "Add..." in it.
4. Type a name for the method that will be invoked when the user selects a new item in the `Choice`; `newItemSelected` is an idea. Press enter, and then click the OK button. NetBeans will write the code and flip you to it. It will look like this:

```
1    private void newItemSelected(java.awt.event.ItemEvent evt) {
2        // TODO add your handling code here:
3    }
```

5. Put some items in the Choice's list of choices, right after `initComponents()` in the constructor. Like this:

```
public BankDBMS() {
    initComponents();
    theChoice.addItem("this");
    theChoice.addItem("that");
    theChoice.addItem("the other thing");
```

6. To test the `Choice`, write the following code in place of line 2 in the preceding code, in `newItemSelected()`:

```
String item = theChoice.getSelectedItem();
System.out.println("new choice from the choice: " + item);
```

7. Execute the program to make sure it's working. Then, the `item` variable can be used as a parameter to whatever method you want `newItemSelected()` to invoke.

CHANGING THE LABEL ON A Button

The default label on Buttons is button1, button2, and so on. To change the label of a Button:

1. Click on the Button.
2. In the Properties pane (on the right, under the Inspector), make sure the Properties button is active (there are three tabs: Properties, Events, and Code); select button1 next to Label (sixth line down).
3. Type the new label myFirstButton, or whatever.
4. Resize the button so you can read the entire label if necessary (click and drag its border).

RENAMING Components

When you create Components, NetBeans gives them names like button1, button2, and so on. To change the name of a Button:

1. Click on the Button.
2. In the Inspector pane (on the right), its name should be highlighted; click on that, once, and wait for it to select the current name.
3. When button1 (or whatever) is selected; type the name you wish to give it instead. Hint: use the class of the component in its name, like testButton. Note: you must press Enter after you finish typing, or the name will not change.

CREATING A CLASS

1. First, have the project you are working on open.
2. Create a new file (File/Add New); a New File window will open.
3. In the New File window:
    a.   Under Categories: select Java classes.
    b.   Under FileTypes: select Java Class.
    c.   Press Next >; a New Java Class window will open.
4. Type the name of the class and press Finish; a text editor window with the shell of the class will open.

CREATING A CLASS WITH A TEST DRIVER

1. First, have the project you are working on open.
2. Create a new file (File/Add New); a New File window will open.
3. In the New File window:
   a.   Under Categories: select Java classes.
   b.   Under FileTypes: select Java Main Class.
   c.   Press Next >; a New Java Class window will open.
4. Type the name of the class and press Finish; a text editor window with the shell of the class will open.

LISTING A.10   An `Account` class shell with a main method.

```
1     /*
2      * Account.java
3      *
4      * Created on June 25, 2004, 2:13 PM
5      */
6     package bankapplet;
7     /**
8      *
9      * @author  levenick
10     */
11    public class Account {
12
13        /** Creates a new instance of Account */
14        public Account() {
15        }
16
17        /**
18         * @param args the command line arguments
19         */
20        public static void main(String[] args) {
21            // TODO code application logic here
22        }
23
24    }
```

SETTING THE MAIN CLASS

1. Right-Click the project node in the Projects window and choose Properties.
2. Click Running Project in the left pane of the dialog box.
3. Use the Browse button to choose the project main class.

CHANGING THE SIZE OF AN Applet

To set the size of the `Applet` to 500x500 pixels, add

```
setSize(500,500):
```

in the body of the `init()` method.

LISTING A.11   `TestApplet.html`.

```
1    <HTML>
2    <HEAD>
3      <TITLE>Applet HTML Page</TITLE>
4    </HEAD>
5    <BODY>
6
7    <!--
8    *** GENERATED applet HTML launcher - DO NOT EDIT IN 'BUILD' FOLDER  ***
9
10   If you need to modify this HTML launcher file (e.g., to add applet
11   parameters),
12   copy it to where your applet class is found in the SRC folder. If you do
13   this,
14   the IDE will use it when you run or debug the applet.
15
16   Tip: To exclude an HTML launcher from the JAR file, use exclusion
     filters in
17   the Creating JAR page in the Project Properties dialog.
18
19   For more information see the online help.
20   -->
21
22   <H3><HR WIDTH="100%">Applet HTML Page<HR WIDTH="100%"></H3>
23
24   <P>
25   <APPLET
```

```
26      codebase="file:/C:/javaText/testApplet/testApplet/build/classes/"
27      code="testguiapplet/TestApplet.class" width=350 height=200></APPLET>
28      </P>
29
30      <HR WIDTH="100%"><FONT SIZE=-1><I>Generated by NetBeans IDE</I></FONT>
31      </BODY>
32      </HTML>
```

This is the HTML code NetBeans generates automatically when you make an Applet called TestApplet.

Lines 25–27: This is the HTML code you could put in any HTML file to start TestApplet. The .class files must be in the directory specified by the codebase. To change the size of the Applet, change the values of width and/or height.

USING THE COLOR EDITOR

In the Visual editor, select a button. Then, in Properties, click the ... to the right of background, select the RGB tab, and slide the sliders

CATCHING MOUSE CLICKS

You can catch mouse clicks in a Frame as follows. Assuming you have a GUI Frame Form (an Applet works the same way), in the Form Editor:

1. Select the Frame.
2. Select Events in the Properties pane.
3. Select mousePressed and click the ellipses box—a Handlers pane will open, click "Add..." in it.
4. Type a name for the method that will be invoked when the user presses the mouse in the Frame; mousePressed is descriptive. Press Enter, and then OK. NetBeans will write the code and flip you to it.
5. Write diagnostic code as in Listing A.12 so that you can be sure that it is catching the mouse presses correctly.

LISTING A.12   Code to handle MouseDown.

```
1    private void mousePressed(java.awt.event.MouseEvent evt) {
2        int x = evt.getX();
```

```
3        int y = evt.getY();
4        System.out.println("Pressed! x=" + x + " y=" + y);
5    }
```

Once you are sure you are getting the correct coordinates when the mouse goes down, you can pass x and y to some other method and do whatever you wanted to do with that information there.

Note that this code will execute when the mouse goes down. You can also handle the event when it goes up (`mouseReleased`), or when it goes down and up without moving (`mouseClicked`), or when it is moved while down (`mouseDragged`).

ADDING JAVADOC COMMENTS

You can add comments to a class from NetBeans by going to Tools/Auto Comment. This will guide you through commenting your code. Then, after you have added the comments you want to all your classes, click on Build and "Generate Javadoc for ..." to create all the files. Try it. It's fun! It's easy! It looks really impressive!

When you have a file open and select Tools/Auto Comment, NetBeans opens an Auto Comment Tool window. All the methods in the current class are listed on the left, each with an icon indicating its status relative to JavaDoc comments. If there is no comment, a red X is displayed; if there are missing tags for elements the tool can detect, a lightning bold is displayed. This is the "autocommenting" the tool does; you, the human, must fill in the comments to make all the methods display the green check icon.

Each method needs a comment, which tells what it does. This is entered in the "Java Comment Text" box at the top. Additionally, methods that have non-`void` return types must have an @return tag, which describes the return value, and methods with parameters require @param tags that describe each parameter.

Notice the four buttons to the right of the list of methods. Autocorrect will insert the tags it can tell you need; click on each to add its description. Best of all, press the Help button for a much more thorough description than is provided here.

COMPILING AND RUNNING JAVA PROGRAMS WITHOUT NETBEANS

This text has relied on the NetBeans IDE for all development. What if you found yourself needing to program in an environment without NetBeans? First, there are a number of other fine development environments available—Eclipse has an excellent reputation; if you search the Web for "free java IDE download," you will find plenty. However, what if, for some reason, you wanted to compile and run Java programs without any IDE at all? Could you? The answer is yes, but until you are familiar with them, the details would be a bit of a problem. This section will describe what you must do to be able to accomplish this. There are a number of issues that must be understood and managed: 1) the command line, 2) if you are running a Windows® box—setting the PATH and CLASSPATH variables, 3) compiling with the javac command, 4) running an application with the java command, and 5) running an applet from a browser. These will be described after a few words about compilation and execution.

When you are using the NetBeans IDE (or any other IDE), to run the current project, you simply push the Run button (or select Run in a menu). This causes a number of things to happen, two of which are compilation of all the classes in the project, and execution of the main class. Executing an application means sending the main() message to the main class. Executing an applet means displaying an HTML file that includes an <APPLET> tag, like the one in Listing A.8.

The next four sections will describe how to compile and run an application and an applet on a Mac or a PC. Before undertaking them, you should understand the concept of a file system.

Disk File Systems and Cyberspace

This section contains some very basic information about computing. Perhaps you already know it; no problem. Perhaps some of the words and phrases are completely foreign. If you encounter phrases or words that are unfamiliar, you should look them up before proceeding! Everything here will be easily found if you Google it.

In all computers, files are organized in a tree-like directory structure, or file system. There is a root directory on each disk, which contains every other directory. Typically, on a PC, it is named c:\, and on a Mac, it is named Macintosh HD. The root directory, like any directory, can contain any number of files and other directories, called subdirectories.

All modern computers have GUI windowing systems, but also include a command-line interface that gives more direct access to the underlying operating system. If you do not use an IDE to run your Java programs, you must use the command line.

When you are using a command-line interface, you are always *in* a particular directory. Often, the current directory is displayed before the command prompt. You can move around the file system by using the change directory (cd) command. This concept of being at a particular place in the directory structure is where the notion of cyberspace came from. These days, you navigate the Web (which is a logical extension of navigating a directory structure) by clicking links; but the idea is the same.

To move down into a subdirectory named code, you type:

```
cd code
```

To move up (oddly, up is toward the root), type:

```
cd ..
```

That's about it.

Compiling and Running Java Classes on a Mac

Two steps are required: 1) go to the directory containing the program you wish to run, and 2) compile and execute your code. Once you are familiar with these, this is easy; the first time, it will take some attention and patience.

These instructions show how to create, compile, and execute a tiny program. If you have already written the classes you wish to run, you can skip the next paragraph and simply move to the directory in which they are stored. Except, you must comment out the package line in each, or these instructions will not work. Compiling and running with packages is covered later. For now, it would be simpler to use this minimal example; if you've been reading the text, you know why!

Create a File Containing the Class You Wish to Run

Use the TextEdit application (under Applications) to create a file named Junk.java containing:

```
public class Junk {
    public static void main(String [] asdf) {
        System.out.println("I did this without an IDE!");
    }
}
```

Notice that there is no package line. NetBeans puts all classes into packages, but it is simpler not to deal with packages right now.

Save the file in a directory named noNB under whatever directory the rest of your programs are in.

Go to the Relevant Directory on the Command Line

Launch the Terminal application. If it is not in your dock, you can find it under Applications. Applications is a directory that is normally in the sidebar of the Finder, but if it is not, it is directly under the root of the Macintosh HD.

When the Terminal starts, you will be in UNIX in your home directory. Type pwd (for print working directory); the screen will say something like:

```
Last login: Thu Apr 14 10:57:27 on ttyp1
Welcome to Darwin!
[cln-403-6850:~] levenick% pwd
/Users/levenick
[cln-403-6850:~] levenick%
```

Navigate to the directory where your program is. You can use the cd (change directory) command for this. The author has a directory in his home directory called javaBook. In that directory is another called code; and in that directory is another called noNB (for no NetBeans). He made it to be able to write this appendix. To navigate there requires the sequence of commands: cd javaBook, cd code, and cd noNB.

After these commands (and a pwd), the Terminal window contains:

```
Last login: Thu Apr 14 10:57:27 on ttyp1
Welcome to Darwin!
[cln-403-6850:~] levenick% pwd
/Users/levenick
[cln-403-6850:~] levenick% cd javaBook
[cln-403-6850:~/javaBook] levenick% cd code
[cln-403-6850:~/javaBook/code] levenick% cd noNB
[cln-403-6850:~/javaBook/code/noNB] levenick% pwd
/Users/levenick/javaBook/code/noNB
[cln-403-6850:~/javaBook/code/noNB] levenick%
```

To see what files and directories are in the current directory, one lists (ls) them. The only file in this directory is Junk.java, which is a tiny test application. Therefore, ls yields:

```
[cln-403-6850:~/javaBook/code/noNB] levenick% ls
Junk.java
[cln-403-6850:~/javaBook/code/noNB] levenick%
```

Compiling with the `javac` Command

Since you are in the noNB directory, and the class you wish to compile is there, you can simply say:

```
javac *.java
```

The * is a wildcard, and matches anything, so this command will compile every file in the current directory that has a .java extension.

Running an Application with the `java` Command

The command to run a Java program is `java`. To run the `Junk` class (i.e., to send the message `Junk.main()`, simply type `java Junk`. The screen will look something like:

```
[cln-403-6850:~/javaBook/code/noNB] levenick% ls
Junk.java
[cln-403-6850:~/javaBook/code/noNB] levenick% javac *.java
[cln-403-6850:~/javaBook/code/noNB] levenick% java Junk
I did this without an IDE!
[cln-403-6850:~/javaBook/code/noNB] levenick%
```

Whew! The second time is easier; honest.

Running an Applet from a Browser

To convince yourself that you can run an applet from a browser without an IDE, save this tiny applet in a file called TinyApplet.java on the noNB directory, as done previously.

```java
public class TinyApplet extends java.applet.Applet {
    public void paint(java.awt.Graphics g) {
        g.drawString("greetings", 50, 50);
    }
}
```

And save this bit of HTML code in a file called tiny.html in that same directory:

```html
<APPLET code="TinyApplet.class" width=350 height=200></APPLET>
```

Compile the applet by `javac *.java` and then run it by navigating to the HTML file from the browser (File/Open File).

Compiling and Running an Application on a PC

There are three steps: 1) set the path and classpath variables, 2) go to the directory containing the program you wish to run, and 3) compile and run the code.

Setting the PATH and CLASSPATH Variables

You will only need to do this once. After that, whenever you restart your computer, these will be set automatically.

1. Click START (lower left) .
2. Select run.
3. Type `command` and click OK. This should get you to the command line.
4. Type `cd c:\` .
5. Type `notepad autoexec.bat` to start the Notepad editor. Add the following two lines at the end:

```
set PATH=%PATH%;C:\Program Files\Java\jdk1.5.0_02\bin;
set CLASSPATH=.
```

Yes, "`CLASSPATH=.`" —dot (.) means the current directory.

This assumes you have jdk1.5.0_02. If you have a newer version, you must type its number instead. Use Explore (right-click Start, choose Explore) to see the name of that directory on your machine—under C:\ProgramFiles\Java).

6. Close Notepad.
7. Restart your computer.

Create a File Containing the Class You Wish to Run

Use the Notepad (as previously) to create a file named Junk.java containing:

```java
public class Junk {
    public static void main(String [] asdf) {
        System.out.println("I did this without an IDE!");
    }
}
```

Notice that there is no package line. NetBeans puts all classes into packages, but it is simpler not to deal with packages right now.

Save it in a directory named noNB under whatever directory the rest of your programs are in.

Go to the Relevant Directory on the Command Line

Get to the command line (as previously) and move to the noNB directory, like this (assuming you keep your code in a directory directly under the root of the c: drive):

```
cd c:\
cd code
cd noNB
```

Compiling with the `javac` Command

Since you are in the noNB directory, and the class you wish to compile is there, you can simply say:

```
javac *.java
```

The * is a wildcard, and matches anything, so this command will compile every file in the current directory that has a .java extension.

Running an Application with the `java` Command

The command to run a Java program is `java`. To run the Junk class (i.e., to send the message `Junk.main()`, simply type `java Junk`.

Running an Applet from a Browser

To convince yourself that you can run an applet from a browser without an IDE, save this tiny applet in a file called TinyApplet.java on the noNB directory, as done previously.

```
public class TinyApplet extends java.applet.Applet {
    public void paint(java.awt.Graphics g) {
        g.drawString("greetings", 50, 50);
    }
}
```

And save this bit of HTML code in a file called tiny.html in that same directory:

```
<APPLET code="TinyApplet.class" width=350 height=200></APPLET>
```

Compile the applet by javac *.java and then run it by navigating to the HTML file from the browser (File/Open File).

Compiling and Executing with Packages

NetBeans uses packages in every project. This makes compiling and executing from the command line a bit more complex. Follow these instructions for a minimal example you can adapt to any project you have built in NetBeans.

Create a Directory with the Name of the Package

Create a directory under your noNB directory, called junk. Copy your Junk.java file to that directory. Add the line

```
package junk;
```

as its first line. The name of the directory and the name of the package must be identical; case matters.

Go to the Directory above It

Move into the noNB directory on the command line.

Compile your code from here by `javac junk/*.java` on a Mac; or `javac junk\*.java` on a PC (what's the difference? slash, or backslash).

Then, execute your code by `java junk/*.java` on a Mac; or `java junk\*.java` on a PC.

On our Mac this looks like:

```
[cln-403-6850:~/javaBook/code/noNB] levenick% javac junk/*.java
[cln-403-6850:~/javaBook/code/noNB] levenick% java junk/Junk
I did this without an IDE!
[cln-403-6850:~/javaBook/code/noNB] levenick%
```

Odds are you will never have to do any of this; but, if you do, it can be very frustrating. Follow this model to learn the pattern, and then remember: 1) the directory must be the same as the package, character by character; 2) you must compile and execute from *above* the package directory.

Appendix

B Documentation, Access, Errors, Exceptions and `repaint()`

DOCUMENTATION

Documentation can be an important part of a program, particularly if it is going to be modified by someone else. In the context of a large software department, good documentation may mean the difference between success and failure. In the context of an introductory class, documentation may be less important.

There is a wonderful tool for documenting Java programs called Javadoc. It generates a copious amount of documentation in an official-looking format with a minimum of labor. How to use it is described in the last section of Chapter 12, "Interfaces and Writing a List Class."

ACCESS MODIFIERS

Methods and variables may have access modifiers preceding them; these control what objects and classes are able to access them. There is one implicit and three explicit access levels.

public

A method or variable (the general term for a method or variable is *member*) declared `public` is, well, public; it is visible from everywhere.

protected

`protected` members are only visible from the class they are defined in, and its subclasses.

private

`private` members are only visible from the class in which they are defined.

`friendly`

If you omit the access modifier, the member is friendly; that means it is `public` within the package, but `private` everywhere else.

Therefore, perhaps the easiest thing for a beginning programmer is to omit the access modifiers, and let all the members be friendly. Ask your instructors what they prefer.

ERRORS

There are at least three types of errors that occur when programming: compile-time errors, runtime errors, and intent errors.

Compile-Time Errors

Compile-time errors are those that happen when the compiler is attempting to translate the source code (the Java code you write) into byte code (which can then be executed to accomplish whatever task you were attempting). The most common are syntax errors.

Runtime Errors

Runtime errors are errors that happen when the program executes. In Java, these are called runtime exceptions, and an `Exception` class deals with them.

Intent Errors

Even after there are no compile-time errors and no runtime errors, there can still be intent errors; cases where a program does not do what the programmer intended. These may be simple mistakes, or reveal deep conceptual misunderstandings.

EXCEPTIONS

The Sun Java tutorial on `Exceptions` (*http://java.sun.com/docs/books/tutorial/ essential/exceptions/index.html*) begins: "If there's a golden rule of programming it's this: Errors occur in software programs. This we know. But what really matters is what happens after the error occurs. How is the error handled? Who handles it? Can the program recover, or should it just die? ... The Java language uses exceptions to provide error-handling capabilities for its programs. An exception is an event that occurs during the execution of a program that disrupts the normal flow of instructions."

Exceptions are very useful for building code that does not break constantly. Beautiful, elegant `Exception` structures can be built; and in a large, commercial software product, they become essential. But, in the context of a first course in Java programming, they are mostly just an annoyance. An interested reader is directed to the Sun tutorial mentioned previously.

`repaint()`, `paint()`, **AND** `update()`

Many Java programmers are befuddled by the three methods `repaint()`, `paint(Graphics)`, and `update(Graphics)`. This is because they are designed to work in a wide variety of circumstances, and they interact in a nonobvious fashion. This happens in several contexts in Java, but GUIs are the most obvious. The designers of Java wanted Java programs to be able to run on any machine that had a Java virtual machine (JVM). For example, a particular program might be running on a desktop machine, or laptop, or a hand-held machine, like a personal digital assistant, or a phone. This presents quite a challenge for the designer of an abstract windows toolkit (AWT). It also makes the job of a novice programmer more difficult than it might otherwise be—so it goes.

public void update(Graphics)

By default, `update(Graphics)` fills the drawable area of a `Component` with its background color, and then sends `paint(Graphics)` to the object. Thus, flicker that comes from redrawing the background over and over can sometimes be fixed by overriding `update()` (see Listing 9.19).

public void paint(Graphics)

Every Java `Component` implements `paint(Graphics)`, either explicitly, or implicitly through inheritance. This method is responsible for painting that component in the `Graphics` context passed in the parameter. When you extend a `Component` (e.g., when you write an `Applet`), if you want to display it differently from its superclass, you override `public void paint(Graphics)`. This was first illustrated in Chapter 3, "Class Design and Implementation."

repaint()

The `repaint()` method is sent to a `Component` when it needs to be repainted. This happens when a window is moved, resized, or unhidden. It also happens when a Web page contains an image and the pixels of the image are arriving slowly down the wire.

When a `Container`, like a `Frame`, is painted, all of its `Components` (`Buttons`, `TextFields`, whatever) must be repainted. This is accomplished (roughly), in Java, by sending `repaint()` to every `Component` in the `Container`, in the order in which they were added to the container.

The action of `repaint()` is to spawn a new `Thread` (see Chapter 9, "Simulation and Animation"), which schedules `update(Graphics)` in 100 milliseconds. If another `repaint()` happens before the 100 milliseconds elapses, the previous `update()` is cancelled, and a new one is scheduled. This is because screen flicker is ugly, and refreshing many times at short intervals (e.g., for every line in an image coming down from the Internet) looks horrible.

paint(Graphics) or repaint()?

When you want to redisplay a component, should you send it `paint(Graphics)` or `repaint()`? The answer is almost always `repaint()`. Only use `paint(Graphics)` if you understand what you are doing, and have a good reason for doing so.

Appendix

C

Answers to Selected Exercises

2.2 `System.out.println()`

2.4 To enclose classes, method bodies, and block statements.

2.6 Keeping things simple.

2.8 Because `String` is a class.

3.2 A class is a template for an object. It is the same as the difference between a cookie cutter and the cookie it makes.

3.4 `something` is an object, `Something` is a class.

3.6 Use an assignment statement.

3.8 name, type, and value

3.10 In the parentheses following the message name.

3.12 `Anything` is the object, `everything` is the message, `something` is the parameter.

4.2 Good design simplifies coding and debugging.

4.4 The context in which you can do graphics.

4.6 To pass information to methods.

4.8 Picture element.

4.10 (x,y) coordinates of the upper left corner, width and height.

4.12 To access variables.

5.2 The hidden parameter that is a reference to the object that received the message that invoked the current instance method.

5.4 So you don't waste your precious cognitive capacity remembering which variable names mean what.

5.6 Class, instance, local, parameter. The entire class, the entire class (except static methods), the local scope, the method.

5.8 `int 17, double 3.141, double 3.0, int 0, int 3, int 4, String "2+2", String "22", int 22, int 3, int 1, String "", String "1", String "(int) 1.414"`

5.10 Is defined as, or, optional, one thing of type, zero or more x's.

6.4 If the classes you have are complicated or do more than one thing.

6.6 `SnowPerson(int, int, int)`

```
   SnowBall(int, int, int)
        FilledCircle(int, int, int, Color)
             Circle(int, int, int)
             FilledCircle:setColor(Color)
   SnowBall(int, int, int)
        FilledCircle(int, int, int, Color)
             Circle(int, int, int)
             FilledCircle:setColor(Color)
   SnowBall(int, int, int)
        FilledCircle(int, int, int, Color)
             Circle(int, int, int)
             FilledCircle:setColor(Color)
   Puddle(int, int, int)
        FilledCircle(int, int, int, Color)
             Circle(int, int, int)
             FilledCircle:setColor(Color)
   adjustSnowBallSizes()
          Circle:getRadius()
          Circle:setRadius(int)
   adjustSnowBallLocations()
          Circle:getRadius()
          Circle:setY(int)
          Circle:getRadius()
          Circle:getRadius()
          Circle:getY()
          Circle:setY(int)
          Circle:getRadius()
          Circle:getRadius()
          Circle:getY()
          Circle:setY(int)
```

6.8 First, the `melt()` message is sent to the base, a `SnowBall`. Next, in `melt`, `getRadius()` is sent to the base, but since it is not declared in `SnowBall`, or `FilledCircle`, it invokes `Circle:getRadius()`. Then the same thing happens with `setRadius(int)` .

7.2 if-else

7.4 if (x > 0) System.out.println("yes"); else System.out.println("no");

7.6

p	q	!p	!p||q	p&&!q	!(p&&!q)	(!p||q) &&!(p&&!q)
t	t	f	t	f	t	t
t	f	f	f	t	f	f
f	t	t	t	f	t	t
f	f	t	t	f	t	t

7.8 For 14: Minor You may not enter! For 41: Major You may not enter! Fix it by putting {}s around the two statements that were supposed to be in the else part.

7.10
```
char gradeForScore (int score) {
    switch ((score-1)/10) {
        case 9: return 'A';
        case 8: return 'B';
        case 7: return 'C';
        case 6: return 'D';
    }
    return 'F';
}
```

8.2
```
String reverse (String s) {
    String returnMe = "";
    for (int i=0; i<s.length(); i++)
        returnMe += s.charAt(i);

    return returnMe;
}
```

8.4
```
boolean isVowel (char ch) {
    return ch=='a' || ch=='e' || ch=='i' || ch=='o' || ch=='u';
}

int countVowels (String s) {
    int count=0;
    for (int i=0; i<s.length(); i++)
        if (isVowel(s.charAt(i))
            count++;

    return count;
}
```

9.2 After `if`, after `while`, in the continuation condition of `for`, on the right-hand side of the assignment operator, as actual parameters.

9.4 They don't. They take turns.

9.6 ! and –, as in –17.

9.8 It sets the bounds of the `Button`.

9.10 See Chapter 11, "Data Structures."

10.2 `hasMoreTokens()` and `nextToken()`

10.4 A class that wraps another class or data (to make it easier to use). Or a method that wraps another method (to rename it).

10.6 To prompt the user to select a file.

11.2 `add()`

11.4 It checks for a vertical bounce and then for a horizontal bounce. Hits the left or the top, hits the right or top, hits the left or bottom, hits the right or bottom, and hits nothing.

12.2 `new Integer(17)`, `anInteger.intValue()`

12.4 So that when your code does not work, you know the problem is in one of the methods you just wrote. It makes it easier to find the bugs.

12.6 It would copy the value at `list[0]` into every other slot in the array!

12.8
```
1    public String toString() {
2        String returnMe="MyIntVectorList: {";
3
4        for (Iterator it=list.iterator(); it.hasNext();) {
5            returnMe += it.next().toString();
            if (it.hasNext())
                returnMe += ", ";
        }
6
7        return returnMe + "}";
8    }
```

13.2 The next smallest element in the unsorted list is repeatedly selected to add to the sorted list.

13.4 See chapter text!

13.8 Assuming you have a `min(int,int)` method:
```
int min4 (int x, int y, int z, int a) {
    return min(min(x,y), min(z,a));
```

Appendix

D

About the CD-ROM

The CD-ROM included with *Simply Java* includes most of the code and projects from the various examples found in the book.

CD-ROM FOLDERS

code: Contains all the code from examples in the book by chapter. Always clean and build projects before you run them.

source: Contains: 1) NetBeans for the Mac, and 2) a PC bundle with Sun's Java™ 2 Platform Standard Edition Development Kit 5.0 and NetBeans for PC.

figures: Contains all of the figures from the book, organized in folders by chapter.

INSTALLATION

On a PC, double-click the "jdk-1…exe" file. On a Mac, just drag the NetBeans icon onto the desktop and double-click it.

The PC software was downloaded from the Sun site at:
http://java.sun.com/j2se/1.5.0/download-netbeans.html

The Mac NetBeans was downloaded from the NetBeans site:
http://www.netbeans.info/downloads/download.php?a=b&p=1

New releases are available periodically; you might want to get a more current one.

Windows 98 or better, or Mac OS X

SYSTEM REQUIREMENTS

- Windows 98 or better, or Mac OS X
- 256 MBs of RAM, minimum 1GB recommended
- Hard disk space?
- Processor speed?
- What is needed to run/access the Java files? The xml files? If it's the JDK, we still need to say so even though it's included on the disc.

Glossary

access modifiers: The keywords `public`, `private`, and `protected` control which methods and variables can be accessed from where. If a method has no access modifier, it is "friendly"; `public` within this package, `private` elsewhere. That's okay to do for most personal programming.

actual parameters: Parameters in the parentheses of a message (may be any expression of a compatible type); compare formal parameters.

API: Application Programmers Interface. The API for a package is the interface that a programmer using that package sees. It is also used to refer to the documentation of that API.

Applet: A Java program that runs in the context of a Web browser. Also a class in the java.applet package.

application: A Java program that runs independently.

argument: Information sent along with a message, which invokes a method; synonym for parameter.

assignment operator: A single equals sign. The semantics of an assignment operator is to evaluate the expression to its right and assign that value to the variable on its left. This is almost the only way to change the value of a variable.

BNF: Backus Naur Form. A metalanguage for describing context free grammars. Commonly used to describe the syntax of programming languages.

bug: An error in a program.

byte code: The intermediate form that the Java compiler converts a class to after that class compiles correctly. It is stored in a .class file, to be interpreted by the Java virtual machine when the program executes.

compile time: During compilation, when the syntax of the program is being checked by the compiler; compare with execute time or runtime.

Component: A generic class in java.awt that includes `Button`, `TextField`, and many other common GUI components.

concatenation: To attach together end to end. If you concatenate "psycho," "the," and "rapist," you get "psychotherapist."

control variable: A variable that controls the execution of an iterative loop.

default value: The value you get if you don't do anything (i.e., by default). Instance variables are assigned zero by default when they are created. If you want to initialize them to something else, you may (e.g., `int x=17;`). Methods and variables in a class definition are instance members by default.

echo a file: To read a file and display it on the screen.

encapsulation: One of the famous attributes of OOP. An object encapsulates its data and methods. A private variable in an object cannot be modified or seen from outside except by the use of an accessor. Thus, if that variable ends up with a bad value, it is (in theory) easier to discern why.

file: Information stored on disk.

file I/O: File input and output.

formal parameters: Parameters defined in a method heading (each must have a type and a name); compare actual parameters.

GUI: Graphical user interface.

hand simulation: Simulating code by hand; performing the semantics of each statement, one by one, to discover how code works; or when it is broken, why it doesn't.

HTML: HyperText Markup Language. An embedded command formatting language commonly used for Web pages.

identifiers: Java names. Must start with a letter and be composed of only letters, digits, and underscores; case matters.

idiom: A sequence of symbols whose meaning cannot necessarily be derived from the individual symbols, and which must be learned as a whole, by rote. Alternatively, a common formulaic usage.

infinite loop: A loop that executes forever.

inheritance: The mechanism by which one class (the subclass) includes the variables and methods of another (the superclass).

instance variable: The default for a variable declared outside of any method; a copy of an instance variable is created for each instance of the class.

invariant: A condition that does not change; something that is known to always be true in some part of an algorithm.

iteration: Another word for *repetition*.

Java virtual machine (JVM): Software that creates the Java runtime environment on a particular machine, and executes byte code.

main method: Where execution begins when your Application runs.

Math.random(): Returns a random `double` in the range [0,1).

null: The value 0, interpreted as a reference (or pointer).

null pointer: A pointer (reference) that is null.

null pointer exception: The `Exception` that is thrown when you try to send a message to a null pointer.

OOP: Object-oriented programming. Also called *object programming*.

object program: Object-oriented program.

package: A package is a collection of related classes and interfaces. You can import packages that other people have written into your program.

parameter: Information sent along with a message, which invokes a method; synonym for *argument*. There are two kinds of parameters, formal (in the method heading) and actual (in the parentheses following a message); they match up one to one, in order.

parameter linkage: When a message is sent with parameters, the values of the actual parameters are copied to the corresponding formal parameters.

pixels: PICTure ELements, the smallest drawable part of the output.

polymorphism: An OOP attribute. The same message, sent to instances of different classes, can have totally different actions. In an `iterator()` loop, the type of the next thing is `Object`, yet you can say `it .next().toString()`; this is an example of polymorphism.

precedence: In an expression with multiple operators, which operator precedes which (e.g., * precedes +).

problem solving: The behavior one engages in when one is stuck and doesn't know what to do next.

prototype: A simplified, preliminary version of something; in this case, a program.

public: An access type; means anyone can see this. Other access modifiers are `protected` (only visible to this class and subclasses thereof), and `private` (only visible to this class). If the access modifier is omitted, the member is "friendly" (`public` to you, the programmer, `private` to anyone else); thus, in casual programming, no access modifiers are necessary.

recursive definition: A definition that uses the thing being defined.

reference: All objects in Java are stored as references; addresses of, or pointers to the `Object`.

reserved word: Words that are part of the Java language and cannot be redefined; they are reserved for the compiler.

scope: The portion of a program where a construct is visible (or defined).

semantics: Meaning, or action; compare syntax.

shadow: To hide a variable, by being named the same thing in a more local scope; most often happens with parameters.

signature: The type and name of a method, along with the number of parameters and their types.

Socket: A mechanism to connect one computer to another (virtually). Also a class in java.network.

spawned: Technical term for *created*; used only for Threads. When a new thread of control is initiated—i.e., begins execution—it is said to be spawned.

static: Modifier that creates class variables or methods instead of instance variables or methods.

String: The Java class whose instances are each a literal series of characters.

syntax: Grammar or form. Every programming construct has both syntax (grammar) and semantics (meaning).

thread of control: (or just thread) The sequence of statements executed when a program executes. A temporal map of where control resides during execution.

toggle: A two-state switch that changes state each time you activate it.

variable: Named memory to store one value of a particular type.

Index